Arun S. Malik

Models
for
Public Systems Analysis

OPERATIONS RESEARCH
AND INDUSTRIAL ENGINEERING

Consulting Editor: J. William Schmidt

CBM, Inc., Cleveland, Ohio

Applied Statistical Methods
I. W. Burr

Mathematical Foundations of Management Science
and Systems Analysis
J. William Schmidt

Urban Systems Models
Walter Helly

Introduction to Discrete Linear Controls: Theory and Application
Albert B. Bishop

Integer Programming: Theory, Applications, and Computations
Hamdy A. Taha

Transform Techniques for Probability Modeling
Walter C. Giffin

Analysis of Queueing Systems
J. A. White, J. W. Schmidt, and G. K. Bennett

Models for Public Systems Analysis
Edward J. Beltrami

Models
for
Public Systems Analysis

EDWARD J. BELTRAMI

COLLEGE OF ENGINEERING AND APPLIED SCIENCE
STATE UNIVERSITY OF NEW YORK
STONY BROOK, NEW YORK

ACADEMIC PRESS   New York   San Francisco   London   1977

A Subsidiary of Harcourt Brace Jovanovich, Publishers

ACADEMIC PRESS, INC.
111 Fifth Avenue, New York, New York 10003

United Kingdom Edition published by
ACADEMIC PRESS, INC. (LONDON) LTD.
24/28 Oval Road, London NW1

Library of Congress Cataloging in Publication Data

Beltrami, Edward J
    Models for public systems analysis.

    (Operations research and industrial engineering
series)
    Includes bibliographical references and index.
    1.   Municipal services—Mathematical models.
I.   Title.
HD4431.B33   352   76-19482
ISBN 0–12–085565–8

PRINTED IN THE UNITED STATES OF AMERICA

To the Memory of My Father,

FRANK BELTRAMI

Contents

Preface

The past several years have been witness to a new interest in the use of mathematical models for solving urgent problems in the public sector. In this book, several classes of such models are reviewed with particular attention centered on questions of how to improve the delivery of urban service systems (sanitation, fire, police, ambulances). The emphasis throughout is on model formulation, by which we mean the translation of significant societal problems into a mathematical framework. Each framework idealizes reality to a lesser or greater degree according to the complexity of the problem. It is important therefore that one discuss the limitations and pitfalls of modeling, and give an appraisal of when its use is appropriate.

In contrast to model formulation little will be said about solution methods. On occasion, however, a particular method is discussed when we feel that it is not adequately covered in standard texts. This particularly applies to our treatment of heuristic algorithms in the last chapter. In an attempt to make the book reasonably self-contained, a set of short appendixes is provided dealing with a review of specific techniques. These give the background for a discussion of the basic models that are interwoven throughout the text in one form or other (notably fixed charge plant location, multiple set covering, and multiservor queueing).

The contents of this book are based on lectures given in the last few years to students in applied mathematics and policy sciences at the State University of New York at Stony Brook, as well as on a number of lectures given elsewhere. By and large the material is standard fare in operations research except that the choice of applications is decidedly not standard. Indeed, many of the references are scattered about in a number of unpublished reports which are not easily accessible to the general reader. Moreover, with the exception of the journal *Urban Analysis*, there appears to be no single scholarly publication that is devoted entirely to the material that is the subject of this book, although a number of important papers are published from time to time in *Operations Research* and *Management Science*.

We have kept the level of mathematics deliberately elementary in order to reach a wide audience of people who include, in addition to operations analysts and applied mathematicians, urban and regional planners, specialists in public administration, and consultants in industrial management. Prerequisite is an ability to work comfortably with quantitatively oriented ideas. First year calculus and some probability and statistics should be all the formal training that is needed to follow most, perhaps all, of the text. We believe the book is useful for self-study. To assist in a review of the material and as an aid to understanding, a few fairly uncomplicated exercises are appended to each chapter. If the book is to be used in a classroom environment, it is recommended that students be asked to code and run some of the material discussed, using standard computer packages such as MPS-X, in order to acquire a feel for the kind of numbers one gets in using such models. This is in fact the way we conducted our own classroom exercises at Stony Brook.

Now for a quick review of the contents. Chapter 1 is essentially a treatment of plant location and siting questions, with a brief overview of water resource modeling. The Federal Water Pollution Control Act of 1972 has brought these ideas to the forefront of public interest. Also included is a formulation of recent models developed at the Brookhaven National Laboratory relating to energy supply and distribution on a regional and national scale. Chapter 2 develops set-covering models for manpower scheduling as a direct outgrowth of the author's experience with the Sanitation Department in New York City. The third and fourth chapters deal with the delivery of emergency services, particularly with models of congestion and delay and of optimal deployment. Here the analysis is probabilistic in nature since both the spatial and the temporal patterns of demand are intrinsically uncertain. This is in contrast to the nonemergency systems dealt with in the other chapters, where deterministic modeling appears to be more appropriate. The tools used are queueing theory and geometric probability. In the last chapter network optimization methods are employed, mainly to explore questions of vehicle routing and scheduling. Such problems occur in a variety of contexts in the public sector. Following this are a few comments on large-scale models of urban growth, these being generally more familiar to the regional planner then to the operations analyst.

Most of the work discussed in the book is based on studies conducted in an operational environment and much, if not all, of it has been implemented with varying degrees of success in a number of municipalities. Thus, for example, the models of Chapters 3 and 4 have been applied in parts of the greater New York City and Boston areas, while the second and fifth chapters relate to work carried out principally (but not exclusively) in New York City. A number of other cities have also benefited from these studies, ranging from Washington, D.C. and Denver to Milan and Zurich. Unfortunately not all this work has been adequately documented and so an overall assessment of what has, and is, being done in the area of public systems analysis is difficult to attain. The purpose of this book is to give an early overview of some of the ideas that have already proven their usefulness.

Acknowledgments

In large measure the models of the second and last chapters follow work done by my colleague, Professor Larry Bodin. He has been a stimulus and an inspiration for much of my own thinking in the field and I want to thank him. Many thanks are also due to Professor Dick Larson and his associates at the Operations Research Center of MIT, and to the collective staff of the Fire Project of the New York City Rand Institute. They provided me with much useful information concerning emergency service systems. In my view, the pioneering efforts of the regrettably now defunct Rand group will long be acknowledged.

A deep sense of appreciation is also due to a number of other colleagues, too numerous to mention, who in one way or the other have influenced the growth of this book or contributed to its contents. Special thanks, however, must go to Professor Stan Altman.

I have also benefited from the opportunity to present this material as a set of lectures in Europe during extended stays at the International Institute for the Management of Technology (Milan), The Techneco Institute (Fano), and the Salzburg Seminar for American Studies. The gracious hospitality shown to me at each of these places was certainly one of the highlights of my experiences in the area of public systems analysis.

Some Thoughts on Mathematics and Public Policy

*Moral: A Word to the Wise Is Not Sufficient
If It Doesn't Make Any Sense*

JAMES THURBER
Further Fables for Our Time

In this book interest is focused on problems related to the delivery of municipal services. Most of the uniformed services, such as sanitation, fire, police, and transit, are all labor-intensive activities. Rising labor costs and increasing demand have in recent years put pressure on the cities to meet or, as it often happens, to close the gap between service levels and actual need. A growing percentage of the municipal budget has correspondingly been allocated to provide for these needs and, to cite the case of New York City, over a quarter of a billion dollars annually is currently budgeted to each of the departments of Sanitation and Fire.

In addition to rapidly increasing labor costs and soaring demand (some of it abusive, as witnessed by the high incidence of false alarms), the delivery of services has been hampered by such factors as a physical armature which has not kept pace with demographic shifts within the city and the existence of powerful and sometimes militant unions who tend to resist changes in long standing but often obsolete labor practices.

As much as 90% of the costs of the services is due to wages and benefits for the workers and therefore one way to effect an improvement in their delivery is to induce changes in manpower utilization so as to *increase productivity for the same level of dollar cost*. These changes are not so much in the

1

direction of new and better equipment, desirable as such capital investments may be, but rather in altering the operational configuration in which both men and equipment are deployed. Admittedly this is a short term tactic, but one which often can relieve visable and pressing needs.

There is a role for analysis here and in this book we briefly survey some of the operational models which have been developed in the last few years for this purpose. Since my own background and experience is principally in New York, I will restrict myself largely to describing work performed there, almost all of it during the recent administration of Mayor John V. Lindsay.

Although our review focuses on some of the modeling questions, it would be a discredit to this kind of analysis not to emphasize that *the real goal is change*. Therefore, the extent to which analysis becomes a tool for this purpose is to be regarded as a measure of its success.

It appears that much well-intentioned work by analysts is relegated to dusty shelves because it does not (and, in all fairness, often cannot) bridge what has been referred to as the "missing chapter" between a set of recommendations and an implemented change. It is characteristic of many otherwise well-trained people to want to believe in a rational approach to problem solving. Unfortunately, urgent city problems often resist the application of "obvious" solutions simply because such solutions fail to account for the institutional mechanisms through which action takes place. Ideas which are acceptable at the upper echelons of urban management either have no impact at all on policy or often reappear in altered guise after percolating down to the day to day operating level. This can happen for a number of reasons. Any change, for example, that threatens long established traditions of the workers or that in any way tends, however inadvertently, to foul them up is an open invitation to low compliance. I recall, to cite an instance, how a negotiated rescheduling of sanitationmen nearly fell through because it ignored the fact that the change could disrupt worker carpools.

We see then that unlike military or even industrial systems, urban systems achieve their goals by satisfying the needs of many different interest groups. Every proposed "optimal solution" to a perceived problem is ultimately altered and modified to suit political, fiscal, and even social expediency. Moreover, even if all parties agree on certain innovations it may turn out that some of the actions are not worth carrying out. Often such pitfalls in the way analysis is transferred is not anticipated until the recommended "optimal" policy is taken out of the hands of the analyst and into the streets.

What this suggests is that in dealing with public sector problems what one generally faces is less a matter of optimization than of accommodation among feasible alternatives, some of which are more or less acceptable than others. It also suggests that successful implementation of quantitative analysis requires a sensitivity to how public institutions actually work and not only of how they should work. For an applied mathematician to be credible in this area he or she should be willing to invest some time and effort working with public agencies on their own turf and playing by their rules. In this way one infiltrates, as it were, the municipal system and becomes an agent for change. Moreover, for the kind of short term operational questions that we are dealing with here the analysis should be action oriented. One thinks in terms of daily, sometimes violent, street terms: ambulances responding to incidents, barges loading garbage at downtown piers. Perhaps I run the risk of overstatement. Surely not all involvement of scientists with the cities requires such an unremitting struggle but I think it important that the pitfalls which lie between mathematical modeling and an effective urban policy not be underestimated.

In the remainder of this book the emphasis is on some of the mathematical questions which were harvested from a few actual case experiences. In discussing these we generally obscure how the analysis was translated into action but let me state my conviction that at least several implementable and, very likely, beneficial results regarding municipal services can be traced to the mathematical arguments that are reviewed here. Although at first sight the organizational, legal, and fiscal constraints which constitute the urban environment would appear to preclude any formal treatment of such questions, mathematical models have in fact sometimes yielded penetrating insights into the operation of these services.

REFERENCES

There are a number of papers which explore the role of analysis in the public arena. To list a few that relate to the study of municipal service systems in New York City let us mention but three:

R. Archibald and R. Hoffman, "Introducing Technological Change in a Bureaucratic Structure," Rand Rep. P-4025 (1969);

P. Szanton, "Systems Problems in the City," Rand Rep. P-4821 (1972);

B. Gifford, "Quantitative Policy Analysis in the City: Limits to Growth," IEEE Section on Systems, Man and Cybernetics, Meeting, Boston (Nov. 1973);

see also

"Making Ideas Work," Introduction to *Third Annual Report*, New York City Rand Inst. (1973).

Plant Location and Optimal Distribution

1.1 A WASTE DISPOSAL PROBLEM

The following material outlines the essential details of a study done for New York City about 1971. It was part of the problem to develop a strategy for the city on waste disposal. Because of antipollution legislation the question examined here is the tradeoff between new incinerator technology and the more traditional landfill disposal methods. We begin with some background material.

New York City disposes of over 25,000 tons of solid waste daily or about 7 million tons per year. The refuse is collected by truck and is either taken to incinerators, or to one of a half dozen sanitary landfills on the periphery of the city, or to one of the transfer stations located on the waters' edge. From the transfer stations, where trucks unload onto waiting barges, the refuse is then hauled by tugboat to a remote landfill known as Fresh Kills (Staten Island, New York).

On-site incinerators in apartments and other buildings as well as from municipal incinerators accounted for about 70% of particulate matter pumped into the atmosphere in New York City in 1965. In the following year an air pollution control bill, known as local law 14, was passed and signed into law.

5

   With regard to municipal incinerators where, at that time, about 30% of all refuse was disposed (or over 2 million tons per year) compliance with the antipollution law meant that New York City would be faced with the prospect of either shutting down or upgrading its low efficiency and high pollution incinerators. The upgrading had been estimated to cost several millions of dollars, a considerable sum even for New York, and in addition would be technologically risky. The alternative, then, would appear to be the shutdown of at least some of these facilities.

   The removal of some of the City's disposal locations has the effect of increasing the cost of collection since the trucks now have to travel longer distances to dump their loads at the remaining sites and, since these locations are likely to be more congested than usual, the collection cost (which already accounts for about 80% of the overall budget for collection–disposal) is increased further.

   Moreover, most of the landfills were nearly exhausted, with essentially no new sites available for development as sanitary landfills, which meant that although the then current disposal cost at a fill was low, the most feasible alternative to landfill—rail haul to disposal sites outside the city—would cost about five times as much in the future. For this reason early depletion of the fills will also result in higher disposal costs. In addition the capacity of the fills and transfer stations is limited to a maximum daily throughput. For example, a typical marine transfer facility can handle no more than about 1800 tons daily.

   It is clear then, that in order to comply with local law 14, at least part of the roughly six–seven thousand tons per day processed by the municipal incinerators would have to go to the remaining facilities. Since these locations are physically limited in the amount of additional load they can absorb, and since the economic drain on both collection and disposal costs is substantial, one is faced with a difficulty. The problem was to develop a strategy for disposal which reduced the impact of these obstacles.

   One possibility suggested at that time was to build a series of small incinerators in the 150–300 tons/day range (the usual size was about 1000 tons/day) which have the effect of dispersing the air pollution over a larger area and in smaller quantities. Indeed in this study we want to evaluate the cost–effectiveness of using a large number of smaller high efficiency pyrolytic incinerators. Such incinerators burn the refuse at extremely high temperatures in the absence of air and they may have a number of useful by-products: notably heavy oil, magnetic metals such as iron fillings, and steam (which can be used for space heating). Moreover the residue from these incinerators is essentially negligible (as we assume in this study) and air pollution is low.

   It should be mentioned, however, that such new facilities cannot be located anywhere. The public is generally reluctant to accept them in their own neighborhoods and political pressure is often sufficient to discourage city administrators from considering certain otherwise desirable sites as potential locations. A community can reject a site because of real or perceived risks to their health, loss of neighborhood status, increase in noise and traffic, and other hazards. However, this possible political pitfall will not be considered further in our study and it is assumed that selected sites are available for construction of new facilities.

The operating costs of these "mini"-incinerators (or, as we shall call them, MI) were estimated to be $10/ton. However, there is the possibility of recycling metal for $2/ton saving and selling steam for another $2/ton. Metal recycling looked more promising at that time than the selling of the steam.

Capital costs of an MI were estimated by the vendors to be in the range of ten to fifteen thousand dollars a day per ton of capacity. Capital costs can be made part of operating costs by amortising repayment of capital costs over a number of years. Assuming 15 years of amortisation at 7% interest, MI capital costs would be between $3.46 and $5.18/ton. Therefore the total per ton cost of an MI was in the range of $9.46–$15.18.

Because of the possibility of adding MIs to the disposal system it is important to carry out an analysis of whether MIs are economically feasible. Note that what is not being discussed is technological feasibility which is a problem of meeting engineering requirements and environmental constraints.

In order to focus the discussion, we have chosen an area in the borough of Queens (New York) which is presently served by one marine transfer station (MTS) as shown in Fig. 1.1. That is, all the refuse generated within the five

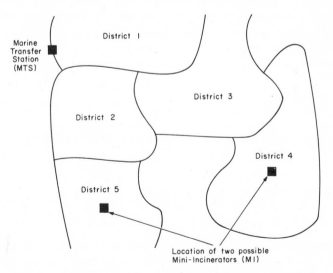

FIG. 1.1   Collection districts in the borough of Queens, New York.

districts of this area is sent to the MTS by trucks and is taken from there by barge to the Fresh Kills landfill.

The intuitive feeling about the economic effects of an MI system is that although the operational–capital cost of an MI will be higher than that of an MTS, having MIs located in certain districts has two potential advantages:

1.   More facilities reduce collection costs since roundtrip travel for the trucks between the sites they service and disposal locations will now be less.

2.   Disposal costs are reduced by virtue of the fact that the present landfill supply can be maintained somewhat longer than if MIs were not available. As we noted above, any alternative to landfill will inevitably cost more.

The question of the economic acceptability of this disposal alternative then becomes an analysis of whether truck travel costs and landfill costs are reduced more than the increase in disposal costs.

One technique to find the cost savings of an MI disposal system is to first calculate what the MI cost per ton would have to be to make this system as costly as the present MTS system.

This *breakeven cost* is calculated below but first it is necessary to give more cost figures (based on 1971 estimates). To begin with, the MTS incurs an operational expense which is calculated to be \$4.33/ton, which includes landfill cost at Fresh Kills. Secondly, the future cost of disposal when present landfill capacity is depleted is roughly taken to be \$10/ton. This figure is based on considering various alternatives to the exhausted landfill supply. The savings that accrue by diverting refuse from the fills to the incinerators is \$10 − \$4.33 = \$5.67/ton, since this prolongs the life of the existing fills. However, this savings will not be realized until later years and so its effect on present cost is discounted (see discussion in the notes at the end of this chapter). This results in a best guess of \$3.32 as the savings per ton of refuse not sent to landfill. The actual saving could lie in a range of between two and five dollars, a point which is taken up again later.

Now consider a ton of refuse diverted from the MTS and sent to an MI. How much more does it cost? Suppose y is the combined operating and capital expense of the MI. Then $y - \$4.33$ is the additional expense. Now consider the savings which result from diverting this same ton. Landfill saving is \$3.32 and there is an additional gain of x dollars because of lower hauling costs. Thus the breakeven cost for y is defined by

$$y - 4.33 = x + 3.22 \qquad [1.1.1]$$

The quantity x is found like this: consider how much it costs to send all refuse daily to the MTS alone. Call this amount α. Now compute how much it costs to dispose refuse when the MIs are available. Call this β. Then $\alpha - \beta$

is the dollar savings generated in transportation costs by diverting refuse. If m tons a day are actually diverted, then $x = (\alpha - \beta)/m$.

Now if the actual cost of an MI is y_0 (dollars per ton) and if $y - y_0 \geqq 0$, then the MI system is economically viable. Therefore one would like to maximize x (that is, minimize β) because that would make the breakeven value of y as large as possible. *The preferred configuration of disposal facilities is the one which makes the left-hand side of* [1.1.1] *as large as possible.*

What we need to do now is to *find the configuration of facilities* (number, location, and disposal capacities) *which minimizes the total transportation cost β.* For simplicity of presentation we restrict our discussion to the five refuse collection districts exhibited in Fig. 1.1, as already mentioned. Moreover the allowed sizes (capacities) of the incinerators will either be 150 or 300 tons/day, and we limit ourselves to building at most one incinerator in either district 4 or 5 or one in both, since these districts are the most remote ones and so are most likely to accrue savings in travel time. Although travel times to a disposal site vary within each district we choose the geographic center in each of them to represent that location having the average travel time. In practice, if the spread of actual travel times is too large, then the district needs to be partitioned into smaller sectors until the average travel time within each sector is sufficiently representative of all travel within it. In our five-district problem no such partitioning was deemed necessary. Roundtrip travel times from the geographic center of each of the districts to the disposal sites are given in Table 1.1 (times are in minutes per truck load and include the time to unload the refuse) together with the refuse that needs to be carted away daily in tons. The figures are obtained from readily accessible operational data available in the files of the city.

TABLE 1.1

District	MTS	Mini-incinerator location		Refuse generation (tons/day)
		District 4	District 5	
1	31	63	50	216.4
2	39	39	36	310.9
3	55	34	34	191.3
4	75	18	34	160.0
5	65	34	18	188.2

It will be convenient to transform this table into values of dollars per ton. We leave it to the reader to convert this table using the following facts: collection costs for a truck crew are \$40/hr and each truck load of refuse to the disposal sites weighs between four and six tons, let us say 4.26 tons. The table of costs (in dollars per ton) should now read as shown in Table 1.2.

TABLE 1.2

District	MTS	Mini-incinerator location		Refuse generation (tons/day)
		District 4	District 5	
1	4.6	9.4	7.5	216.4
2	5.8	5.8	5.4	310.9
3	8.2	5.1	5.1	191.3
4	11.2	2.7	5.1	160.0
5	9.5	5.1	2.7	188.2

From this table one readily computes the total cost, labeled as α previously, in sending all refuse to the MTS alone. It is only the computation of β and m that require any concern. To do this we employ a linear programming formulation in the special format of the transportation problem (see background discussion in Appendix A). Let c_{ij} be the cost per ton of collecting and hauling refuse by truck between district i (the origin) and disposal site j (the destination) and let x_{ij} be the actual tonnage assigned to sink j from source i. The cost to be minimized by appropriately choosing the values of $x_{ij} \geqq 0$ (the value of β) is

$$\text{cost} = \sum_{i=1}^{5} \sum_{j=1}^{3} c_{ij} x_{ij} \qquad [1.1.2]$$

where $j = 1$ denote the MTS in district 1, and $j = 2, 3$ are incinerators in districts 4 and 5, respectively. To give a specific example, assume that a 300-ton incinerator is built in district 4 and a 150-ton incinerator in district 5. Since all refuse generated daily is to be collected one must have

$$\sum_{j=1}^{3} x_{ij} = q_i, \qquad i = 1, \dots, 5 \qquad [1.1.3]$$

where $q_1 = 216.4$, $q_2 = 310.9$, etc. Also the capacity of each disposal location cannot be exceeded and so

$$\sum_{i=1}^{5} x_{ij} \leqq m_j, \qquad j = 1, 2, 3 \qquad [1.1.4]$$

where $m_1 = 1500$ (assumed maximum daily throughput at MTS), $m_2 = 300$, $m_3 = 150$. In order to take advantage of the standard solution techniques it is mathematically convenient to have a *balanced problem* in the sense that $\sum q_i = \sum m_j$. However, in our case there is an excess of disposal capacity and so one introduces a *dummy district* (labeled $i = 6$) whose daily refuse generation exactly equals this surplus of 883.2 tons. Note, incidentally, that when the problem is posed in balanced form the inequalities of [1.1.4] become equalities and the sum runs up to $i = 6$. The dummy variables x_{6j} can therefore be thought of as slacks. In an optimal solution the dummy source is then subtracted out and this reveals the optimal assignment for the remaining districts.

As noted in Appendix A, these linear programs can be solved by using standard computer codes. In some of these an initial basic feasible solution is required. The simple approach given below is one of the accepted ways of obtaining an initial vertex without having to use artificial variables. However, the full algorithm for completing the solution will not be described here since it is documented in all the standard references as well as in Appendix A.

The initial solution is obtained by a simple device which can be applied to any linear programming problem in the transportation framework. To begin with, write down in tabular form the sources (including the dummy source) and destinations, each with supplies or capacities, as shown in Table 1.3.

TABLE 1.3

INITIAL ASSIGNMENT USING NORTHWEST CORNER RULE

Districts (i)	Disposal sites (j)			Refuse generated (tons/day)
	1	2	3	
1	216.4			216.4
2	310.9			310.9
3	191.3			191.3
4	160.0			160.0
5	188.2			188.2
(Dummy) 6	433.2	300	150	883.2
	1500	300	150	

Note that the sum of the supply column is the same as the sum of the capacity row. Now begin an assignment of refuse from the first district to each site in turn. Since it needs to dispose of 216.4 tons and the MTS is capable of receiving it, all of it goes to site 1. Next, the second district sends all of its 310.9 tons also to site 1, since the MTS capacity is not yet saturated. This continues until we get to the dummy source which can send only 433.2 tons of its refuse to the MTS since together with the other assignments this saturates the MTS capacity. Of the remaining refuse, 300 tons is sent to site 2 (no more is possible) and the remaining 150 tons to site 3. Since the problem is balanced, all sources are satisfied and all sinks are saturated. Because we started at the top left-hand corner of Table 1.3, it is called the *northwest corner rule*. This gives us an initial basis with $m+n-1 = 6+3-1 = 8$ basic variables and 10 non-basic ones (see Appendix A). The final solution turns out to be the assignment of refuse depicted in Table 1.4.

TABLE 1.4

OPTIMAL ASSIGNMENT

Districts	Disposal sites (j)		
(i)	1	2	3
1	216.4	0	0
2	310.9	0	0
3	89.5	101.8	0
4	0	160.0	0
5	0	38.2	150
6	883.2	0	0

Thus, $x_{11} = 216.4$, $x_{12} = 0$, etc. We see that all refuse in districts 4 and 5 is sent to the MIs within those sectors (as expected intuitively) and that even district 3 sends some of it to an incinerator. The rest goes to the MTS. Since the dummy district sends all of its load to the MTS we interpret this to mean that in an optimal assignment the MTS is not saturated and that it has surplus capacity. That is, the first constraint of [1.1.4] contains a positive slack variable x_{61}. If some of district 6 had gone to sites 2 or 3 it would mean that these facilities are also underutilized. As it happens, this is not the case.

The solution to the transportation problem can also be viewed as a network in which the optimal assignments are visually depictable as linkages between sources and sinks, as in Fig. 1.2.

In order to conclude the analysis, let us mention that a number of possible configurations were examined and the optimal transportation network obtained for each. Table 1.5 summarizes the results, including the computation of the breakeven value of y. Note, incidently, that the number of diverted

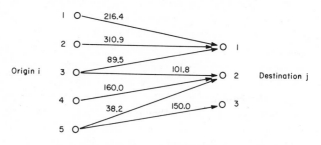

FIG. 1.2   Optimal source–sink assignments.

tons per day, a quantity denoted above by m, is also part of each optimal solution. For instance, in the problem treated above, $300 + 150 = 450$ tons are diverted away from the MTS.

TABLE 1.5

Capacity of MI (tons/day)	Number of MIs	Location of MIs (district)	Breakeven cost of MI (dollars/ton)
150	1	4	15.87
300	1	4	14.04
150, 150	2	4, 5	15.05
300, 150	2	4, 5	14.04
300, 300	2	4, 5	13.27

A large portion of the benefits achieved using MIs is due to saved truck time. It is crucial to recognize that these savings will only be realized by utilizing the time saved to make the truck routes longer and, therefore, reduce the number of roundtrips necessary to pick up the same amount of refuse.

We saw that the actual operating (and capital) cost of an MI ranges between $9.46 and $15.18/ton. If it costs $15.18 then the MI would not result in much savings while at the lower range the savings could be substantial. In order to illustrate how these yearly savings are computed, consider the case of a 300 ton/day incinerator located in district 4. The breakeven value is, as we know, $14.04. If the actual cost is $9.46 then the difference is $4.58/ton, which is multiplied by the 300 tons/day capacity of that incinerator. This gives a daily saving of $1374 which is then multiplied by 301 working days per annum of the New York Sanitation Department to give a final annual savings of $413,574.

Of all the values used in our analysis, that of landfill savings appears to be the least secure. For this reason it is recommended that one vary this quantity in the range of $2.00–$4.00 to see what effect this has, if any, on the answers obtained previously. This means that all the computations have to be repeated for each new value of the landfill savings (for a total, say, of three values in the range given) but the information gathered may be of utmost importance. This is called *sensitivity analysis* since it allows one to gauge whether or not it is worth the trouble to get a more precise estimate of the landfill savings (which would be the case if the breakeven value y is severely affected by changes in this landfill cost) or whether the results of the analysis retain a certain validity in spite of a possible poor estimate of this value. Sensitivity analysis is a way, then, of determining how vulnerable an optimal policy is with regard to changes in certain parameters which determine that policy.

1.2 OPTIMAL LOCATION OF FACILITIES

In the plant location study just completed, it was seen how to use a transportation network format in order to determine the optimal assignment of refuse from donor districts to the selected facilities. However this approach suffers from the defect that one has to choose in advance both the number and location of incinerator sites. An obvious question here is whether or not a different selection of sites for the (at most) two facilities can possibly improve the cost effectiveness of the overall system. However, an explicit enumeration of the possibilities is quite large and not very convenient. In fact, with five districts the choice of having none or a 150-ton or 300-ton incinerator leads to $3^5 = 243$ alternatives to evaluate, each of them requiring their own optimization analysis as already shown.

What is needed is an implicit way of evaluating the alternatives and so a more sophisticated approach will be described now. There is a price, however. The optimization model we give is one in which the computational difficulties are more pronounced than with the simple transportation network scheme present earlier.

We continue to label refuse districts by i and possible disposal location by j. Transportation cost between i and j and the amounts transported (in tons) are, as before, c_{ij} and x_{ij}—both of them nonnegative. Now, however, one introduces a *decision variable* y_j which is defined as

$$y_j = \begin{cases} 1, & \text{if } j\text{th facility is built} \\ 0, & \text{otherwise} \end{cases} \qquad [1.2.1]$$

If $j = 1$ is the label of the marine transfer station (MTS), then y_1 is set to one since that facility exists and is not anticipated that it be closed. On the other hand, if certain other sites are determined from exogenous factors to be unsuitable, then the corresponding y_j are set to zero.

Now let f_j be the fixed daily cost of having a facility at location j ($j = 1, \ldots, 6$). It is determined as the capital expense of construction amortized at a given interest rate over the loan period and then computed on a daily basis. In addition to this *fixed charge* there is a *variable cost* which is proportional to the amount actually disposed of at location j. If h_j is the cost per ton of disposal due to crew wages, stack scrubbing, burner maintenance, and process heat, then the variable cost on a daily basis is

$$h_j \sum_{i=1}^{5} x_{ij}, \qquad \text{if the } j\text{th facility is built}$$

$$0, \qquad\qquad\qquad \text{otherwise}$$

By letting $\delta_j = \sum_{i=1}^{5} x_{ij}$ then the total cost at facility j can be written as

$$f_j + h_j \delta_j, \qquad \text{if } \delta_j > 0$$
$$0, \qquad\qquad\quad \text{if } \delta_j = 0$$

which can be restated as

$$f_j y_j + h_j \delta_j \qquad [1.2.2]$$

for in any optimal solution it is necessarily true that $y_j = 0$ whenever $\delta_j = 0$ and $y_j = 1$ if $\delta_j > 0$ (why?). Thus the *total cost to be minimized is*

$$\text{cost} = \sum_{i=1}^{5} \sum_{j=1}^{6} c_{ij} x_{ij} + \sum_{j=1}^{6} (f_j y_j + h_j \delta_j) \qquad [1.2.3]$$

There are some constraints to be observed, however. Analogous to the previously discussed transportation approach one requires that

$$\sum_{j=1}^{6} x_{ij} = q_i \qquad [1.2.4]$$

where q_i is the daily refuse generated in district i, and

$$\delta_j = \sum_{i=1}^{5} x_{ij} \leqq m_j y_j \qquad [1.2.5]$$

where m_j is the installed capacity of facility j (in tons per day). We multiply m_j by the decision variable to ensure that no refuse is sent to a facility which is not to be built.

The optimization problem of minimizing [1.2.3] subject to [1.2.1], [1.2.4] and [1.2.5] is known as the *fixed charge problem* and is a special kind of integer program (see Appendix B) in which some of the optimizing variables (namely, the y_j) are to be integer—zero or one—while the other variables x_{ij} need only be nonnegative. For this reason such models are examples of what is also referred to as *mixed-integer programs.*

In the above formulation the plant capacities m_j are prespecified. However, by a slight modification of the model it becomes possible to select these plant sizes optimally. Suppose, in fact, that two incinerators are being considered. One, at 150 tons daily capacity, has a fixed charge of f_{j1} and the other, at 300 tons, has a fixed cost of f_{j2}. Let y_{jk} be a new decision variable $(k = 1, 2)$ defined by

$$y_{jk} = \begin{cases} 1, & \text{if a 150 ton } (k = 1) \text{ or 300 ton } (k = 2) \text{ unit is built at } j \\ 0, & \text{if no unit is built} \end{cases} \qquad [1.2.6]$$

Since at most one facility can be constructed at j we additionally constrain by

$$y_{j1} + y_{j2} \leqq 1 \qquad [1.2.7]$$

Assuming for simplicity that the variable cost does not depend in any substantial way on capacity, then the new total cost to be minimized is

$$\text{cost} = \sum_{i} \sum_{j} c_{ij} x_{ij} + \sum_{j} \sum_{k} (f_{jk} y_{jk} + h_j \delta_j) \qquad [1.2.8]$$

where [1.2.4] remains the same but now [1.2.5] is replaced by

$$\delta_j = \sum_{i=1}^{5} x_{ij} \leqq \sum_{k=1}^{2} m_{jk}\, y_{jk} \qquad [1.2.9]$$

Here m_{jk} is defined as

$$m_{jk} = \begin{cases} 150, & \text{if } k = 1 \\ 300, & \text{if } k = 2 \end{cases} \qquad [1.2.10]$$

The integer program described by the minimum of [1.2.8] subject to [1.2.5] through [1.2.10] yields, in addition to the optimal assignment of refuse from sources to sinks, the least cost choice of the number, size (i.e., capacity) and location of incinerators, and as such, it offers a substantial improvement over the model derived in Section 1.1. It would be unfair, however, not to point out that the numerical solution of such program requires the use of algorithms which are sufficiently complex as to warrant the use of carefully designed computer codes. Many such codes are variants of the branch and bound idea outlined in Appendix B. By contrast, the transportation format of Section 1.1 can, for a reasonably sized problem, be solved manually or with the use of a desk calculator quite easily.

The total cost at a facility, as given by [1.2.2], is displayed graphically in Fig. 1.3.

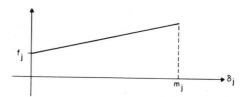

FIG. 1.3   Linear cost at a facility.

In many problems a more realistic variable cost would reflect economies of scale in which case such cost would not necessarily be proportional to tonnage handled (the variable δ_j) but might be some *concave* function such as shown in Fig. 1.4.

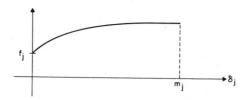

FIG. 1.4   Convex cost at a facility.

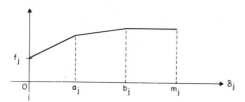

FIG. 1.5 Piecewise linear cost at a facility.

In such cases the objective function would no longer be linear in the x_{ij} variables and the linear program becomes a nonlinear one (see Appendix D), a kind which is notably more difficult to handle. One way to circumvent this inherent nonlinearity is to replace the concave function by a *piecewise linear* approximation as exhibited in Fig. 1.5, in which the objective is now described by linear pieces between 0 and a_j, a_j and b_j, and b_j to m_j. We forego the details.

Another conceivable extension of the model occurs when at least some of the facilities are *transshipment points*. This would occur, for example, if the incinerator residue (ash and incompletely combusted charred materials) are sufficient as to warrant their further transportation by truck to the marine facility and onto the barges. Indeed in older, nonpyrolytic incinerators as much as 25% of the ingoing refuse remain as residue. In such cases the model must account for transportation costs not only between source i and (intermediate) sink $j > 1$ but also for the transportation of residues between $j > 1$ and the final destination $j = 1$.

Assuming, in fact, that exactly .25 of refuse burnt at the incinerators remains as residue, then the transportation cost term in [1.2.3] is augmented to read now as

$$\sum_{i=1}^{5} \sum_{j=1}^{6} c_{ij} x_{ij} + \sum_{j=2}^{6} \hat{c}_{j1} \hat{x}_{j1}$$

where $\hat{x}_{j1}$ (for $j > 1$) is the amount of residual waste carted to the MTS from each incinerator, and $\hat{c}_{j1}$ is the associated dollar cost per ton. But then the variable cost of operating the facilities also needs to be modified to account for the additional load placed on the MTS. We do this by redefining the δ_j as

$$\delta_j = \begin{cases} \displaystyle\sum_{i=1}^{5} x_{ij}, & \text{if } j = 2, \ldots, 6 \\[2ex] \displaystyle\sum_{i=1}^{5} x_{i1} + \sum_{l=2}^{6} \hat{x}_{l1}, & \text{if } j = 1 \text{ (MTS)} \end{cases}$$

Finally one needs a balance equation which says that the amount trans-shiped to the MTS from incinerator j is .25 of the amount going into that incinerator

$$\hat{x}_{j1} = .25 \sum_{i=1}^{5} x_{ij}, \qquad j = 2,\dots,6$$

Also

$$\delta_1 + \sum_{j=2}^{6} x_{j1} \leqq m_1$$

At this point it would be appropriate to ask whether such plant location models as discussed in this section are suitable in other contexts. Well, in the next section a variant is applied to power plant siting but when it comes to the location of emergency facilities (fire stations, hospitals, and the like) in an urban environment such models have notable shortcomings. We can list several objections. First, assume that travel time between i and j is c_{ij} and that q_i is the average daily number of incidents in district i which require service, while m_j is the capacity of the facility j in terms of available units to dispatch. Then the analogue of the waste collection problem is one in which the objective is to minimize total travel time and in which districts are the sources of alarms. But total travel time is not a measure which is necessarily consistent with the goal of responding to an incident (a fire or accident) as quickly as possible and a better objective might be to minimize the maximum travel time between incidents and responding units.

A second objection is that even if the cost function is modified to minimize a maximum (such problems are often referred to as of the "bottleneck" type), in actual urban emergency work there is considerable interdistrict cooperation and this is a significant feature which is not captured by the plant location model. In a later chapter, the concept of mutual aid will be elaborated on.

A third hesitation in using the existing model is that it does not account for the stochastic nature of demand. As we will see later, a doubling of average demand does not necessarily require a doubling of capacity to meet that demand, whenever calls arrive at random. However, our deterministically formulated model would match a doubling of total demand by a doubling of requiste capacity.

A fourth reservation about the model is that even if it accounts for response time, it ignores workload as well as other measures of performance. It is possible for one unit to work harder on the average than another, an inequity which labor leaders would not fail to recognize. Finally, one can object to using average travel times c_{ij} since actual times depend on a number of factors such as rush hour traffic congestion.

1.3 MORE ON OPTIMAL PLANT SITING

By a slight extension of the model given in Section 1.2, it is possible to describe the optimal location of nuclear power plants. Our treatment is based essentially on a recent analysis of power distribution in the Pacific Northwest in which 13 possible sites for a nuclear plant are considered as acceptable for environmental and other reasons. A paper which details this study is given in the references and here it suffices to sketch out the main features of the model itself. Once again however it is necessary to caution the reader that as in the incinerator problem, the location of public facilities is in general a political issue and the use of models can at best only illuminate the effectiveness of alternative configurations in terms of cost. It can happen that an optimal configuration is rejected because the "solution" ignores the fact that other, economically less satisfactory, options may nevertheless require the expenditure of less political credit for their implementation.

Costs here are to be assigned in two ways. The capital expenditures necessary for construction of generating plants and of transmission facilities are based on the ability to satisfy peak electric load (measured in megawatts, MW) whereas operating costs are associated with energy (in megawatt-hours, MWh) delivered annually by the plant. These operating costs are variable (pumping, cooling, water treatment, and maintenance) that depend linearly on the energy load. It is assumed that the market for electricity is concentrated in a small number of load centers (eight of them) analagous to the concentrated waste collection districts of the previous sections. Label these destinations by the index j and let d_j be the annual demand for peak (MW) with e_j the annual demand for energy (MWh). The amortized annual capital-construction costs, under an assumed interest rate, is given by f_i at site i and h_i is the operating cost in dollars per MWh. The annual transmission costs between plant location i and demand site j are c_{ij} (dollars per megawatt). If x_{ij} is the annual MWh of energy and y_{ij} the average MW of peak, delivered from i to j, then the total cost to be minimized is

$$\sum_{i=1}^{13} \sum_{j=1}^{8} c_{ij} y_{ij} + \sum_{i=1}^{13} (f_i y_i + h_i \delta_i)$$

where

$$\delta_i = \sum_{j=1}^{8} x_{ij}$$

and

$$y_i = \begin{cases} 1, & \text{if nuclear power plant at location } i \text{ is built} \\ 0, & \text{otherwise} \end{cases}$$

In order to consider the remaining constraints it is necessary to digress a bit.

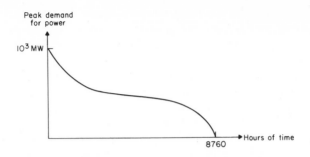

FIG. 1.6   Load duration curve of a typical generating plant.

Demand for electricity varies considerably because of daily, weekly, and seasonal factors for each customer. If one looks at the distribution of aggregate demand over a variety of customers, each with its own differing requirements of long or short duration, then the power output of a generating plant which is, let us say, rated to have a maximum peak output of 10^3 MW, would typically look like that shown in Fig. 1.6.

Power output is a measure of the rate at which energy is delivered to the aggregate demands. Thus energy is power integrated over time and so, for example, the area under the curve is total energy delivered in one year (there are 8760 hrs in a year). The above *load duration curve* is a profile of the number of hours during which the aggregate power demand *equals or exceeds* a given level. Notice that even though the plant is nominally rated as being able to deliver 10^3 MW, in actual fact it delivers something quite a bit less during most of a year. The ratio of the *average* annual power output to the peak output for which the plant is rated is called the *plant factor* (*PF*) and is the ratio of the area under the load duration curve to the area of the rectangle with sides of length 10^3 and 8760. In our study it is assumed that each plant has a *PF* of .9 and so a crude approximation to the load duration curve (a better approximation is used later in Section 1.5) is given by Fig. 1.7, where $.9 \cdot 10^3$ MW is to be interpreted as the *average* power output of a plant during the year. The plant factor is a measure of the utilization of a plant. On the

FIG. 1.7   Crude approximation to load duration curve of Fig. 1.6.

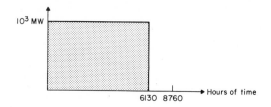

FIG. 1.8 Total energy delivered in a year (shaded area).

average, therefore, the plant has an idle capacity of $.1 \cdot 10^3$ MW which could be used to satisfy off-peak demands—that is to say, those demands that can be met during any time period in which the plant is not being fully utilized to satisfy the primary loads. This point will be taken up again in Section 1.5 with an example of an off-peak demand given there. Note that a plant is built to have a specified peak capacity in expectation of peak power demands of that magnitude and that is why capital costs are associated with peak. On the other hand, operating costs is a measure of the expense required to meet a power demand over time, which is energy.

A plant is also occasionally inoperative due to fuel replenishment and maintenance. In our case it is assumed that a plant is operating only 80% of the year. Therefore the total energy delivered in a year is $.9 \cdot 10^3 \cdot 8760$ MWh minus $(.2 \cdot 8760) \cdot 10^3$ which is $.7 \cdot 10^3 \cdot 8760 = 6130 \cdot 10^3$ MWh as shown in the shaded area of Fig. 1.8. Since d_j is the demand for peak at location j then the energy demand e_j is given by $6130 \cdot 10^3 d_j$ and one therefore has

$$\sum_{i=1}^{13} y_{ij} = d_j$$

$$\sum_{i=1}^{13} x_{ij} = e_j$$

[1.3.1]

Let m_i denote the nominal peak rating of plant i (we assume here that m_i is 10^3 MW throughout). Then, since $.9 m_i$ represents the (average) peak power output of plant i, it follows that total aggregate demand for power cannot exceed this value at each plant

$$\sum_{j=1}^{8} y_{ij} \leq .9 m_i y_i$$

[1.3.2]

Correspondingly, total energy demand cannot exceed $6130 m_i$ and so

$$\sum_{j=1}^{8} x_{ij} \leq 6130 m_i y_i$$

[1.3.3]

The capacity bound of $.9 m_i$ is in fact an upper bound on plant utilization assuming a plant factor which is a generous national average. While this

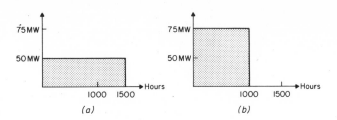

FIG. 1.9   Two ways of meeting the same energy demand.

utilization may in fact hold true for any of the proposed power plants, it could also happen that some plants would deliver lower average peak power loads and so the constraints [1.3.2] and [1.3.3] are inequalities rather than equalities. On the other hand, to exceed these upper bounds would suggest that a plant is capable of an average output with *PF* greater than .9, which is not consistent with our assumptions.

There are many ways of meeting an energy demand. For example, the energy in Figs. 1.9a and 1.9b is the same but that in Fig. 1.9b is at a higher power output and with a shorter total duration. The *load factor* (*LF*) is a measure of the fraction of total time that a load persists. In Fig. 1.9b the *LF* is clearly smaller than in Fig. 1.9a. In the present model the overall load factor for each plant is given by .7 as we can see from Fig. 1.8.

Incidently, one would want the total annual energy output of a plant to equal $.7(8760) \cdot 10^3$ times the total average power output of that plant. This will certainly hold true, for otherwise, one would have

$$\sum_i \sum_j x_{ij} \neq 6130 \cdot 10^3 \sum_i \sum_j y_{ij}$$

But this is not possible in view of Eqs. [1.3.1] and the fact that $e_j = 6130 \cdot 10^3 d_j$. Therefore a separate constraint to ensure this is not required.

As a final set of constraints note that if of two plants one of them has a higher variable cost than the other but a lower capital cost, then the tendency would be to optimize by having peak loads satisfied by the plant with lower capital cost and energy by the other one. In order to offset this possibility and to ensure that energy transmission occurs along the same lines that are used for peak loads, one imposes the restriction that

$$x_{ij} \leq .8(8760)\, y_{ij} = 7008 y_{ij}$$

which means that since the plant is in operation only .8 of the year, the total energy delivered cannot exceed the amount $7008 y_{ij}$. If the load at j is of shorter total duration than 7008 hrs, the x_{ij} would be less than this maximum, as

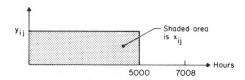

FIG. 1.10   Relation between the variables X_{ij} and Y_{ij}.

in Fig. 1.10. Also, in order to ensure that in an optimal solution there be no peak delivered when energy is zero, let

$$y_{ij} \leq x_{ij}$$

The last two inequality constraint sets ensure, in particular, that either x_{ij} or y_{ij} is zero whenever the other one is zero. Of course one must not forget the constraint

$$x_{ij} \geq 0$$

which automatically guarantees that $y_{ij} \geq 0$.

Thus we see that the nuclear power plant and solid waste disposal plant models are basically similar in character, consisting of sources and sinks with costs based on fixed charges due to capital investment, transportation (transmission) costs, and variable operating expenses. In the next section we see yet one more example of such problems and in one of the later lectures such problems will arise again not only in the context of facility location but also in terms of optimal districting for each plant.

As for energy, some of the model formulation utilized previously will be reintroduced in Section 1.5.

1.4   SEWAGE TREATMENT IS ALSO A PLANT LOCATION PROBLEM

The area of water quality management is another candidate for plant location analysis. A prototype situation, and one of many possible variants is this. A stream or river contains a number of points indexed by i at which effluents are discharged due to industrial activity or simply as sewage outfalls. These effluents contain bacterial activity which deplete the river of its oxygen (biochemical oxygen demand, or BOD). A standard measure of the health of a body of water is, in fact, its dissolved oxygen (DO) content and so BOD is ranked as a pollutant. Suppose that DO is recorded at several locations j along the river and that a_{ij} is a coefficient which measures the DO at j due to removal of x_j tons of BOD per day at site i. That is, a_{ij} indicates the improvement in water quality at j due to pollution abatement measures taken at i. There is at least one classical way of evaluating such "transfer" coefficients, known as the Streeter–Phelps Equation, and it utilizes the fact that stream aeration tends to re-oxygenate the water over time with the consequence that the downstream flow has a different DO content than at the source i. We will assume here that the a_{ij} are known, using this equation or some other means.

The x_i tons/day removed is a result of waste treatment plants located at i. Once again the cost of such treatment involves a fixed charge and a variable cost and so can be written as

$$f_i + h_i x_i$$

There is no zero–one decision variable since every outfall is assumed to be treated. If the minimum desired improvement at site j is b_j, then one requires that

$$\sum_i a_{ij} x_i \geqq b_j \qquad [1.4.1]$$

The b_j are determined from federal or local water quality standards and are measured in parts per million (ppm). The objective is to minimize the total cost of water treatment

$$\text{cost} = \sum_i (f_i + h_i x_i) \qquad [1.4.2]$$

by choosing x_i subject to [1.4.1] and the fact that

$$0 \leqq x_i \leqq u_i \qquad [1.4.3]$$

where u_i is the maximum amount of wastes (BOD) which can be removed at the source due to limitation in plant size and type of treatment. In this case then, the model is described by a linear program.

Several comments are in order. To begin with, the choice of cost as an objective function is not at all an obvious one and must be regarded as a proxy for the goal of improving water quality by a suitable mix of abatement alternatives. Second, the costs and the transfer coefficients are often nonlinear in character and the linear version given here may not be appropriate. Also note that implicit in the model is the assumption that the river has reached a steady state with regard to the mix of wastes. Waste loadings are taken to be uniform from day to day and we ignore any uncertainties of streamflow that would affect the value of a_{ij}. Finally since x_i is nonnegative, it means that it is not possible for a source to reduce its treatment level and so if water quality at i is high, new industry or sewage outfalls could be added, with no abatement, and without violating the DO standards. However, the present model does not account for this. Additionally, if the cost of treatment at i is high, then even if pollution there is high, the optimization procedures will tend to force other low cost facilities to abate even further.

One minor extension of the model is to allow u_i, the level of treatment at site i, to be a variable (much as incinerator capacity was a variable in our previous discussion). But then the charge depends on u_i. Assuming that the dependence is linear, the cost [1.4.2] may be modified accordingly. Because of [1.4.3], u_i is automatically nonnegative.

In the above model, cost and water quality can be viewed as conflicting objectives. Ideally one would like to minimize cost and, simultaneously, maximize each of the water quality measures on the left side of [1.4.1]. However, this would imply the use of a multidimensional objective function. For each set of x_i values, the objective would in this case no longer be a single number. But this precludes being able to obtain a uniquely defined optimum since the ordering of one quantity as greater than another is restricted to scalars. Mathematical convenience therefore dictates a preference for scalar-valued functions. In the present case, a choice was made to consider cost, although one could equally have decided to maximize aggregate water quality subject to a restriction on cost.

In environmental problems of this kind, as indeed in many of the models encountered in this book, one is frequently faced with multiple and conflicting objectives in which several social goals are traded off against each other. For example, in managing water resources, national interests may not coincide with regional needs, or to cite a case to be discussed in a later chapter, equity of coverage in urban fire protection is not necessarily the same goal as efficiency of coverage in terms of response time to alarms. If one wishes to be able to handle problems with multidimensional objectives, then the notion of an optimum solution is to be replaced by some other concept.

To be precise, consider the particular instance of two objectives given by $z_1(x)$, $z_2(x)$ where $x = (x_1, \ldots, x_l)$ denotes all vectors which lie in some feasible set S, defined by specifying a number of linear constraints imposed by the needs of the problem (it is not necessary here to identify S further). Suppose now that one wishes to maximize z_1 and z_2 simultaneously over S

$$\text{maximize}\quad [z_1(x), z_2(x)] \qquad\qquad [1.4.4]$$

As we know, [1.4.4] *is not meaningful in itself* and so we replace it by defining a *feasible solution* x' to be *inferior to some other feasible* x^0 whenever

$$z_1(x^0) \geqq z_1(x')$$
$$z_2(x^0) \geqq z_2(x') \qquad\qquad [1.4.5]$$

with at least one of the two inequalities in [1.4.5] being strict. *Noninferiority* of x' therefore means that there is no other x^0 for which [1.4.5] is true and a *surrogate for* [1.4.4] *is then that of finding the set of noninferior points in S.* This notion also occurs in welfare economics as that of *Pareto optimality* which is a social state in which no one can be made better off without making someone else worse off. A little thought will convince the reader that the noninferior set must constitute a portion of the boundary of S since every interior point is necessarily inferior.

There is a way of generating noninferior points which happens to coincide in practice with the usual procedure of choosing a single scalar-valued objective, relegating the other objective to playing the role of a constraint. In fact, the solution of the problem to maximize $z_1(x)$ subject to $z_2(x) \geqq \gamma$ for some constant γ, must be noninferior. Suppose, on the contrary, that x^0 provides the maximum and that there exists some other x' for which $z_1(x') > z_1(x^0)$ and $z_2(x') \geqq z_2(x^0)$. Then x' also satisfies $z_2(x) \geqq \gamma$ and yields an even higher maximum of z_1, which is not possible. Thus, if one varies γ upward over a range in which feasible solutions exist, the corresponding optima constitute the noninferior set. This will be illustrated in one of the exercises at the end of the chapter.

In most instances, as we noted above, one chooses a single value for γ and the resulting solution can be considered as a proxy for the entire set. Note, incidentally, that one can also maximize z_2 subject to $z_1 \geqq \gamma$. By way of illustration let us reconsider the sewage treatment problem. If, for simplicity, there were only one constraint of the type [1.4.1], namely $z_2(x) = \sum a_i x_i \geqq b$, then b is what we labeled as γ above, with x being the vector having components x_i. Letting $z_1(x)$ equal the cost given by [1.4.2], we see that the model posed earlier is equivalent, when b is allowed to vary, to finding the set of noninferior x relative to the simultaneous goals of minimizing z_1 and of maximizing z_2 (or, if one prefers, of maximizing both z_2 and the negative of z_1). In this example it is clear that the range of values that b can take is from zero to $\sum a_i u_i$ (why?).

In Chapter 4, noninferiority will be reintroduced in the context of optimal dispatching of emergency vehicles.

1.5   ENERGY MODELS

In this section we wish to take a look at a problem of *optimal distribution in contrast to the optimal plant location* problems considered earlier. What is to be considered here is energy distribution and our treatment is a simplified version of some models that have been explored at Brookhaven Labs (see references for details). As will be seen, the modeling is again in terms of linear programming and so it offers another illustration of the versatility of this mathematical tool.

Energy demand on a regional basis is considered, for simplicity, to consist of only the following (aggregated) categories: space heating, air conditioning, process heat (for industrial manufacture), private transportation, and miscellaneous electric uses. A fixed time period of one year has been chosen for the analysis and within that period the demands are assumed known and independent of energy price or supply. The extent to which elasticity of demand is accounted for, implicitly by the model, is commented on later. Notice that these demand categories are not necessarily the best characterizations of the way a region uses energy and an alternative way would be to treat demand in terms of acres of residential, commercial, and industrial development.

Energy supply is limited in our model to the primary fuels of oil and coal and to electricity. Each supply can serve several demand sectors and each demand can be serviced by a few supply sectors, as illustrated in Fig. 1.11. The electrical supply sector is disaggregated into three types. There are oil- and coal-fired electric generating plants and oil-fired turbines. The latter represents a low efficiency way of meeting peak electric demands without major capital investments, whereas the first two are relatively more efficient but require substantial plant construction. Efficiency, incidently, is a measure of the energy loss in the process of converting fossil fuels to electricity. In the present version of the model, nuclear plants are excluded as are gas, geothermal, solar, and other possible sources.

The miscellaneous electric demand section can also be disaggregated according as to whether it is a peak load or base load (see Section 1.3 for the appropriate jargon).

A base load is an electrical demand which is operative throughout the region during all of the $.8(8760) = 7008$ hrs of the year that a plant is not shut down due to maintenance, whereas a peak load is determined by occasional, intermitent, and usually short term uses. In Section 1.3 we gave an example of a typical load duration curve and a simple straight line approximation to it was given there. Here we continue to use a simple but more accurate representative of that curve as shown in Fig. 1.12. As before, these approximations reflect average loads and are uniformly distributed throughout the period in which they are operative. As one can see, about 50% of the load is sustained continuously and it is this part we call base. The remaining part is comprised of a peak load which lasts about 10% of the time and an intermediate peaking load which lasts 50% of the time. The load factor (see

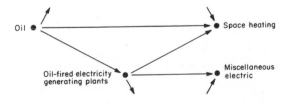

FIG. 1.11 Segment of the energy supply–demand network.

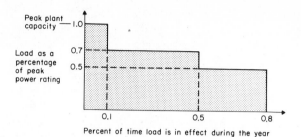

FIG. 1.12   An approximation to the load duration curve of Fig. 1.6.

Section 1.3) of the base is .8, that of intermediate is .5 and the peak has a $LF = .1$. Base and intermediate are primarily (but not exclusively) serviced by oil- or coal-fired steam electric plants, each of which represent a high capital investment, while peak is typically (but not exclusively) handled by gas turbines or diesels which require stripped down and otherwise marginal plant facilities.

Incidently, the plants with load curves shown in Fig. 1.13 would require the same capital cost (power) but operating cost (energy) in the second plant is twice that of the first plant.

In addition to these supply and demand categories there is one called pumped storage in which water is pumped uphill during hours in which the plants are idle and then released again to drive the electric generating equipment during peak load periods. Thus pumped storage is a supply category when it moves downhill and is a demand when water moves uphill. Pumped storage is an example of an off-peak demand. Notice that the source–sink energy network sketched above is a transshipment model in which certain categories (pumped storage and miscellaneous electric) are intermediate sources. However, as is typical in such models, one can reformulate it as a transportation network without transshipment points by simply treating each such point in two ways, once as a source and again as a sink. Details of how this is done were demonstrated in Section 1.2 and we will do this once more below.

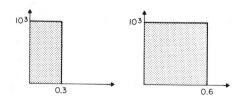

FIG. 1.13   Load curves with the same power but different energy output.

TABLE 1.6

ENERGY SUPPLY–DEMAND NETWORK

	Space heating	Air conditioning	Base loads LF = .8	Intermediate loads LF = .5	Peak loads LF = .1	Process heat	Private trans-portation	Pumped storage	Index i
Primary fuels									
Oil									1
Coal									2
Central electric									
Oil–steam (electric plants)									3
Coal–steam (electric plants)									4
Oil-fired turbines									5
Pumped storage									6
Index j	1	2	3	4	5	6	7	8	

The supply–demand network for our problem is given in the Table 1.6. The blocked out entries are inadmissable linkages between a particular source i and sink j.

Let $x_{ij} \geq 0$ be the amount of energy delivered annually between i and j measured in Btu (1 Btu equals 3413 kWh) and define it as zero if an i, j link is blocked. Supplies in each category are limited annually (either by the cost of extraction, or by refinery capacity, or by the generating capacity of the electric plants) and so we have supply constraints of the form

$$\sum_{j=1}^{8} \frac{1}{e_{ij}} x_{ij} \leq S_i, \qquad i = 1, \ldots, 6 \qquad [1.5.1]$$

where e_{ij} is the conversion efficiency in going from a primary fuel to an intermediate form, and S_i is the maximum amount of supply type i available in one year (measured in 10^{15} Btu, on a national scale).

Thus, for example, in converting oil or coal to electricity in steam generating plants, the value of e_{ij} is .31 since roughly 70% of the energy in the raw fuel is dissipated in the process. Thus $e_{ij}^{-1} = 3.2$ in this case, which means that each Btu of intermediate electric demand requires 3.2 Btu of the primary fuel supply.

The value of e_{ij}^{-1} is 5.0 in converting oil or coal to electricity by means of the less efficient gas turbines. Refinery losses give an efficiency of .9 for oil. However what would normally be a conversion coefficient of $e_{ij}^{-1} = 1.1$ in this case is simply factored through the first, third, and fifth constraints of [1.5.1] (each involving oil) and absorbed in the corresponding supplies S_i $(i = 1, 3, 5)$. That is, actual oil supply is diminished by dividing it with 1.1. The energy loss in pumped storage is such that of the energy used to pump water uphill is available for peak use, and the corresponding e_{ij}^{-1} is taken to be 1.4. Thus the inequalities [1.5.1] can be explicitly written as

Oil: $\qquad\qquad \sum x_{1j} + 3.2 \sum x_{3j} + 5.0 \sum x_{5j} \leq S_1$

Coal: $\qquad\qquad \sum x_{2j} + 3.2 \sum_{4j} \qquad\qquad \leq S_2$

Oil–electric: $\qquad\qquad 3.2 \sum x_{3j} \qquad\qquad \leq S_3$

Coal–electric: $\qquad\qquad 3.2 \sum x_{4j} \qquad\qquad \leq S_4 \qquad [1.5.2]$

Oil turbine: $\qquad\qquad\qquad 5.0 \sum x_{5j} \leq S_5$

Pumped storage: $\qquad 1.4 \sum x_{6j} \qquad\qquad \leq S_6$

Notice that in the first equation of [1.5.2] the total oil required is the oil used as raw fuel directly together with the oil which needs to be converted into intermediate energy forms with an accounting for the loss in efficiency. Similarly for the second constraint. We see from [1.5.2] that the electrical sector is treated as a demand as far as the primary fuels are concerned. The third constraint says that $S_3/3.2$ is the maximum amount of electrical energy that can be generated annually from oil-fired power plants in order to satisfy all demand categories (except for $j = 7$) and similarly for the fourth and fifth constraints.

Associated with each possible link between i and j is the total cost c_{ij} in dollars per 10^6 Btu associated with extraction, refining, conversion, and transportation, as well as for final conversion prior to utilization. These include capital recovery and operating costs. In our model the objective is to minimize the overall cost of meeting an exogenously determined demand for energy

$$\text{Cost} = \sum_{i=1}^{6} \sum_{j=1}^{8} c_{ij} x_{ij} \qquad [1.5.3]$$

where x_{ij} can be thought of as a particular energy path or trajectory between the collection of sources and the set of sinks.

Let D_j denote the demand categories, $j = 1, ..., 8$. Since there are conversion efficiencies in transforming energy at the users' end (for example, in converting oil into mechanical energy in private transportation, or in obtaining thermal energy in home burners from electric sources), one writes

$$D_j = \sum_{i=1}^{6} d_{ij} x_{ij}$$

where D_j are measured in 10^5 Btu. Now oil converts into space heat at an efficiency of .7, given a typical home with *average insulation*. However, electrically heated homes generally have better than average insulation and so *relative to other homes* the conversion efficiency of electricity to heat is found to be roughly 1.4. It is greater than one only in this relative sense and among homes of equal insulation it would only have an efficiency of something less than (but close to) one. The value of 1.4 also reflects the fact that electric heaters are more efficient than oil burners. In the case of air conditioning the efficiency is 3.0, also greater than one. This is because the removal of 3 Btu of warm air from inside a room to the outside only requires about 1 Btu of electrical energy. The air conditioning is simply a device for moving warm air out of a room and is not an energy converter. As for private transportation, 1 Btu of energy delivered to the wheel drive requires about 5 Btu of oil energy and so the conversion efficiency here is .2. Coal conversion as a fuel is about similar to oil, with a coefficient of .65. Leaving aside for the moment the electrical demand sector, our demand constraints read as

Space heating: $\qquad .7x_{11} + 1.4 \sum_{i=3}^{5} x_{i1} = D_1$

Air conditioning: $\qquad 3.0 \sum_{i=3}^{5} x_{i2} = D_2 \qquad [1.5.4]$

Process heating: $\qquad .7x_{16} + .65x_{26} + \sum_{i=3}^{5} x_{i6} = D_6$

Private transportation: $\quad .2x_{17} \qquad\qquad\qquad = D_7$

As for miscellaneous electric uses, *the model defines peak load* ($LF = .1$) *endogeneously* by saying that it is constituted as some fraction of other demands. Specifically, the model stipulates that .05 of base load and .1 of intermediate load and .2 of air conditioning is what in fact the peak load is made up of. Therefore one has this defining constraint

$$\sum_{i=3}^{5} x_{i5} = .05 \sum_{i=3}^{5} x_{i3} + .1 \sum_{i=3}^{5} x_{i4} + .2 \sum_{i=3}^{5} x_{i2} \qquad [1.5.5]$$

Thus, $D_5 = x_{35} + x_{45} + x_{55}$ is not specified exogenously, but is determined internally to the model once the other demands are chosen. Since part of the energy required by D_3 and D_4 is reassigned to peak needs, the demand constraints for these miscellaneous electric uses are written as

$$(1 + .05) \sum_{i=3}^{5} x_{i3} = D_3$$

$$[1.5.6]$$

$$(1 + .1) \sum_{i=3}^{5} x_{i4} = D_4$$

We mentioned earlier that oil-fired turbines are an economical way of meeting short term peak demands since they require little in the way of capital expenditure. Pumped storage is another device for meeting peak loads. In order to ensure that the optimal solution conforms to the usual practice of employing these conversion devices largely (but not exclusively) for peak loads, we impose a constraint that requires the turbines and storage facilities to be used first to satisfy such loads before other conversion plants be drawn upon

$$x_{35} + x_{45} \leqq x_{55} + x_{65} \qquad [1.5.7]$$

Pumped storage is an off-peak demand in that energy is delivered to it only when other requirements for electricity have been met. Therefore the amount of energy which is available to satisfy pumped storage needs can never exceed the energy available through idle plant capacity. That is, if one examines the load duration curve again as displayed in Fig. 1.14, it will be seen that only

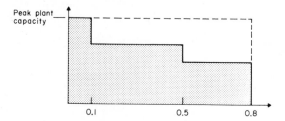

FIG. 1.14   Idle plant capacity (unshaded area).

the unshaded area can be used for off-peak uses since this area represents the total energy which the power plants could deliver but which, because of varying loads, remains un-utilized (if the *PF* were 1.0 then there would be no idle plant capacity throughout the year, but that is not the case here).

Consider, for example, the load duration curve for the third supply: oil–steam electric plants. Since power is the rate of energy use per unit time, the maximum combined plant capacity over all such plants is $C_3 = (S_3/3.2 \div 7008)$ in units of 10^{15} Btu/hr and we can compute unused energy as shown in Fig. 1.15. Thus, the annual energy, x_{38} sent to pumped storage must satisfy

$$x_{38} \leq 7x_{35} + .6x_{34} \qquad [1.5.8]$$

Similarly, for other central electric conversion plants one has

$$x_{48} \leq 7x_{45} + .6x_{44}$$
$$[1.5.9]$$
$$x_{58} \leq 7x_{55} + .6x_{54}$$

Since conversion of electricity to pumped storage has an efficiency of 1.4, one also requires the following self-evident balance equation, which relates the dual roles of storage as both a supply and a demand

$$1.4 \sum_{j=4}^{6} x_{6j} = \sum_{i=3}^{5} x_{i8} \qquad [1.5.10]$$

Finally let us deal with environmental restrictions. Each Btu of different energy forms results in a variety of noxious emissions and other pollutants, such as particulate matter, thermal energy (from nuclear reactors), radioactive wastes, hydrocarbons, carbon monoxide, and nitrous oxide. Here we consider only two such wastes from just a few sources. They are

Carbon dioxide (CO_2) from coal-fired plants, measured in 10^{11} lb/10^{15} Btu:

$$5.4 \sum_{j \neq 7} x_{4j} \leq E_1 \qquad [1.5.11]$$

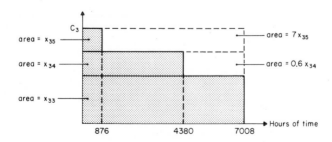

FIG. 1.15 Idle plant capacity: detailed breakdown of Fig. 1.14.

Sulfur dioxide (SO_2) from oil-fired plants and oil fuel, measured in 10^9 lb/10^5 Btu:

$$.37\left(\sum_{j \neq 7} x_{3j} + \sum_{j \neq 7} x_{5j}\right) \leq E_2 \qquad [1.5.12]$$

where E_1, E_2 are maximum levels of the emissions that one wishes to tolerate on a *regional* level.

The energy distribution model can easily be extended to include a greater variety of energy sources and demands but the version given here captures at least some of the main features of the existing system, especially in the description of the electrical supply sector based, as it is, on the use of different load factors. One could perhaps quarrel with the use of cost as an objective function but cost does at least reflect, to some degree, market conditions which prevail in a competitive economy. In fact cost may be taken as a surrogate for price (if one assumes a constant mark-up or value added) and so a small change in supplies can, through the use of dual variables (see Appendix A), indicate the marginal increase or decrease in price due to that change.

Under actual market conditions the relationship between supply, demand, and price is typically that as shown in Fig. 1.16.

This kind of interaction is not reflected directly in the model since demand is exogenously determined independent of cost. However, as fuels become scarcer (supply decreases), eventually a point is reached in the model at which demand switches to alternate supplies. This happens whenever a particular supply bound is met, which means that additional demands for that fuel must be satisfied by other sources at a higher price (cost). Also, since the essence of the model is to find that mix of primary and processed fuels which meets a given demand profile at least cost, the best (i.e., in terms of price) interfuel substitutions would occur to meet that demand. Therefore the model accounts for cross elasticities of demand.

It would also be possible to account for the increased cost of extraction and importation of scarce fuels by having a given source appear several times at different costs. For example, if oil is thought of as domestic (known reserves), domestic (future reserves and shale), and imported, then each would

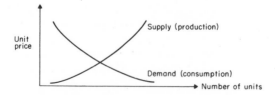

FIG. 1.16   Relation of supply to demand.

be available at a different cost and with its own supply constraint. The optimization procedure would then satisfy all oil needs at the lowest cost until supply at that cost is depleted, at which point more expensive fuel would become available. In this way, supply as a function of price would be modeled. A satisfactory context for this procedure will be described after we make a few more comments. The only link that appears to be missing is how total demand itself is dependent on price. The model now says that as a particular source becomes scarce and expensive, an alternate source is utilized. When all sources become scarce and expensive, then demand itself is expected to decrease (demand elasticity). This feedback linkage has not been modeled. Whereas in actuality a scarce commodity could increase in price, thereby suggesting that either other fuels be substituted or demand decreased, in our model a scarce resource (when a supply bound is met) effectively causes an infinite price increase and so fuel substitution is mandatory. When all fuels become scarce, then total price is infinite and demand can no longer be met. In this case either a lower demand is called for or the solution is infeasible.

To summarize, the model yields the least cost (capital recovery and operation) match of energy demands in any particular target year accounting for conversion, transmission, and utilization efficiencies, environmental constraints on emissions, with the possibility of substitutions between fuels, and it describes the technical aspects of how the electrical supply sector responds to varying load throughout the year. A slight extension of the model would allow one to assess the impact of introducing new supply and conversion technologies (such as the breeder reactor, solar energy, or coal gasification) and, as such, could be considered a useful tool for national or even regional energy policy.

What we want to discuss next is a refinement of this model which reveals the *optimum investment* in energy production over time. As such, the model begins to capture some of the particulars of how to design an energy policy which responds to changing needs in a dynamic way without being tied to a particular target year.

To begin with, then, assume one is dealing with a 5-yr planning horizon (any number of years will do) and that investments in new electric conversion plants occur on a year-by-year basis. In order to properly account for costs it is necessary, as in Section 1.3, to separate capital investments, to meet peak demands, from operating expenses.

Let $x_{ij}(t)$ be the amount of energy (Btu) delivered from source i to sink j in year t $(t = 1, ..., 5)$. As energy sources we consider only domestic and imported oil (the latter at a higher cost) and two types of oil conversion plants, as shown in the Table 1.7. Demands are similarly restricted. We also introduce variables $Y_l(t)$ as the electrical plant capacity to be built in year t, measured in 10^9 Btu/yr (which is equivalent to some fraction of a MW power

TABLE 1.7

ENERGY SUPPLY–DEMAND NETWORK IN A TIME-DEPENDENT MODEL

	Space heating	Air conditioning	Miscellaneous electric LF = .8	LF = .5	LF = .1	Index i	Index l	Index k
Oil (domestic)	1					1		1
Oil (imported)		2				2		2
Oil–steam (electric plants)						3	1	
Oil (turbine plants)						4	2	
Index j	1	2	3	4	5			

rating), with $l = 1, 2$. Also $Z_k(t)$ denotes the amount of primary fuel (oil, in our case) to be extracted and refined in year t, $k = 1, 2$. As before some linkages are blocked, as shown in Table 1.7. The objective to minimize is the total cost given by

$$\sum_{i=1}^{4} \sum_{j=1}^{5} \sum_{t=1}^{5} c_{ij}(t) x_{ij}(t) \Big/ (1+\rho)^t + \sum_{l=1}^{2} \sum_{t=1}^{5} \bar{c}_l(t) Y_l(t) \Big/ (1+\rho)^t$$

$$+ \sum_{k=1}^{2} \sum_{t=1}^{5} \hat{c}_k(t) Z_k(t) \Big/ (1+\rho)^t \qquad [1.5.13]$$

where c_{ij} is the annual energy cost in dollars per 10^6 Btu, as determined by operational expenditures, $\bar{c}_l$ are capital construction costs in dollars per 10^9 Btu/yr, $\hat{c}_k$ is the expense of extraction and refining (dollars per 10^6 Btu), and ρ is an interest rate. The factor $1/(1+\rho)^t$ represents the value of an expenditure in year t at the beginning of the first year given the intervening opportunity for alternate uses of the capital funds (see notes to this chapter for a discussion of discounting).

There are two types of constraints in the model—interperiod and intraperiod. The first refers to activities across several time periods and the second relates to activities within a single year.

Interperiod Constraints

Consider the first year in which there already exists an inventory of conversion plants (capacity already installed) whose total power rating is given by $S_l(1)$, with $l = 1, 2$. Since $Y_l(1)$ is the new generating capacity installed in that year, then one set of supply constraints is

$$\frac{x_{31}(1) + x_{34}(1)}{.5} + \frac{x_{33}(1)}{.8} + \frac{x_{35}(1)}{.1} \leqq Y_1(1) + S_1(1) \qquad [1.5.14]$$

for oil–steam generating plants, and

$$\frac{x_{41}(1) + x_{34}(1)}{.5} + \frac{x_{43}(1)}{.8} + \frac{x_{45}(1)}{.1} \leqq Y_2(1) + S_2(1) \qquad [1.5.15]$$

for oil turbines.

For later time periods $t > 1$ one correspondingly has

$$\frac{x_{31}(t) + x_{34}(t)}{.5} + \frac{x_{33}(t)}{.8} + \frac{x_{35}(t)}{.1} \leqq S_1(t) + \sum_{u=1}^{t} Y_1(u) \qquad [1.5.16]$$

$$\frac{x_{41}(t) + x_{44}(t)}{.5} + \frac{x_{43}(t)}{.8} + \frac{x_{45}(t)}{.1} \leqq S_2(t) + \sum_{u=1}^{t} Y_2(u)$$

These relations come about from the following argument. If a particular plant delivers, let us say, 10^6 Btu during the year at a load factor of .5, then this represents a power output of $10^6/.5 = 2 \cdot 10^6$ Btu/yr (or some equivalent units of megawatts) assuming, as before, that the load is uniformly distributed during the period in which it is active (i.e., we work with average load). It makes a difference in power requirements—that is, in power plant rating— whether a given amount of energy is delivered at a load factor of .8 or .5 or .1. For example 10^3 Btu at $LF = .8$ and .5 looks like that shown in Fig. 1.17. As we see from these illustrations, needed plant capacity is $2 \cdot 10^3$ Btu/yr in one case and only $1.25 \cdot 10^3$ Btu/yr in the other (note, incidently, that 10^9 Btu/yr is approximately $\frac{1}{3}$ of a megawatt, so a plant of 10^3 MW rating has an output of about $3 \cdot 10^{12}$ Btu/yr). Space heat load is assumed to have a 6-month duration ($LF = .5$). Air conditioning, since it has virtually no temporal overlap with space heating, is safely ignored. Indeed, since a plant's capacity is designed for the greatest peak load throughout the year, one needs to consider only those loads during the whole year which have the

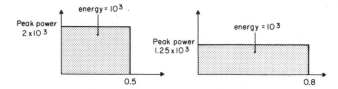

FIG. 1.17   Power output at different load factors.

greatest peak demand (in our case, this is assumed to be heating). For instance, if the demand for heating is 10^5 MW from mid-October to mid-April and 10 MW thereafter, whereas air conditioning is 10^4 MW from June through September (and none thereafter), then it suffices to install a plant whose peak rating is 10^5 MW in order to satisfy both space conditioning requirements throughout the year. Incidentally, if an off-peak demand had also occurred in our model, it would be ignored in [1.5.16] since no new plant capacity is needed to meet such demands, as we saw earlier in this section.

Since the above constraints represent actual power requirements, no conversion efficiency factor is needed. That is to say, we are not here accounting for the conversion of oil to electricity as in our previous analysis. It should be mentioned that whereas $\bar{c}_l(t)$ represent new capital outlays or investment for generating equipment and facilities in the tth year (and this includes transmission line costs, as in Section 1.3), the capital expense of the already emplaced (inherited) plants is taken to be part of the operational expenses $c_{ij}(t)$, as in the previously worked out static model of this section.

Supply constraints, like costs, take several forms. In addition to peak power supply, as previously discussed, one must consider electrical energy supply

$$\sum_{j=1}^{5} x_{3j} \leqq \sigma \left[S_1(t) + \sum_{u=1}^{t} Y_1(u) \right]$$

$$\sum_{j=1}^{5} x_{4j} \leqq \sigma \left[S_2(t) + \sum_{u=1}^{t} Y_2(u) \right]$$

[1.5.17]

These constraints state that total energy from each plant type ($l = 1, 2$) cannot exceed available plant capacity in 10^9 Btu/yr multiplied by the average fraction of a year, which we call σ, during which the plant is actually in operation (that is, not shut down for maintenance). As before, this percentage of non-downtime is taken to be .8. The product of σ with power capacity is total available electrical energy of type l in year t. An example is illustrated in Fig. 1.18.

Since newly installed plant capacity is not expected to change radically from year to year, one imposes the constraint that total capacity (new plus inherited) in year t does not exceed total available capacity in year $t-1$, times a growth factor α. If $\alpha > 1$, then this represents expansion whereas $\alpha \leqq 1$ denotes retrenchment (because of plant obsolescence—an item to be discussed later—together with lack of investment)

$$S_l(t) + \sum_{u=1}^{t} Y_l(u) \leqq \alpha(t) \left[S_l(t-1) + \sum_{u=1}^{t-1} Y_l(u) \right] \qquad \text{for} \quad t > 1$$

[1.5.18]

$$S_l(1) + Y_l(1) \leqq \overline{Y}_l$$

($\overline{Y}_l$ forces an upper bound on any initial investment in plant construction).

Now consider raw fuel supply. Total oil which can be extracted ($k = 1$) or imported ($k = 2$) is designated as R_k and so

$$Z_k(t) \leqq R_k$$

[1.5.19]

One can also bound [1.5.19] below by some factor r_k in order to ensure that there be minimal oil consumption commensurate with nondiscretionary demands, but we will not include this here. If $\beta_k(t)$ is a factor which represents the growth in extraction and refining operations, then

$$Z_k(t) \leqq \beta_k(t) Z_k(t-1)$$

[1.5.20]

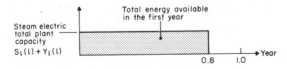

FIG. 1.18 Relation of power to energy in time-dependent models.

When $\beta_k > 1$, it means that more can be extracted in the tth year than in the previous one, whereas $\beta_k \leq 1$ means that the resource of type k is being phased out. For a scarce resource it could happen that β_k increases for a few years and then eventually decreases in later years or either that resource is depleted or as the need for it is replaced by alternate fuel technologies (such as breeder reactor). Deliberate import quotas to lessen dependence on foreign oil is another reason why β_k could decrease.

Intraperiod Constraints

Let $D_j(t)$ be exogenously determined energy demands in year t in 10^{15} Btu. Then, accounting for conversion efficiencies, one has in similar fashion to before

Space heating: $.7[x_{11}(t)+x_{21}(t)] + 1.4[x_{31}(t)+x_{41}(t)] = D_1(t)$

Air conditioning: $3.0[x_{32}(t)+x_{42}(t)] \qquad\qquad\qquad = D_2(t)$

Miscellaneous electric $(LF = .8)$ $(1+.05)[x_{33}(t)+x_{43}(t)] \qquad\qquad = D_3(t)$

Miscellaneous electric: $(LF = .5)$ $(1+.1)[x_{34}(t)+x_{44}(t)] \qquad\qquad = D_4(t)$

Peak demand: $(LF = .1)$ $\begin{aligned} x_{35}(t) + x_{45}(t) &= 0.5[x_{33}(t)+x_{43}(t)] \\ &\quad + .1[x_{34}(t)+x_{44}(t)] \\ &\quad + .2[x_{32}(t)+x_{42}(t)] \end{aligned}$

The time dependence of demands reflects estimated changing needs in the future as projected from present trends. For example, if one detects a decrease in electrically heated homes, this would be described by introducing a new constraint which states that electric space heating is limited to some maximum amount $D_1'(t)$ which is diminished in value over time. Since conversion efficiency in this case is 1.4, the constraint can be written as

$$1.4[x_{31}(t)+x_{41}(t)] \leq D_1'(t)$$

We have already expressed a constraint on total fuel supply over the whole five years. On a year by year basis, one describes fuel resources in terms of conversion efficiencies

Domestic oil: $x_{11}(t) + 3.2 \sum_{j=1}^{5} x_{3j}(t) + 5.0 \sum_{j=1}^{5} x_{4j}(t) = Z_1(t)$

[1.5.21]

Imported oil: $x_{21}(t) + 3.2 \sum_{j=1}^{5} x_{3j}(t) + 5.0 \sum_{j=1}^{5} x_{4j}(t) = Z_2(t)$

Among the other intraperiod restrictions is, as before, that oil turbines should be used to deliver peak loads prior to other generating equipment

$$x_{35}(t) \leqq x_{45}(t)$$

(or one can simply block the cell involving x_{35} so that steam plants can never service peak loads).

Finally there is an environmental constraint on sulfur dioxide emissions

$$.37\left[\sum_{j=1}^{5} x_{3j}(t) + \sum_{j=1}^{5} x_{4j}(t)\right] \leqq E$$

where E is in 10^{11} lb/10^{15} as an annual measure.

There is one hidden flaw with the model as presented here which is that investment decisions on capital equipment undertaken in year t do not immediately result in the availability of such plants. There is an average lag time of 2.5 yrs before construction is complete and the new facility is operational. Also significant changes in supply levels or demand patterns may not occur on a year-by-year basis, but would be noticeable over a more extended time period. Therefore let us revise the model to think of each t as representing a 5-yr period so that the entire planning horizon of five units is actually 25 yrs. Assume that investment decisions for plant construction are made at the beginning of each 5-yr time slot, while other expenditures are computed at the midpoint of each period and then discounted back to the middle of the first five years. Thus [1.5.13] needs to be modified by replacing the factor $(1+\rho)^t$ by $(1+\rho)^{5t}$ for the first and third terms and by $(1+\rho)^{5t-2.5}$ in the second one. Since interest is usually accrued on an annual basis, these changes reflect discounted costs on expenditures taken every five years except in the case of capital investment which, as we noted, has a lead time of 2.5 yrs. The cost terms in [1.5.13] are dollars per 10^6 Btu in time period t (for c_{ij} and $\hat{c}_k$) and dollars per 10^9 Btu/yr of capacity built in period t (for $\bar{c}_l$). The x and Z variables represent energy flows, and Y the Btu/yr to be built— within a designated 5-yr period.

Constraints [1.5.17] remain unchanged with this new interpretation, but [1.5.16] should be restated by dividing the left-hand side of the inequalities with a five. The reason is that since the $x_{ij}(t)$ now refer to energy throughout a 5-yr span, the terms obtained by dividing these x_{ij} values by appropriate load factors exaggerate the need for plant capacity by a factor of five. This becomes clear when we recall that plant capacity measures peak power output as determined from an annual load duration curve. Thus, a 10^9 Btu/yr generating station delivers $.5 \cdot 10^9$ Btu to an annual demand of $LF = .5$ when taken over one year and it provides $2.5 \cdot 10^9$ Btu to the same demand when taken over a 5-yr span. Conversely, a $2.5 \cdot 10^9$ Btu demand at $LF = .5$ during a 5-yr period converts to $(2.5 \cdot 10^9)/.5 \cdot \frac{1}{5} = 10^9$ Btu/yr power requirement.

Alternatively, one can say that a 5-yr demand of $2.5 \cdot 10^9$ Btu operates at a total 5-year load factor of 2.5, which results in power demand of $(2.5 \cdot 10^9)/2.5 = 10^9$.

Similarly, [1.5.17] should be modified by dividing through the left side by five, for the same reason as above. All other constraints remain as before except for the new meaning of t.

One by-product of the modified model is that it now makes sense to allow for the deterioration and eventual obsolescence of capital equipment. If, for example, the effective lifetime of a plant is 20 yrs, then the sums $\sum_{u=1}^{t}$ in constraints [1.5.16]–[1.5.18] are to be replaced by $\sum_{u=t-4}^{t}$.

The model can be further extended to account for investments in other aspects of energy production such as refineries. Oil which is available for conversion to other forms would then be constrained by the availability of existing plus new refinery installations, similar to what was done for the electrical sector in the above model. We leave this to the reader to work out.

If the optimal solution were to saturate the supply of domestic oil by, let us say, the third time period, then this would suggest that new deposits be explored. Since this would probably mean development of less assessible and more costly oil sources, it would also indicate that perhaps other techno-logical alternatives should be investigated. On the other hand, the optimal solution could well indicate using imported oil at higher prices in the first four years in order to conserve domestic supplies for later use. The possibility of switching from one fuel type to another in successive time periods and of changing the interfuel mix to meet changing demands and changing price levels (or increasing scarcity) is the primary attraction of this kind of modeling. As such, it can be used to evaluate policy alternatives on energy production by varying such parameters as β_k, R_k, and α.

1.6 EXERCISES

1.6.1 Transfer Table 1.1 (Travel time per truck load) into Table 1.2 (Costs, in dollars per ton).

1.6.2 Referring to the problem given in Section 1.1, of minimizing trans-portation cost when a 300-ton incinerator is placed in district 4 and a 150-ton incinerator in district 5, (Equations [1.12]–[1.14]), solve it using the North-west Corner rule by the method introduced in Appendix A.

1.6.3 As another example of linear optimization, consider a very special case of a study performed in Los Angeles in which pupils in a ghetto area are to be transported to schools in more affluent areas where there are idle classrooms. The cost to be minimized is total bus time between schools.

Suppose bus travel time, in minutes, between schools A and B in the first area to schools C, D, and E in the second area are those given in the accompanying tabulation. Suppose also that A, B have, respectively, two and three classes of ghetto children to transport, and that schools, C, D, E can each receive at most two classes. Formulate this problem as a linear program and solve it using a hand calculation, along the lines suggested in Appendix A.

	C	D	E
A	11	7	8
B	7	15	11

Once the transportation scheme has been worked out, there is still more to the problem if one is to pursue it to an implementable conclusion. For there are many ways of getting pupils between two locations and one wants a least cost way of doing it. To be specific, suppose each classroom has 30 pupils and that buses can be rented by the school district at a cost which depends on their seating capacity (see tabulation). Buses whose capacity exceeds 30 can possibly pick up at both A and B before going to the destinations and similarly can drop off passengers at one or several of the schools C, D, or E. Travel time between A and B or between C and D, C and E, or D and E is 4 min. Moreover, travel time cannot exceed 15 min per pupil. For example, a 60-passenger bus can start at A, pick up 30 pupils, and then go to B for another 30. From there the only school it can go to is C for a total travel time of $4 + 7 = 11$ min. At this point, the 30 boys and girls from A could be dropped off and then the bus could proceed to either D or E, unless all 60 children got off at C.

Capacity	Cost/Month
30	$1000
45	$1300
60	$1500

Quite frankly, there is no single codified procedure for handling this routing problem although a number of possible approaches will be discussed in Chapter 5. Perhaps the best procedure here is to "eyeball" the solution by working out a number of trial routes and then comparing them. The solution to the first part of this exercise is to be used as a guide to determine which classes in the ghetto area to match up with recipient schools in the more affluent zone.

A report on the full study done by the Rand Corporation in Los Angeles is referenced in the notes, but it will not help you do this exercise.

1.6.4 Consider the optimization problem of maximizing $z_1 = x_1 - x_2$ and $z_2 = x_2$ subject to the conditions $x_1 \leq 15$, $x_1 + x_2 \leq 20$, and $x_1, x_2 \geq 0$ (see Section 1.4 for a discussion of multidimensional objective functions). Draw the feasible set and find the noninferior subset S within it by maximizing z_1 subject to the above constraints together with $z_2 \geq \gamma$. Show that the resulting noninferior set is the same as if z_2 is maximized subject to the additional constraint of $z_1 \geq \gamma$. Finally, establish that the interior point $(5, 5)$ is inferior.

1.7 NOTES AND REMARKS

1.1 The study sketched in this section is in no way to be interpreted as either a condemnation or an endorsement of New York City's policy toward the problem of solid waste disposal and is to be thought of only as a case exercise on how such problems can be modeled. The material in this section is based in part on an unpublished report by the author and Mr. Jim Moar (one-time staff member of the New York City Environmental Protection Administration). Background material on local law 14 can be found in two article written as case studies for the Harvard Business School:

J. Russell, "Incineration and Local Law 14," *Urban Anal.* 1 (1973), 249–264; 2 (1974), 145–154.

For those not familiar with the concept of *discounting*, as used to compute landfill savings, a brief review is included here. Recall that if an amount I_0 is invested in one time period at an interest rate α, then in the kth period the total return, after compounding, is $(1 + \alpha)^k I_0$. On the other hand, if the amount I_0 is not invested until the kth period, then the *present value* of that later investment is only $I_k = I_0/(1 + \alpha)^k$ for one has lost the opportunity to accrue interest during the intervening k periods. I_0 is precisely the amount that initial investment of I_k would be worth k time slots later since $(1 + \alpha)^k I_k = I_0$. It is the same way with expenditures. A cost C_0 incurred k years from now is treated as only $C_0/(1 + \alpha)^k$ at present because the opportunity to invest $C_0/(1 + \alpha)^k$ with interest now will, after k periods, provide the needed C_0 to expend in the future. That is, one discounts future costs by an amount equal to what is actually needed to be put away at present in order to meet that future need. One can view in the same way a dollar benefit S_0 which accrues k years from now. It is only worth $S_k = S_0/(1 + \alpha)^k$ at present because current investment (at $\alpha\%$ interest) of S_k will grow to produce the same value of S_0 in the future.

In the case of landfill savings we saw that this was determined as \$5.67/ton but that since this benefit is not accrued until later years its effect on the present must be discounted. Its present worth was determined to be only

$3.32. Similarly, in the objective function of [1.5.13] the eventual total cost of expenditures for energy producing facilities during the tth year is discounted to the present for the same reason.

We will see in this book that in a number of public sector questions it is possible to choose some measure of performance as a goal or objective. If the objective is a social "benefit" we want to maximize it and if the objective is dollar cost, then one seeks a minimum. However the choice of feasible alternatives over which to optimize are either difficult or expensive to evaluate. This occurs, for example, when a system is sufficiently complex that the only effective way to get a handle on it is to use computer simulation (this technique will be discussed in Chapter 3). In such cases only a finite number of alternatives are available for comparison. An instance of this was uncovered in Section 1.1 in which both costs and benefits were interpreted in dollar units as respectively, the expense of mini-incinerator investments on one hand and the savings due to decreased truck travel and landfill depletion on the other. The number of alternatives was limited to a few different facility configurations.

In such problems one is confronted with a question of tradeoffs. As the alternatives increase in complexity both cost and benefits grow. As long as the benefits increase more rapidly than cost we are willing to adopt increasingly more costly alternatives. When this ceases to be true then the costs outweigh the benefits. That is, the *marginal benefit should never be less than the marginal cost*: $\Delta B - \Delta C \geqq 0$ where ΔB is the net change in benefit between two alternatives and ΔC is the corresponding change in cost. Or, to put it another way, one should require that $\Delta B/\Delta C \geqq 1$. The *breakeven cost* occurs when $\Delta B = \Delta C$. If one plots the benefit–cost ratio $\Delta B/\Delta C$ in terms of increasing complexity of alternatives (which is generally synonymous with increasing cost of implementing each option) then quite typically a curve like the one shown in Fig. 1.19 would result. Note that the benefit–cost reaches its maximum before the breakeven value. Beyond this maximum, *benefits accrue at a decreasing rate* (*the law of diminishing returns*). In some situations one is only

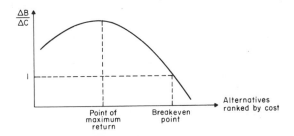

FIG. 1.19 Benefit–cost curve.

interested in achieving a specified goal represented by some fixed benefit level. In this case all alternatives which achieve this same level of performance are compared only in terms of cost, and the best one chosen. This is *cost–effectiveness* analysis and can be thought of as an evaluation of the set defined by benefit = constant, consisting of all equally effective ways of achieving the goal. The mini-incinerator example is again an instance of this in which the fixed benefit level is that of having all refuse removed from the given five districts. Each different configuration of mini-incinerators in terms of location and size (including the option of no such facilities) provided the alternatives. Another example of cost–effectiveness analysis will be provided in Chapter 3.

1.2 An extended version of the mixed integer programming formulation of the incinerator location problem can be found in the report by

W. Walker, M. Aquilina, and D. Schur, "Development and Use of a Fixed Charge Programming Model for Regional Solid Waste Planning," Rand Rep. P-5307 (1974).

One of the best general surveys of facility location models in general is the article by

C. Revelle, D. Marks, and J. Liebman, "Analysis of Private and Public Sector Location Models," *Management Sci.* **16** (1970), 692–707.

1.3 The study of this section follows the paper by

R. Dutton, G. Minhan, and C. Millham, "The Optimal Location of Nuclear Power Facilities in the Pacific Northwest," *Operations Res.* **22** (1974), 478–487.

In practice there usually are impediments to the location of a nuclear plant which often lead to lengthy litigation. An interesting discussion of some of the difficulties is available in the book by

D. Nelkin, *Nuclear Power and Its Critics*, Cornell Univ. Press, Ithaca, New York, 1970,

which is based on a controversial siting question in Cayuga Lake, New York. Another article on the same case is that by

D. Sipper, "Nuclear Power of Cayuga Lake," in *Patient Earth* (J. Harte and R. Socolow, eds.), Holt, New York, 1971.

1.4 We drew our material for the first part of this section from the survey article by

D. Marks, "Operations Research and Water Quality Management," *Urban Anal.* **2** (1974), 3–20.

A specific case illustration of such modeling is to be found in the paper by

J. Liebman and W. Lynn, "The Optimal Allocation of Stream Dissolved Oxygen," *Water Resources Res.* **2** (1966), 581–591, which is based on a study of waste treatment plants on the Williamette River in Oregon. Other appropriate references include the papers by

A. Converse and D. Freyberg, "Watershed Carrying Capacity as Determined from Water-borne Waste Loads," *Urban Anal.* **2** (1973), 826–836;

J. Cohon and D. Marks, "Multiobjective Screening Models and Water Resource Investment," *Water Resources Res.* **9** (1973), 826–836.

This last reference contains a discussion of multidimensional objective functions.

Referring to Eqs. [1.4.4] one notes that if x lies in a noninferior set S then corresponding to these feasible vectors is a set of z_1, z_2 values that lie in the plane. In general the tradeoff between z_1 and z_2 is similar to that which is displayed in Fig. 1.20 where we see that an increase in z_1 implies a decrease in z_2 and conversely. It is apparent from Fig. 1.20 that in the vicinity of the point A, a marginal increase in the value of z_1 can substantially degrade the performance of z_2. The same is true if the roles of z_1 and z_2 are reversed. For this reason the locations B, C on the curve can be viewed as less favorable choices than that at A even though all three correspond to Pareto optimal noninferior policies. In such a case, the value of x which gives rise to z_1^*, z_2^* at A can be construed as "optimal" in this heuristic sense.

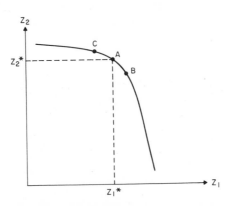

FIG. 1.20   Tradeoff between objectives Z_1 and Z_2.

1.5   Our basic reference for energy modeling is a report by

K. Hoffman, "A Linear Programming Model of the Nation's Energy System," Rep. BNL-EASG-4, Brookhaven Natl. Lab. (1973).

Versions of this report have appeared elsewhere, for example,

M. Searle, ed., "Energy Modelling," Rep. EN-1, Resources for the Future, Washington, D.C. (Mar. 1973).

The time-dependent version of the model is due to

W. Marcuse, L. Bodin, E. Cherniavsky, and Y. Sanborn, "A Dynamic Time-Dependent Model for the Analysis of Alternative Energy Policies," presented at IFORS meeting, Tokyo, 1975,

and is available in the proceedings of the conference.

The models discussed in Sections 1.4 and 1.5 are rich in policy implications that are only hinted at in this short survey. Nor have we touched on other significant questions having to do with resources in general, many of which are susceptible to the kind of treatment explored in these sections. We cannot resist, however, a brief outline of one such modeling study that was carried out as a tool for water resource management of a South American river basin (Rio Colorado). Details are worked out in the paper by

D. Marks and J. Cohon, "An Application of Linear Programming Alternatives," in *Studies in Linear Programming* (H. Salkin and J. Saha, eds.), North-Holland Publ., Amsterdam, 1975.

Along the river in question, a number of sites have been designated as possible locations at which one can build either reservoirs, hydroelectric power plants, or irrigation basins. Many configurations are possible and one would like to allocate the rivers' water and capital investments along it so as to maximize some national planning objective such as net economic benefit. However, since the river passes through several geographically and politically distinct subregions, one could also be concerned about equity of water use in each region, a goal which need not be consistent with national interests. This implies the possible use of a multidimensional objective function.

In tracing water flow through the system, an important constraint must be observed which is that the total water mass be conserved at each point where it is stored or diverted. One assumes here that the streamflow can be represented by a seasonal mean in which fluctuations are averaged out. As an illustration of how the mass continuity equations are worked out consider, for example, a schematic of a segment of the river along which two reservoirs are located at sites s and $s-1$ as shown in Fig. 1.21. The basic relation is that storage in the reservoir at s in season $t+1$, $R_{s,t+1}$, equals the storage in the preceding season plus any additions in the present season (river inflow $Q_{s,t}$ and any imports $I_{s,t}$) minus deductions (reservoir release $D_{s,t}$ and any diversions $E_{s,t}$)

$$R_{s,t+1} = R_{s,t} + Q_{s,t} + I_{s,t} - E_{s,t} - D_{s,t}$$

Now the upstream inflow $Q_{s,t}$ depends on natural streamflow and the amount released from the upstream reservoir at $s-1$. That is,

$$Q_{s,t} = D_{s-1} + \Delta F$$

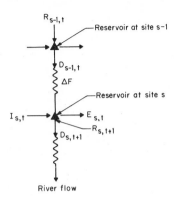

FIG. 1.21   Schematic of water uses along a river.

where ΔF is the increment of natural streamflow between sites $s-1$ and s. If the second equation above is substituted in the first, one obtains

$$R_{s,t+1} - R_{s,t} + D_{s,t} - D_{s-1,t} + E_{s,t} - I_{s,t} = \Delta F$$

in which all variables on the left side represent policy decisions (decision variables over which to optimize) while ΔF is a known entity. There is a set of such equations for each s and t. Of course other constraints must also be included which represent limitations on reservoir use, irrigation for crop production, and on water for power generation. For example, if V_s is the maximum storage capacity of a reservoir at s then, clearly, $R_{s,t} \leq V_s$ for each s and all t. As for hydroelectric generation one constraint is analogous to that of [1.3.3] in that total energy output $P_{s,t}$ in MWh at site s must satisfy $P_{s,t} \leq 2190\gamma H_s$, where H_s is peak plant capacity (MW), γ is the plant factor, and 2190 is the number of hours in a season. Another energy production constraint is based on physical considerations which make the value of $P_{s,t}$ dependent on flow through the turbines in the plant $D_{s,t}$ and on the height ("head") of the reservoir level $A_{s,t}$. We do not write it here since it involves additional discussion which goes beyond the purpose of these few comments.

1.6   Exercise 1.6.3 is based on a study documented by

R. Fulkerson, A. Horelick, L. Shapley, and D. Weiler, "A Transportation Program for Filling Idle Classrooms in Los Angeles," Rand Rep. P-3405 (July 1966).

2

Manpower Scheduling

2.1 A NONLINEAR ALLOCATION MODEL

In the previous section we were concerned with linear models. Now our first intrinsically nonlinear model will be introduced. Consider an urban area that wishes to improve efficiency of its household refuse collection service by the appropriate allocation of work crews throughout the week. Suppose to begin with, that the crews work one shift a day for six days a week (Sunday excluded). The average refuse available curbside on the jth day (with $j = 1$ being Monday, $j = 2$ is Tuesday, etc.) is denoted by f_j and is measured in tons. Although it is difficult to measure the quality of a garbage collection service (a neighborhood perception of good service depends on such hard to quantify factors as noise during collection, frequency of service, and promptness and courtesy of sanitation workers, and so on) a surrogate measure of bad performance is the amount of refuse that remains uncollected at the end of a day. Let m_j be the *missed* tonnage of refuse on the jth day. Then our objective would be to minimize the sum $m_1 + m_2 + \cdots + m_6$. Now if p is the average productivity of the work crews (each crew works one garbage collection truck), given in tons collected per day, and if n_j is the number of crews assigned to work on the jth day, then

$$m_{j+1} = m_j + f_j - pn_j \qquad [2.1.1]$$

which accounts for the fact that the backlog of uncollected garbage on day j becomes part of the refuse inventory on day $j+1$. However [2.1.1] is not quite correct since m_{j+1} must necessarily be nonnegative whereas this equation allows for m_{j+1} to be less than zero. Therefore the correct definition of m_{j+1} should be

$$m_{j+1} = \max(m_j + f_j - pn_j, 0) \qquad [2.1.2]$$

which is a nonlinear relation. If σ_j denotes $m_j + f_j - pn_j$ then m_{j+1} can be alternately described as the ramp function given by

$$m_{j+1} = \begin{cases} 0, \sigma_j < 0 \\ \sigma_j, \sigma_j \geq 0 \end{cases}$$

Therefore the objective function

$$\sum_{j=1}^{6} m_j \qquad [2.1.3]$$

is nonlinear in the variables $n_1, \ldots, n_6$ even though it appears to be linear at first sight. The problem, which we label as I, is to choose the $n_j \geq 0$ subject to several linear constraints given below so as to minimize [2.1.3]. To begin with, n_j can never exceed either the available number of trucks M or the total number of crews in the total workforce N. Since M is usually less than N,

$$0 \leq n_j \leq M \qquad [2.1.4]$$

Assume also that union regulations limit each crew to work at most five of the six days. Then, since $r_j = N - n_j$ is the number of crews not working on day j, and since each of the N available crews gets at least one day off a week (besides Sunday), it follows that $\sum_{j=1}^{6} r_j \geq N$ or, to put it another way,

$$\sum_{j=1}^{6} n_j \geq 5N \qquad [2.1.5]$$

It would be tempting to reformulate the above problem as a linear program. This can be done as follows.

Consider the m_j as independent of the n_j variables and enlarge the optimization problem by choosing the set of $n_1, \ldots, n_6$ and $m_1, \ldots, m_6$ so that

$$\sum_{j=1}^{6} m_j \qquad [2.1.6]$$

is minimized subject to the constraints [2.1.4] and [2.1.5] used above and, additionally,

$$m_{j+1} \geqq 0 \qquad\qquad [2.1.7]$$

$$m_{j+1} \geqq m_j + f_j - pn_j \qquad\qquad [2.1.8]$$

Let us call this problem II.

The objective is now clearly linear in the optimizing variables and it remains to show that I and II are equivalent.

If superscript zero denotes the optimal value of a variable then whenever $n_j{}^0$, $m_j{}^0$ satisfy II it must be true that at least one of [2.1.6] or [2.1.8] are strict equalities. Otherwise a new set of values for m_j can be chosen with $m_j \leqq m_j{}^0$ for which [2.1.7] and [2.1.8] are still satisfied and which give [2.1.6] an even smaller value for [2.1.6]. But this contradicts optimality. Therefore m_{j+1} must be equal to the larger of zero and $m_j + f_j - pn_j$, which is the same as saying that [2.1.2] holds. Conversely, [2.1.2] certainly implies [2.1.7] and [2.1.8]. Since the other constraints are automatically satisfied in both I and II we have established the equivalence of the linear and nonlinear problems.

Neat as the above formulation is, one can easily develop intrinsically non-linear versions of the problem for which the trick we used no longer works. For example, one can argue that since large missed collections are more serious than small ones, one would like to penalize large violations more severely than small ones. This can be done by choosing the following non-linear objective function to minimize: $\sum_{j=1}^{6} m_j{}^2$ or, in the most conservative case, one might prefer to minimize the largest violation by minimizing the maximum of the m_j. In addition the constraints themselves can be nonlinear. Consider a simple extension of our model in which there are two shifts a day. In this case one can allocate n_{ij} crews on the ith shift and jth day ($i = 1, 2$; $j = 1, ..., 6$) subject to constraints of the same type as before and, in addition, the constraint that as many as possible crews be assigned to the first, or day, shift before any are allocated to the second, or night, shift. We actually encountered this restriction in a study performed in New York City, which was imposed for essentially two reasons: one was the night shifts are paid more under union regulations and so would cost the city more; the other was the noise and inconvenience to the residents in having evening service. Mathematically our requirement is translated in this way. Since at most M crews can be assigned on any one shift, the optimal solution should provide that

$$n_{2j}{}^0 = \begin{cases} 0, & \text{if } n_{1j}{}^0 + n_{2j}{}^0 \leqq M \\ n_{1j}{}^0 + n_{2j}{}^0 - M, & \text{otherwise} \end{cases} \qquad [2.1.9]$$

This means that if the optimum allocation can meet the daily needs within a single shift, then that shift is not the second one, whereas if more than one shift is needed then M crews should be allocated to the first shift and the remainder to the second. Another way of stating [2.1.9] is by the following single nonlinear relation, as a little thought will show

$$n_{2j}(M - n_{1j}) = 0 \qquad [2.1.10]$$

Notice that if in an optimal solution $n_{1j}{}^0 < M$ then no further reduction in the objective function can be achieved by further increasing the assignment of crews on either shift since [2.1.10] then forces $n_{2j}{}^0$ to be zero.

One immediately recognized failing of the allocation model is it does not explicitly account for dollar cost. Indeed [2.1.3] or any of its variants is only a measure of social cost. If weekly cost to the municipality is

$$C = \sum_{j=1}^{2} \sum_{j=1}^{6} c_{ij} n_{ij}$$

(allowing for night shift pay differential) then one possibility is to mix apples and oranges and to form a composite objective function

$$\sum m_j + \delta C \qquad [2.1.11]$$

where $\delta \geqq 0$ is some measure of the relative significance of social to dollar cost. In our experience this is generally a less satisfactory procedure than to simply minimize $\sum m_j$ subject to the addition constraints of $C \leqq \bar{C}$ or, alternatively, to minimize C with an upper bound on $\sum m_j$. The reason is that the mixed form [2.1.11] does not delineate the opposing goals as sharply as in the case where one goal is treated as a constraint. The conflict between dollar and social cost could also be resolved in principle by looking at the problem as one with a two dimensional objective function, as discussed in Section 1.4. In practice, however, it is generally expedient to treat one of the goals as a constraint, as previously done.

There is at least one other type of nonlinear objective function that can be refashioned into a linear format. Whenever the scalar $\bar{w}$ is some desired performance level and w is the actual level, then $|w - \bar{w}|$ measures the discrepancy between the two, and one seeks to minimize this absolute difference subject, in general, to a variety of other constraints. Even if the variable w is assumed to be some linear function of a set of decision variables $x_1, ..., x_l$, the expression $|w - \bar{w}|$ is itself nonlinear. By way of illustration, suppose one has p regions, each utilizing a water resource in some amount w_i, and that $\bar{w}$ is the average annual use. The most equitable allocation of that resource to each of those regions (subject to a number of restrictions that we need not specify here) might well be construed as that which minimizes the deviation from the average. If each w_i is dependent on some nonnegative variables $x = (x_1, ..., x_l)$ lying in a suitable feasible region, then one seeks x so as to obtain

$$\min \sum_{i=1}^{p} |w_i - \bar{w}| \qquad [2.1.12]$$

Introduce new nonnegative variables u_i, v_i and rewrite [2.1.12] in linear form as

$$\min \sum_{i=1}^{p} (u_i + v_i) \qquad [2.1.13]$$

subject to the *additional constraints* that

$$u_i \geq w_i - \bar{w}$$
$$v_i \geq -(w_i - \bar{w}) \qquad [2.1.14]$$

This procedure is similar to that displayed before in which [2.1.3] is replaced by [2.1.6] together with [2.1.7] and [2.1.8]. For each value of x the difference $w_i - \bar{w}$ is either greater than (or equal to) zero or it is negative. Suppose that at the optimum one has $w_i - \bar{w} \geq 0$. Then it must be true there that

$$u_i = w_i - \bar{w}$$
$$v_i = 0 \qquad [2.1.15]$$

(since u_i and v_i are both nonnegative). Indeed if even one of the relations [2.1.15] is an inequality, then [2.1.13] can be further reduced, which is not possible at a minimum. Similarly, if $w_i - \bar{w} < 0$, then for the same reason one must have

$$u_i = 0$$
$$v_i = -(w_i - \bar{w})$$

Therefore,

$$u_i = \begin{cases} w_i - \bar{w}, & \text{if } w_i - \bar{w} \geq 0 \\ 0, & \text{otherwise} \end{cases}$$

$$v_i = \begin{cases} -(w_i - \bar{w}), & \text{if } w_i - \bar{w} < 0 \\ 0, & \text{otherwise} \end{cases}$$

Or, in all cases, at an optimum one has

$$u_i - v_i = w_i - \bar{w}$$
$$u_i + v_i = |w_i - \bar{w}|$$

This means that the nonlinear [2.1.12] is equivalent to the linear version given by [2.1.13] together with [2.1.14].

Problems of this type will be met again in later chapters in connection with political districting and the delivery of emergency services.

2.2 WHO IS TO PICK UP ALL THE GARBAGE?

They do not pick up the garbage on Sunday in New York City. So there is even more on Monday.

New York's Sanitationworker's Union—a well-organized body with strong leadership—has for over 40 years worked according to something called the "chart day schedule." What it does is to put exactly the same number of workers on the streets ever day, Monday through Saturday. The schedule operates on a rotating basis in which each of the roughly 11,000 workers is assigned to one of six "charts" or groups. This is shown in Table 2.1, from which we see that every six weeks each worker receives a 3-day weekend for recreation. This is due to the fact that the chart repeats itself beginning with the seventh week.

TABLE 2.1

SIX-WEEK ROTATING SCHEDULE DISPLAYED OVER SIX WEEKS[a]

	Mon- day	Tues- day	Wednes- day	Thurs- day	Fri- day	Satur- day	Sun- day
1	×						×
2		×					×
3			×				×
4				×			×
5					×		×
6						×	×

[a] × indicates day off. This table can be read either as the 6-week assignment for a typical group (or "chart") of men or, equivalently, as the profile of the groups that are off on any given week.

Since the Sunday garbage backlog was too much for the Monday crews—and maybe for the Tuesday crews, too—it sat there on into the week with its attendant smells and hazards. At one point in 1969 this led to riots in the Brownsville section of Brooklyn. It was clear that something had to be done to eliminate the mismatch between the uneven work demand and the unwavering constant workforce. One solution was to hire more workers at an annual cost of several million dollars. A better one, as we soon realized was to divide the workers into a large number of groups or charts and to use a larger period for the rotating schedule.

This meant a restructuring of the work schedule so that more workers were available on peak days and fewer on slack days. But with a different number of workers on the street every day, some of them might have to work more than others—or get more overtime pay. The possibilities were hardly appealing to the union. Moreover, there had not been a work practice change in over 40 years.

At this time a group of us from the State University of New York at Stony Brook were asked to look at this "chart day" problem. The first thing to be done was to decide how many workers were actually required on a day-by-day basis. A model of the situation was worked out and is discussed in Section 2.1. What was found is that if all workers in the department were divided equally into 30 equal groups or "brackets," as they came to be called, then on Monday 28 of the 30 brackets should be working, 27 on Tuesday, and 26, 23, 23, 23 for the rest of the week. Everyone gets Sunday off. This contrasts sharply with the constant 25 brackets available each day under the chart system ($\frac{5}{6}$ of 30 is 25). Indeed on Monday the difference between 28 and 25 represents a service squeeze of three out of 30 brackets, or $\frac{1}{10}$ of the workforce. At an average annual wage (1971 rates) of about $11,000 per worker, this represents a savings of about 13 million dollars in personnel that one does not have to hire.

Having done this it was still necessary to assign personnel to specific days in such a way that a satisfactory rotating schedule is maintained which guarantees a certain minimum number of days of rest and recreation. This problem of scheduling is discussed in terms of a suitable model in Section 2.3, but for now a heuristic discussion will suffice.

As Table 2.2 shows, it is possible to guarantee that each bracket actually gets two days off each week and, in fact, in nine out of 30 weeks, all workers get a weekend off while maintaining the required work profile. This is done on a rotating basis and the figure can be read as the schedule of days off for a typical bracket over 30 consecutive weeks. On the 31st week the schedule starts to repeat itself. It can also be read as the day-off assignment for all 30 brackets in the department on any given week and with this interpretation it is clear that 28 brackets are working on Monday, 27 on Tuesdays, and so on.

By permuting rows in Table 2.2 a variety of other schedules can be constructed as shown in Tables 2.3 and 2.4. Notice that in Table 2.3 there are nine 3-*day* weekends off in 30 weeks! However the price for this, as one can see, is that it also requires that each bracket work nine 6-day work weeks. Because of union overtime regulations this option would cost the city more to implement.

That this analysis could successfully provide a service—a solution to the chart day problem—was evident on November 30, 1971, when the City of New York and the Sanitationworker's Union announced an agreement on a new contract. According to the agreement, there would be a change in work practice as described by the manpower rescheduling shown in Table 2.2. According to the New York Times, "City officials described the new pact as a 'major breakthrough in labor relations in the city' because salary increases were linked to specific provisions to increase productivity." The schedule provided nearly twice as many weekends off for each sanitationworker as he had had before and at the same time it has saved the city money.

We have told this story in order to illustrate how a relatively simple analysis can lead to far reaching results in improving the delivery of municipal

REVISED CHART SYSTEM—MAXIMIZE 2-DAY WEEKENDS—30 WEEKS[a]

	Monday	Tuesday	Wednesday	Thursday	Friday	Saturday	Sunday	Comment
1						×	×	2-day weekend
2		×					×	
3		×					×	
4		×					×	
5	×						×	2-day weekend
6			×				×	
7			×				×	
8	×						×	2-day weekend
9			×				×	
10			×				×	
11						×	×	2-day weekend
12				×			×	
13				×			×	
14						×	×	2-day weekend
15				×			×	
16				×			×	
17				×			×	
18						×	×	2-day weekend
19				×			×	
20				×			×	
21						×	×	2-day weekend
22					×		×	
23					×		×	
24						×	×	2-day weekend
25					×		×	
26					×		×	
27					×		×	
28						×	×	2-day weekend
29					×		×	
30					×		×	
No. of brackets off each day	2	3	4	7	7	7	30	

[a] × indicates day off.

TABLE 2.3

REVISED CHART SYSTEM—MAXIMIZE 3-DAY WEEKENDS—30-WEEK ROTATING SCHEDULE, INCLUDING 6-DAY WORK WEEKS[a]

	Monday	Tuesday	Wednesday	Thursday	Friday	Saturday	Sunday	Comment
1							x	6-day work week
2					x	x	x	3-day weekend
3				x			x	
4							x	6-day work week
5	x	x					x	3-day weekend
6			x				x	
7							x	6-day work week
8					x	x	x	3-day weekend
9							x	6-day work week
10					x	x	x	3-day weekend
11				x			x	
12		x					x	
13							x	6-day work week
14					x	x	x	3-day weekend
15				x			x	
16							x	6-day work week
17					x	x	x	3-day weekend
18			x				x	
19							x	6-day work week
20	x	x					x	3-day weekend
21			x				x	
22				x			x	
23							x	6-day work week
24					x	x	x	3-day weekend
25				x			x	
26							x	6-day work week
27					x	x	x	3-day weekend
28				x			x	
29				x			x	
30			x				x	
No. of brackets off each day	2	3	4	7	7	7	30	

[a] x indicates day off

REVISED CHART SYSTEM—30-WEEK ROTATING SCHEDULE DISPLAYED OVER 30 WEEKS[a]

	Monday	Tuesday	Wednesday	Thursday	Friday	Saturday	Sunday	Comment
1						×	×	3-day weekend
2	×						×	
3		×					×	
4		×					×	
5		×					×	
6						×	×	2-day weekend
7			×				×	
8			×				×	
9			×				×	
10						×	×	2-day weekend
11			×				×	
12				×			×	
13				×			×	
14						×	×	2-day weekend
15				×			×	
16				×			×	
17				×			×	
18						×	×	3-day weekend
19	×						×	
20				×			×	
21				×			×	
22					×		×	
23						×	×	2-day weekend
24					×		×	
25					×		×	
26					×		×	
27						×	×	2-day weekend
28					×		×	
29					×		×	
30					×		×	
No. of brackets off each day	2	3	4	7	7	7	30	

[a] × indicates day off.

services. Moreover, the situation is not unique with the sanitation department. Most public or municipal services require their employees to work more than five days a week in situations where workload requirements usually vary from day to day (firemen, policemen, nurses, ambulance drivers, subway transit workers, etc.) and therefore the kind of analysis presented here and in the next section is applicable in a number of settings.

2.3   A MODEL FOR MANPOWER SCHEDULING

We now make the discussion of the previous section more formal by discussing a scheduling model that incorporates a number of special cases.

Let us agree that the basic work period is one week and that each week is partitioned into a number of consecutive time periods which we call *shifts*. A variety of legal, organizational, and operational constraints together act to determine the number of workers that can be assigned to each shift so as to best match a demand profile that typically varies with time of day and day of week. Mathematically this is often equivalent to solving an appropriate nonlinear program and indeed in the sanitation problem, as we saw in Section 2.1, it was the weekly inventory of missed refuse collections that was to be minimized by allocating an appropriate number of work crews (or more appropriately, a number of *brackets*, as defined in Section 2.2). Another example is outlined in the notes. Having done this one knows the number n_i of worker brackets to deploy on the ith shift and if N is the total available brackets (the workforce) then $N - n_i = r_i$ is the number which can be allowed off for rest and recreation.

Labor practices, union regulations, and the requirements of management contribute to the determination of what constitutes a feasible arrangement of shifts off for a bracket. For example, Monday 8 a.m.–Tuesday midnight and Thursday 4 p.m.–Saturday 4 p.m. might be acceptable periods of no work for a typical bracket and as such constitutes a feasible recreation cluster. Another might be simply Thursday 4 p.m.–Monday 8 a.m. The problem now is to determine *who* is to work in each shift given that we know *how many* are required to work. *This is the question of scheduling in contrast to the problem of allocation considered earlier.*

Let A be a matrix whose entries a_{ij} are zero or one, with one indicating that the jth feasible recreation cluster contains the ith shift, and zero otherwise. Assume that each time off arrangement has a value of worth v_j. These numbers are arrived at by consultation with the employee's union and with management and it might well be agreed, for example, that the second of the two clusters given above is twice as desirable as the first one. Alternatively one can think of the dollar costs c_j required to have men in a bracket work a week in which the jth recreation schedule is in operation. Such cost comprised hourly wages including differential for nighttime and weekend work, and overtime pay for work in excess of certain negotiated time periods.

If x_j is a nonnegative integer variable which indicates how many times the jth recreation schedule is to be picked in a week (equivalently, x_j is the number of brackets whose assignment is to share the same jth work schedule each week), then our problem is to maximize total worth

$$v_1 x_1 + \cdots + v_m x_m \qquad [2.3.1]$$

or to minimize total cost

$$c_1 x_1 + \cdots + c_m x_m \qquad [2.3.2]$$

where m is the number of feasible recreation clusters one wishes to consider. However there is a constraint to impose, namely that the ith shift must appear on some cluster or other exactly r_i times a week which in turn assures us that, as required, n_j brackets are available for work on that shift. This is formulated as

$$\sum_{j=1}^{m} a_{ij} x_j = r_i \qquad [2.3.3]$$

where $i = 1, \ldots, s$, and s is the total number of shifts in a week. More abstractly [2.3.1] with [2.3.3] can be written as

$$\text{maximize} \quad v'x$$

subject to

$$Ax = r \qquad [2.3.4]$$

with x, r being m- and s-dimensional vectors, respectively. As we will see, this problem is generally ill-posed in that nonnegative and integer feasible solutions to [2.3.3] do not always exist and one may have to relax the recreation and rest requirement by stipulating that each shift i appear on some recreation cluster or other *at most* r_i times each week. That is, one would replace [2.3.3] by

$$\sum_{j=1}^{m} a_{ij} x_j \leqq r_i \qquad [2.3.5]$$

The problem of maximizing [2.3.1] or minimizing [2.3.2] subject to [2.3.3] is an integer programming problem (see Appendix B) known as a "multiple set covering." That this nomenclature is not fanciful can be seen by considering a finite set S from which a collection of possible overlapping subsets has been defined. For each subset there is some associated "cost" for picking it. The problem is to choose in a least cost way, a number of these (not necessarily disjoint) subsets in such a way that every element of S appears in some subset or other a specified number of times—that is, this minimal cost selection of subsets is a complete multiple covering for S. In our case, the *set S consists of shifts and the subsets are groups of shifts* formed into daily schedules.

We now consider a few examples. Let us begin by reformulating the sanitationmen problem. There, each day constitutes a shift (so that $s = 7$) and the A matrix is given by

Feasible recreation clusters

$$
\begin{array}{c}
\text{Monday} \\
\text{Tuesday} \\
\text{Wednesday} \\
\text{Thursday} \\
\text{Friday} \\
\text{Saturday} \\
\text{Sunday}
\end{array}
\left[
\begin{array}{ccccccccc}
1 & & & & & & & & 1 \\
 & 1 & & & & & & & 1 \\
 & & 1 & & & & & & \\
 & & & 1 & & & & & \\
 & & & & 1 & & 1 & & \\
 & & & & & 1 & 1 & & \\
1 & 1 & 1 & 1 & 1 & 1 & 1 & 1 & 1
\end{array}
\right]
\qquad [2.3.6]
$$

with all unspecified or blank entries interpreted as zero. Here m is 9, corresponding to possible day-off arrangements. Notice that Sunday is always a day off and the ninth column means that only Sunday is a day off, which is equivalent to specifying a 6-day work week. Columns 7 and 8 are 3-day weekends, and columns 1 and 6 are 2-day weekends.

Suppose, for purposes of illustration, that management decides that each bracket is to work an *average* of five days a week (that is, some brackets may actually work four or six days). Since there are N brackets, a total of $5N$ of them work each week. That is,

$$
\sum_{j=1}^{7} n_j = 5N \qquad [2.3.7]
$$

and, since $r_i = N - n_i$, then

$$
\sum_{i=1}^{7} r_i = 2N \qquad [2.3.8]
$$

In our case, since everyone gets Sunday off, $r_7 = N$ and so

$$
\sum_{i=1}^{6} r_i = N \qquad [2.3.9]
$$

The constraint equations [2.3.3] can, in view of [2.3.6], be written out as

$$
\begin{aligned}
x_1 & & & & & & & + x_8 & & = r_1 \\
& x_2 & & & & & & + x_8 & & = r_2 \\
& & x_3 & & & & & & & = r_3 \\
& & & x_4 & & & & & & = r_4 \qquad [2.3.10] \\
& & & & x_5 & + x_7 & & & & = r_5 \\
& & & & x_6 & + x_7 & & & & = r_6 \\
x_1 + x_2 + x_3 + x_4 + x_5 + x_6 + x_7 + x_8 + x_9 & & & & & & & & & = r_7
\end{aligned}
$$

In view of [2.3.9] and the fact that $r_7 = N$ one sees that

$$x_7 + x_8 = x_9 \qquad\qquad [2.3.11]$$

which says that there are as many brackets working 6-day work weeks as there are brackets working 4-day work weeks. It is also clear from the last equation that as many recreations clusters are chosen as there are brackets available. This is a significant fact since it means that a recreation schedule can be constructed over an N week horizon for each bracket using each of the nine clusters each of them occurring x_j times during the N weeks. But this is the basis for forming a rotating schedule since the N-week schedule can now simply be assigned to each of the N brackets on a rotating basis.

To make the problem more specific suppose one wishes to maximize the number of 2-day weekends. To do this assign a positive value, let us say unity, to the first and sixth clusters, $v_1 = v_6 = 1$, and set all other v_j to zero. Then one needs to maximize $x_1 + x_6$ (from [2.3.1]) and from the first and sixth equation in [2.3.10] this means that one wants to maximize $r_1 + r_6 - x_7 - x_8$. Since x_7, x_8 are nonngative in an optimal solution, the largest value clearly occurs when $x_7 = x_8 = 0$. But then $x_9 = 0$ from [2.3.11] and this implies that every crew works exactly five days a week. From [2.3.10] one also sees that the optimal solution is then $x_i = r_i$ for all $i = 1, ..., 6$ and the optimum number of 2-day weekends is $r_1 + r_6$. In the sanitation problem of Section 2.2 the r_i were 2, 3, 4, 7, 7, 7 so that there are nine weekends and the jth recreation cluster occurs exactly the number of times exhibited in Table 2.2 For example, the Wednesday–Sunday cluster occurs $x_3 = 4$ times. Finally, note that since $\sum_{j=1}^{6} x_j = 30$, one can piece together a weekly assignment for each of the 30 brackets so as to form a 30-week rotating schedule. Indeed by repeating each of the columns in [2.3.10] exactly x_j times and then turning the entire array on its side, the schedule presented in Table 2.2 is reproduced except for a suitable permutation of the resulting rows. This simple device for obtaining an N-week rotating schedule will be true in all the examples to be discussed. The only missing ingredient is how to permute the rows so as to obtain a favorable distribution of days off during the N-week period, but this is an exercise which we leave to the reader.

To make the sanitation problem more interesting, assume now that labor and management jointly decide that three 2-day weekends are worth (or equally desirable to) two 3-day weekends. Then $2v_7 = 3v_1$ and if v_7 is arbitrarily given a unit value then $v_1 = \frac{2}{3}$. Thus $v_1 = v_6 \cdot \frac{2}{3}$ and $v_7 = v_8 = 1$ with all other $v_j = 0$. The objective now is to maximize $\frac{2}{3}(x_1 + x_6) + x_7 + x_8$. Using [2.3.10] this is recalculated to be $r_1 + r_6 - \frac{1}{3}(x_1 + x_6)$. Since x_1, x_6 are nonnegative in an optimal solution, the temptation is to do as before and to set them to zero since this yields the largest possible value to the objective function. However, there is a subtlety here which we chose to ignore in the example just given, but that now we need to point out. The problem is this: one must check whether setting x_1 and x_6 to zero is consistent with the remaining equations in [2.3.10]; but this depends on the values of r_i. Thus, since $x_2 = r_2 - r_1 + x_1$ and $x_5 = r_5 - r_6 + x_6$, then the requirement that x_2 and x_5 be nonnegative means that the smallest possible values of x_1, x_6 are

$$x_1 = \begin{cases} r_1 - r_2, & \text{if } r_1 > r_2 \\ 0, & \text{otherwise} \end{cases}$$

$$x_6 = \begin{cases} r_6 - r_5, & \text{if } r_5 > r_6 \\ 0, & \text{otherwise} \end{cases}$$

In our example the r_i are such that x_1 and x_6 can freely be taken to be zero, but it is not at all the case in general. So, one now has that 2-day weekends are ignored and that a maximum number of $r_1 + r_6 = 9$ 3-day weekends are obtained. Since $r_1 + r_6 = x_7 = x_8 = x_9$ in this solution, then there are also nine 6-day work weeks. One can solve [2.3.10] for the remaining values to obtain, besides $x_1 = x_6 = 0$, that $x_2 = 1$, $x_3 = 4$, $x_4 = 7$, $x_5 = 0$, $x_7 = 7$, $x_8 = 2$. The rotating schedule corresponding to this solution is exhibited in Table 2.3.

We saw earlier that the maximum number of 2-day weekends is given by $r_1 + r_6$. One can also show, and we leave this to the reader, that the maximum of 3-day weekends for any given set of r_i values, is given by

$$\min(r_1, r_2) + \min(r_5, r_6) \qquad\qquad [2.3.12]$$

For another example let us assume that a "weekend" is any consecutive 2-day period and that each day is again a shift. In this case, the A matrix is as follows, with blank spaces again denoting zeros:

Feasible recreation schedules

Monday	1						1
Tuesday	1	1					
Wednesday		1	1				
Thursday			1	1			
Friday				1	1		
Saturday					1	1	
Sunday						1	1

Following an example cited in the literature (see notes at end of chapter), let the r_i values be 1, 2, 3, 3, 2, 5, 6 (for $i = 1, ..., 7$). With each bracket working an average of five days a week, then $\sum_{i=1}^{7} r_i = 2N$ and so there are $N = 11$ brackets to consider.

The constraint equations [2.3.1] can be written out for this example as

$$
\begin{aligned}
x_1 & & & & & & + x_7 &= r_1 \\
x_1 + x_2 & & & & & & &= r_2 \\
& x_2 + x_3 & & & & & &= r_3 \\
& & x_3 + x_4 & & & & &= r_4 \qquad\qquad [2.3.13] \\
& & & x_4 + x_5 & & & &= r_5 \\
& & & & x_5 + x_6 & & &= r_6 \\
& & & & & x_6 + x_7 & &= r_7
\end{aligned}
$$

Since these equations always possess a unique solution (the reader should verify this) there is no question of optimization for such problems. Indeed in the case of the r_i given above, the solution turns out to be $x_1 = 0$, $x_2 = 2$, $x_3 = 1$, $x_4 = 2$, $x_5 = 0$, $x_6 = 5$, $x_7 = 1$, which leads to the 11-week rotating schedule exhibited in Table 2.5. This schedule is constructed in a completely analogous way to those of Tables 2.2 and 2.3. The × again denotes a day off and one notes that Saturday–Sunday pairs are about as evenly spaced as is possible. This however is not the end of the story. The unique solution to [2.3.13] is not necessarily nonnegative and integer valued in all cases. For example, if r_j happens to be greater in value than $r_{j-1} + r_{j+1}$ (mod 7) then as is readily verified a feasible solution does not exist. Thus $r_j \leqq r_{j-1} + r_{j+1}$ (mod 7) is necessary for nonnegative solutions but it is still not sufficient.

TABLE 2.5

ELEVEN-WEEK ROTATING SCHEDULE[a]

	Mon-day	Tues-day	Wednes-day	Thurs-day	Fri-day	Satur-day	Sun-day
1		×	×				
2						×	×
3		×	×				
4						×	×
5			×	×			
6						×	×
7				×	×		
8						×	×
9				×	×		
10						×	×
11	×						×
	$r_1 = 1$	$r_2 = 2$	$r_3 = 3$	$r_4 = 3$	$r_5 = 2$	$r_6 = 5$	$r_7 = 6$

[a] × denotes day off.

Consider, for example, r_i all equal to 1 except for $r_5 = 2$. Then x_3 turns out to have noninteger value of $\frac{1}{2}$ even though the necessary condition is satisfied. Therefore the problem is reformulated by replacing [2.3.13] by the condition

$$\sum_{j=1}^{7} a_{ij} x_j \leqq r_i \qquad [2.3.14]$$

which means that each shift (or day, in our case) is to appear in some consecutive 2-day recreation cluster or other at most r_i times. However, one can enrich the feasible set by inserting additional brackets consisting of single days off. To put it another way, one adds slack variables $y_i \geqq 0$ to [2.3.14] to once again make it into a set of equality constraints. This can be written out as

$$
\begin{array}{llll}
x_1 & + x_7 + y_1 & & = r_1 \\
x_1 + x_2 & + y_2 & & = r_2 \\
x_2 + x_3 & + y_3 & & = r_3 \\
x_3 + x_4 & + y_4 & & = r_4 \\
x_4 + x_5 & + y_5 & & = r_5 \\
x_5 + x_6 & + y_6 & & = r_6 \\
x_6 + x_7 & & + y_7 & = r_7
\end{array}
$$

$$[2.3.15]$$

A nonnegative integer value solution to [2.3.15] now always exists (indeed $x_j = 0$ is one such possibility) but the problem is that recreation clusters of nonconsecutive days off represented by the y_i are not especially desirable and so an appropriate optimization problem now consists of assigning negative values to each "slack" variable, with zero values to the other variables. Normalizing each negative value to -1 leads to maximizing:

$$-\sum_{i=1}^{7} y_i \qquad [2.3.16]$$

subject to [2.3.15]. For example, if $r_1 = 5$, $r_3 = 6$, $r_7 = 1$, $r_2 = r_5 = 2$, $r_4 = r_6 = 3$, then the optimum solution is $x_1 = x_5 = 2$, $x_2 = x_4 = x_7 = 0$, $x_3 = 3$, $x_6 = 1$ with $y_i = 0$ except for $y_1 = y_3 = 3$. This is interpreted as saying that there are two brackets off on Monday–Tuesday, two off on Friday–Saturday, three off on Wednesday–Thursday, and one on Saturday–Sunday. In addition, three other brackets are assigned to nonconsecutive day pairs given by Monday–Wednesday for a total of 11 brackets. This means that a simple rotating schedule based on the original 11 brackets is still possible in this case except it must include some work clusters other than those originally desired.

When $\sum_{i=1}^{7} y_i$ is zero in an optimal solution, it clearly signifies that [2.3.13] possesses a feasible integer valued solution. Note also that by adding the equations in [2.3.13] one obtains $2 \sum_{j=1}^{7} x_j = 2N$ provided everyone works an average of five days a week. Therefore, as many clusters are chosen as there are brackets of men and so a simple rotating schedule is always possible in such cases, as in the sanitationmen problem. However, when $\sum_{i=1}^{7} y_i \neq 0$, it is no longer clear that a simple rotating schedule can be devised, even though in the example above this turned out to be possible. Suppose that y_3 had the value of 1 instead of 3 in that problem. Then with three Mondays and one Wednesday to assign, one Monday–Wednesday pair can be formed with only two isolated Monday clusters left over. With 11 brackets to assign this would require one of them to work a 6-day week (with Monday off) and another bracket would be given Monday plus, let us say, Friday–Saturday off. This device would then preserve the appearance of a rotating schedule. Note, incidently, that even if $\sum y_i$ is nonzero, it is always an even number (why?).

Let us look at one final example. Up to now we have been describing weekly schedules. Suppose the time period is actually a single day which is broken down into a variety of time periods or shifts. This could be of interest in problems in which manpower requirements vary throughout a day but do not change from day to day. As an illustration, consider the following six shifts and the men needed on each:

Shift	Men needed
midnight–2 a.m.	6
2 a.m.–8 a.m.	4
8 a.m.–noon	5
noon–4 p.m.	6
4 p.m.–6 p.m.	8
6 p.m.–midnight	10

If each man works consecutive 8-hr periods, then there are only four feasible recreation clusters. Unlike the previous problems, it is now more convenient to consider an A matrix of feasible work clusters because such a matrix is more sparse and easier to work with than a corresponding matrix of recreation (why?). Therefore we write A as

$$
\text{Shifts} \;
\begin{array}{c}
1 \\ 2 \\ 3 \\ 4 \\ 5 \\ 6
\end{array}
\overset{\text{Work clusters}}{
\begin{bmatrix}
1 & & & 1 \\
1 & & & \\
 & 1 & & \\
 & 1 & & \\
 & & 1 & \\
 & & 1 & 1
\end{bmatrix}}
$$

In order to ensure nonnegative integer valued solutions, we require that the ith shift is to appear on some work cluster or other at least n_i times. That is, $Ax \geqq n$ which can be written out as

$$
\begin{aligned}
x_1 \quad\quad\quad + x_4 &\geqq 6 \\
x_1 \quad\quad\quad\quad &\geqq 4 \\
x_2 \quad\quad\quad &\geqq 5 \\
x_2 \quad\quad\quad &\geqq 6 \\
x_3 \quad\quad &\geqq 8 \\
x_3 + x_4 &\geqq 10
\end{aligned}
\qquad [2.3.17]
$$

The objective function in this case is to minimize the total cost in terms of the number of men required to handle the day's requirements:

$$
\min \sum_{j=1}^{4} x_j \qquad [2.3.18]
$$

The solution turns out to be $x_1 = 4$, $x_2 = 6$, $x_3 = 8$, $x_4 = 2$. Notice that if [2.3.17] had been written as equality constraints (insisting on ith shift appearing exactly r_i times in some work cluster or other) then the problem would be infeasible since $x_2 = 5$ and $x_2 = 6$ are inconsistent.

The solution requires 20 men each day. If each man works exactly five days a week, then it means that a total workforce of 28 men is needed with eight off each day. Indeed if the required workforce is N, then since $r = N - 20$ is the number not working each day, one has from [2.3.8] that $r = \frac{2}{7}N$ and so $\frac{5}{7}N = 20$. The result then follows.

2.4 EXERCISES

2.4.1 As an alternate approach to the one given in the text for converting a nonlinear objective $|w - \bar{w}|$ into linear form, show that $\min |w - \bar{w}|$ is equivalent to $\min(u + v)$ with $u, v \geqq 0$ and $u - v = w - \bar{w}$.

2.4.2 Develop a 12-week rotating schedule in the case in which there are $N = 12$ brackets and the r_i have been determined as $r_1 = 0$, $r_2 = 2$, $r_3 = 4$, $r_4 = 4$, $r_5 = 6$, $r_6 = 6$, and $r_7 = 2$ (with r_1 corresponding to Monday). Prepare the schedule as in Tables 2.2–2.5, with the condition that 2-day weekends be maximized. A weekend is defined (as usual) as any consecutive 2-day period involving Saturday and Sunday. Note that: $\sum_{i=1}^{7} r_i = 2N$.

2.4.3 Show that the maximum possible number of 3-day weekends in any rotating schedule is given by $\min(r_1, r_2) + \min(r_5, r_6)$ (relation [2.3.12] in the text).

2.4.4 Show that the system of Eqs. [2.3.13] always possesses a unique solution.

2.5 NOTES AND REMARKS

2.1   The basic model of this section is due to

S. Altman, E. Beltrami, S. Rappaport, and G. Schoefle, "A Nonlinear Programming Model of Crew Assignments for Household Refuse Collection," *IEEE Trans. Systems, Man, Cybernetics* **SMC-1** (1971), 289–293.

The linear version of this model was presented by

E. Ignall, P. Kolesar, and W. Walker, "Linear Programming Models of Crew Assignments for Refuse Collection," Rand Rep. D-20497 (1970).

Another example of a nonlinear manpower allocation model is to be found in a study done for the St. Louis Police Department by

N. Heller, "Proportional Rotating Schedules," Ph.D. Dissertation, Univ. of Pennsylvania (Aug. 1969).

One version of Heller's model is roughly this. Suppose that the hourly requirements for police in one day are given by f_i, $i = 1, ..., 24$, and that men are assigned to one of three consecutive 8-hr shifts. If n_j is the number assigned on the jth shift ($j = 1, 2, 3$) and if N is the total available workforce, then the problem is to minimize the discrepancy between manpower and service needs:

$$\min \left\{ \sum_{i=1}^{8} (f_i - n_1)^2 + \sum_{i=9}^{16} f_i - n_2)^2 + \sum_{i=17}^{24} (f_i - n_3)^2 \right\}$$

subject to $n_1 + n_2 + n_3 = N$ and $n_j \geqq 0$.

An objective function of the type [2.1.12] occurs in the water resource modeling study by Cohon and Marks quoted in Section 1.4.

2.2   The Stony Brook group entered into the public affairs of New York City at a time when leverage for change was highest; namely during a period in which city administrators worked in a near-crisis atmosphere to induce the unions to *increase productivity in return for added wages and benefits*. The usual and time honored response of labor was that increased public demand for services could be met by hiring more workers, while the Lindsay administration countered by asking for changes in work practices that would achieve the *same goal at less cost*. The role of the analyst was clear—to propose simple and workable changes that would meet minimum levels of acceptability by both labor and management. The solution of the "chart day" problem was an example of such analysis. Other illustrations will appear elsewhere in these notes. A thorough chronicle of the events leading to the adoption by the union of the revised 30-week chart in the contract negotiations of 1971 between the sanitation union and the city, is given by

J. Mechling, "A Successful Innovation: Manpower Scheduling," *Urban Anal.* **2** (1974), 259–313.

It is a fascinating account of how analysis gets utilized by public agencies and it includes a description of the very real difficulties encountered in implementing the new schedules, which did not occur on a city wide basis until 1972. An equally engrossing account of another rescheduling problem, this time for New York City Police, is told in an article by

M. Moore, G. Allison, T. Bates, and J. Downing, "The Case of the Fourth Platoon," *Urban Anal.* **2** (1974), 207–258.

The celebrated "fourth platoon" case, which also occurred during the tenure of Mayor Lindsay, is one in which the Policeman's Benevolent Association (PBA) opposed what would have appeared to have been a viable rescheduling of the police, designed to increase their effectiveness during high crime hours.

The *New York Times* quote is from an article which appeared on November 17, 1971, ("Sanitation Union Wins Raise . . . Accord Links Pay to Better Service"). As it happens, in the subsequent administration of Mayor Beame, the 30-week schedule was downgraded somewhat to one of 25 weeks with a slight loss of coverage on Mondays (see *New York Times*, "Productivity Programs in the City Changed Drastically by Beame," February 23, 1975).

In the notation of Section 2.1, the number N of brackets is 30 and the n_j are 28, 27, 26, 23, 23, 23, 0 with corresponding r_j of 2, 3, 4, 7, 7, 7, 30. There was nothing magical about the number 30. The larger the number of brackets the better is the fit which is possible to the required daily service profile. The old system of six brackets (or "charts," as they were called) allowed for no compromise on matching Monday's demands except by having either all groups work Monday (too many) or using five out of six (too little). But with 30 there was more maneuverability in how men could be matched to demand. The best fit of course occurs when each work crew constitutes a bracket, but then the corresponding time horizon necessary for a rotating schedule consists of too many weeks. Thirty brackets gave a good match and provided an acceptable 30-week rotation. As it happens the number of brackets could have been some what more or less and still provided essentially the same allocation.

Other implemented rotating schedules are documented in studies by

N. Heller and W. Stenzel, "Design of Police Work Schedules," *Urban Anal.* **2** (1974), 21–50; J. Howell, "Cyclic Scheduling of Nursing Personnel," *Hospitals: J. Hospital Assoc.* **40** (1966).

2.3   The basic modeling reference here is two papers by Bodin:

L. Bodin, "Towards a General Model for Manpower Scheduling," *Urban Anal.* **1** (1973), 191–208, 223–246.

An instructive and simple-to-read special case is treated by

G. Monroe, "Scheduling Manpower for Service Operations," *Indust. Eng.* (1970), 10–17.

Another study for the New York City Transit Authority is by

L. Liu, "Manpower Scheduling in Transportation Systems and the Multiple Set Covering Problem," Ph.D. Dissertation, SUNY, Stony Brook (July 1973).

Liu's analysis was complicated by a set of rigid regulations regarding coffee breaks and end of work shift. Since the trains do not remain idle while the crews take a break, the subway schedule is decoupled from the assignment of workers and this necessitates the use of overlapping and even concurrent shifts.

3

Models for Deploying Emergency Services I: Response Delays

3.1 MODELS OF CONGESTION

No doubt everyone has at some time or other experienced the inconvenience and frustration of waiting on lines to be serviced. Cars waiting to get through toll booths, airplanes in a holding pattern before landing, people standing on line at a post office or bank—the examples are numerous. Abstractly, one can think of each queue (or waiting line) in terms of an arrival stream of "customers" or calls for service, followed by one or more "servers." Cars, airplanes, and people form the arrival stream in the cases just cited, whereas the toll booths, the runway, and the bank clerks form the servers.

In the public sector some of the most significant examples deal with an emergency response system in which calls arrive for service at a central dispatcher who then screens and processes the calls. The dispatcher assigns one of n response units (if not all are busy) to the scene of the incident or call. The response units are typically ambulances, police cars, and fire trucks, and together they form n parallel servers. However, if all are busy, then calls being handled by the dispatcher must be held until a unit becomes available, thereby backlogging the system.

Congestion in such systems occurs because of the unpredictable pattern of the arrival stream and because the service time is itself variable. If one arrival occurs exactly every 10 sec and if service is exactly 8 sec per customer, then clearly, no waiting line forms. But if arrivals are random with an *average* interarrival time of 10 sec and if service time is also uncertain with an *average* of 8 sec per call, then sometimes the server is idle and there will be no line while at other times there is a rapid buildup of customers waiting in queue. A fundamental problem is to determine the average time a customer needs to wait in line before getting served or, if one prefers, the average time between arrival and departure after service. If this time is unacceptable then what should the average service time be or, if that is not changable, how many servers should there be, in order to bring service to within acceptable limits? Of course if there are enough servers or if service time is decreased (both of them costly alternatives), then no significant queue buildup will ever develop. However, there is a tradeoff here between providing adequate service and the cost necessary to maintain it as we see in Fig. 3.1. Here the cost of service is held proportional to the level provided and "cost" to a customer is some measure of inconvenience or loss which is expressed in the same units as service cost.

Prior to discussing delays in emergency services in more detail we examine briefly the analytical structure of a simple queue:

Assume that one is in a municipal office which processes monthly un-employment checks (a time example in 1976). During office hours people arrive at random according to a Poisson distribution to collect their payment, at the average rate of 9/hr. Let λ denote this arrival rate. The single server is a municipal employee who can process each claim for payment at the average rate, call it μ, of 12/hr. However, the exact service time is also an unknown, indeed a random quantity and is exponentially distributed. From Appendix C we know that as long as the ratio λ/μ is less than one, the average time a "customer" spends waiting on line for service is given by

$$\lambda/\mu(\mu-\lambda) \qquad\qquad [3.1.1]$$

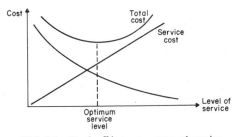

FIG. 3.1   Tradeoff between cost and service.

in the "steady state" and that the average time spent on line and in being served together is 1 divided by $\mu - \lambda$. If the ratio λ/μ is greater than or equal to one, the queue is unstable in the sense that it eventually grows longer and longer without bound.

As we know, the number λ/μ is the fraction of time in which the server is busy. In our example λ/μ is $\frac{3}{4}$ so that on the average the clerk is handling clients 45 out of every 60 min. The average time spent by the person in line is $\frac{1}{4}$ of an hour, or 15 min. We now state a result which goes against the intuition of some people who hear it for the first time. Suppose that ten clients arrive on the average every hour, instead of nine. This represents a roughly 10% increase in the arrival rate and one would expect the average waiting time in line to be correspondingly modest. In fact, as our formulas show, the average waiting time is now 25 min—a 67% increase in the average delay! When 11 customers arrive per hour the delay is 55 min and for 12 customers the waiting line is infinite. Note a curious fact here: even though the average delay before service is 25 min (when ten people arrive each hour) the fraction of time the clerk is busy is $\frac{10}{12} = \frac{5}{6}$ or during $\frac{1}{6}$ of his time (10 min out of each hour) he is idle! Such is the nature of randomness.

Going back to the original example, let us decide that a 15-min wait is too long. What can be done about it? Well, one can add another clerk who then handles arrivals at a separate line (much as is done in banks, for example) or the two clerks can work together from the same queue or one can replace the tired and disinterested clerk by a highly efficient individual who can process on the average, let us say, 24 customers/hr (an unlikely possibility, but please overlook it in order to simplify our discussion). The three possibilities can be exhibited schematically in Fig. 3.2.

What would you guess represents the best alternative? The first case is equivalent to having two distinct queues in which the arrival rate is exactly half of the single line rate. Since $\lambda/2 = 4.5$, then each queue has an average waiting time in line of 3 min. Note another curious consequence of randomness here: if jockeying between lines is not permitted (that is, if each arrival picks a line at random and stays on it), then it may happen that some lines are occasionally shrunken to zero while the other is backlogged. Incidently, this writer pessimistically believes that whatever line he chooses to stand on *always* turns out to be the longest. In the second case, the two clerks work

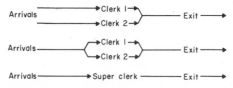

FIG. 3.2   Three service possibilities for a queue.

from the same line and so here the formulas given above will not suffice. Reference to Eq. [C.23] of the Appendix C shows that in this case the average waiting time in line is now 48 sec. The third case is where μ is doubled to the value of 24 so that λ/μ is now $\frac{3}{8}$. In this case, formula [3.1.1] gives an average customer delay of 1.5 min.

One is tempted to conclude that the best service alternative is to have two clerks work together. However, suppose service is judged in terms of how long the person must wait until service is completed. In order to compute these times it suffices to add to the waiting times the average time it takes for a clerk to complete service. In the first and second cases this time is 5 min/customer ($\frac{1}{12}$ of 60 min) but it is only 2.5 min for the third alternative, as the reader readily appreciates. The total waiting times in the system are now, respectively, 8 min, 5 min and 48 sec, and 4 min. Quite clearly having an efficient clerk works best in this case.

One more counterintuitive result should be mentioned here. When the arrival rate λ increases, so does the workload. In order to match this increasing demand for service, it would appear reasonable to let the service rate also increase in proportion to λ. Although this is not usually possible to accomplish without increasing the number of servers, let us suppose, for simplicity, that we are dealing with a single server queue. Formula [3.1.1] shows that if, for example, λ and therefore μ are doubled, then the average time in line is halved. What this means is that a policy of allocating service in proportion to demand leads to an overallocation during periods of peak demand. From the point of view of cost, this is not an efficient use of resources. Instead, let us consider a better procedure. To be specific, look again at the problem of a single clerk handling unemployment checks. If 15 min is the maximum acceptable delay, what should the service rate be to match an increased demand of 12 arrivals/hr? What one wants, in fact, is that value of μ for which λ divided by $\mu(\mu - \lambda)$ is $\frac{1}{4}$ (when $\lambda = 12$). This leads to the quadratic equation given by $\mu^2 - 12\mu + 48 = 0$ whose solution is roughly $\mu = 15$. Therefore instead of increasing μ by $33\frac{1}{3}\%$ (to match a similar increase in λ) it suffices in this case to increase it by 25%. Notice also that the utilization of the server (that is the probability λ/μ that it is busy) is now .8 in contrast to .75 before. Therefore a higher λ requires a better use of the server in order to achieve the same service level. The point of our remarks is simply to demonstrate that the analysis of queues typically involves many considerations and that careful study of a congestion problem often reveals features that are not apparent to intuition alone. Unfortunately some queuing situations are sufficiently complex as to defy the usual analytical tools and for this reason more expensive methods must be employed as a substitute. The most useful tool is called computer simulation and we will comment on it later.

Let us now examine waiting lines in a different context. Suppose one has a region serviced by a single hospital and that calls for service occur at random, averaging 9 calls/hr. A dispatcher then sends an ambulance (if one is available) to the incident. Assuming no dispatcher delays, what is the average time a patient must wait before the ambulance arrives? In order to answer this one must first observe that ambulance response time depends on the size and shape of the region, unlike the previous example in which service time depended only on the clerk's efficiency. It will be convenient to make some simplifying assumptions here concerning the region. Restrict the area to be square shaped with each side a length of d miles. The hospital itself is taken to be in the geographic center of the region. As it happens, these assumptions do not seriously invalidate the kind of conclusions that follow from a queuing analysis and are again made only to simplify the arguments used.

It can be established that the average response distance (as we show later in Chapter 4) is $d/2$ miles and so, if vehicle speed is assumed constant, mean travel time is proportional to $d/2$. However the distribution of this travel time is no longer exponential (as we will also show in the next chapter) and so the average waiting time before arrival of the ambulance is no longer found by the formula given earlier for the case of a single ambulance (single "server") assigned to the hospital. Nonetheless, it can be computed and is given by

$$W_q = \lambda/2\mu^2 \left[(\mu^2 V + 1)/(1 - \lambda/2\mu) \right] \qquad [3.1.2]$$

where V is the variance of the service time distribution. Note that if service time is indeed exponential then, since $V = 1/\mu^2$ in this case, [3.1.2] reduces to [3.1.1]. At the other extreme, *if service time is a constant*, $1/\mu$, then the variance is zero and [3.1.2] becomes

$$\lambda/[2\mu(\mu - \lambda)] \qquad [3.1.3]$$

which is half the expected waiting time which occurs under exponential service. This again demonstrates the role of uncertainty as a source of delay.

Suppose, for the sake of argument, that W_q, as computed from [3.1.2], is not acceptable. In order to improve response time it is suggested that the hospital's area of responsibility be halved so that one now expects $\lambda = \frac{9}{2}$ calls|hr. This is similar in spirit to splitting at random the waiting line of the earlier example into queues handled by two distinct clerks. However, a smaller area also affects the average travel time of the emergency vehicle since it has less distance to travel to reach an incident. A curious fact now emerges which illustrates once again that intuition can be a fallible guide. A number of people, I imagine, would hazard a guess that this travel time is itself halved. Not so. In fact, since the area of the square is d^2, then half the area is $d^2/2$ and for a square this means that each side is of $d/\sqrt{2}$. But then the average travel time is one half of $d/\sqrt{2}$. Thus, a 50% reduction in area results in only a 30% reduction in response time! A question now arises as to whether it is better to halve the response area or to double the number of ambulances in the system. Judging from the analysis used in an earlier example, it would appear that doubling the vehicle fleet size is a better option, but since halving an area also reduces travel time, as we saw, then the alternative is less clear. It is in problems of this kind that analytical methods could be used to advantage. Unfortunately, an analogue of formula [3.1.2] is not known for $s > 1$ servers and one must use a surrogate measure of performance, as explained in Section 3.2. Note incidently, that both alternatives cost about the same since halving the area means that an equal number of vehicles be assigned to give the remaining half area equal coverage.

In modeling of emergency service a number of assumptions are implicitly or explicitly made. It is appropriate to review some of them here. To begin with, the typical analysis revolves around a queuing system which is observed in a steady state and in which the arrival rate is a constant λ. However, λ does vary over time, both daily and weekly, and so one must agree that the analysis is used for a peak arrival period or any other period during which λ is indeed roughly constant. The trouble is that such time spans may be short enough so that transient effects cannot be ignored. That is, in practice a system may rarely be observed in equilibrium and so the steady-state assumption is only more or less an approximation. Another assumption is that of a constant mean service rate. This can be violated in a number of contexts. For example, as an emergency fire service becomes backlogged in a heavy demand period, the response units get to the scene of an incident less promptly than normal (average travel time would increase if distant vehicles need to be called in to augment the already hard pressed units) and this delay can escalate the incident and thereby increase the time required for service at the scene. Therefore μ depends on the number of busy units in such cases. A more serious problem is that the service time may not be exponentially distributed.

A typical time profile of an emergency response looks like the one shown in Fig. 3.3. Now response time is usually measured from t_2 to t_4 but it could be from t_2 to t_5 or even t_2 to t_6 in some cases (such as an ambulance which

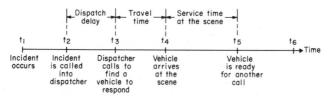

FIG. 3.3 Time profile of an emergency service system.

brings the patient back to hospital). The sum of these delays need not be exponential. In practice, t_2-t_3 is often ignored, and in police or fire work t_3-t_4 is generally small in comparison to t_4-t_5. In such cases the extent to which time spent at the scene of an incident is exponential, is the measure of how well the formulas of Appendix C can be used. In ambulance work, on the contrary, t_3-t_4 is likely to be more significant than time at the scene, and here, as we saw above, the exponential assumption is generally not valid. For ambulances, t_4-t_5 is usually short and fairly constant, while t_5-t_6 is close to t_3-t_4. These remarks apply primarily to *urban emergency* systems in which travel distances are short and alarm rates are high. In suburban or rural areas, t_3-t_4 would tend to be significant for all emergency services, whereas t_2-t_3 would be less important because of lower call rates and increased availability of vehicles.

It is apparent from the diagram above that the total delay is formed by several *queues in tandem*. In fact t_2-t_3 is itself two service blocks that look like those in Fig. 3.4, and we see that if all of the *s* vehicles are temporarily

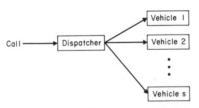

FIG. 3.4   Example of queues in tandem.

unavailable then the call is held by the dispatcher until a unit can be sent from an adjacent district or until one of the original *s* vehicles again becomes available (at time t_6). If the average service time of the dispatcher is $1/\mu$, when a unit is available for dispatch, this time will increase whenever entry of the call into the second queue is blocked by all *s* servers being occupied. This phenomenon of blocking when one queue tries to empty into another is roughly what happens also in a telemedical network which consists of a hierarchal queueing system for which there are *s* primary neighborhood health centers staffed by physician assistants or nurses. A secondary level of treatment is available through a physician who is linked by television to the *s* centers. After consultation at the primary level a patient may be referred to the physician for further treatment. However if this secondary level is busy, the patient is blocked for a while; see Fig. 3.5.

A final example of such in tandem hierarchal systems is that of garbage trucks arriving at a disposal site which consists of a weighing station (where a waiting line sometimes occurs as the loaded trucks are weighed one by one

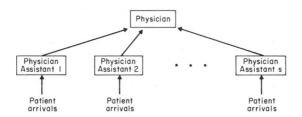

FIG. 3.5 Schematic of a hierarchial medical system (in-tandem queues).

on a drive-on–drive-off scale) followed by a platform with open bins into which the trucks unload their haul of refuse (this is the actual situation at the New York City marine transfer stations). When all the bins are occupied, any truck at the weighing station must wait for an opening before it can move onto the platform area, thereby increasing the likelihood of congestion at the arrival end of the disposal facility. Schematically, one has the following configuration displayed in Fig. 3.6.

The platform area can be thought of as an n-service queue with each of the n bins as a server working in parallel with the others. The weighing scale is a single server which precedes the platform.

To illustrate how the analysis of this kind of queue can be used for policy recommendations imagine that a municipality is about to decide between diverting part of the truck arrivals away from a congested facility to another dump site much further away (thereby increasing transportation costs) or of renovating the existing structure to include an additional disposal bin. One knows the costs of each alternative but the benefits become apparent only after an analysis of how much congestion is relieved when λ is reduced or when the number of servers is increased. All these examples are difficult to treat analytically, unless the several service blocks can be usefully combined and then viewed as a single service block. This is largely the way such problems will be handled in the following sections.

Before proceeding, however, it will be useful to digress somewhat by reconsidering the in-tandem queue of garbage trucks waiting to unload. If one could observe hundreds of typical arrivals and record their progress through

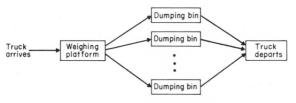

FIG. 3.6 Schematic of a garbage truck dump station (in-tandem queues).

the disposal facility, then it is possible to arrive at an estimate of the average waiting time until the completion of service simply by totaling the times of each and every truck and then dividing by the number of trucks which were observed. However if the objective is to evaluate how the system behaves under a proposed change—for example, a new weighing mechanism is installed or some of the dumping bins are closed down or more trucks are allowed to use the facility than before—then there is nothing to observe until after the change takes place. Therefore one either uses analytical formulas of the kind discussed earlier (when they are available) or resorts to the device of simulating actual behavior in order to determine whether or not the change is worthwhile. In our case since the in-tandem system may involve blocking of service in one queue because of congestion in the other, analytical results are not easy to come by and so what we would like to do is to create typical case histories of a truck working its way through the facility. The essential ingredient is the ability to reproduce a facsimile of a random arrival or of random service or dump time and then to use these times to simulate an actual truck arrival and departure. If repeated often enough (a simple bookkeeping task performed quickly and accurately on a computer) then tolerably good estimates of how the queue behaves can be obtained. This procedure is called *computer simulation* and if the program is written cleverly enough then one can quite readily, for example, vary the number of disposal bins until acceptable truck disposal times are obtained or, in another instance, it would be possible to quickly simulate waiting times under a variety of arrival and service rates.

We can illustrate the essential logic of the method in a simple hand-computed example based on a study carried out for New York City in which a particular marine transfer station was observed for an extended period of several days at those hours during which congestion was at a peak. Interarrival, weighing, and dumping times were all recorded for about 100 trucks (details of the sampling are available in a reference cited in the notes) and the standard statistical tests (chi-squared and Kolmogorov–Smirnov) applied to determine whether or not the data fit certain theoretical distributions within acceptable confidence levels. As it happened, the truck arrivals followed' a Poisson distribution with a mean interarrival time of 72.45 sec, whereas weighing was a constant 35 sec *plus* a variable time given by the gamma distribution with $n = 2$ and a mean of 16 sec (see Appendix C for a discussion of such distributions, especially Eqs. [C.8] and [C.9]). Dumping time was, similarly, a constant 80 sec followed by a variable amount also given by a gamma distribution with $n = 4$ and a mean of 31 sec. In order to perform the simulation one needs to pick "typical" arrival, weigh, and dump times for succeeding trucks according to the probability distributions which were obtained from observations. If the probability function is denoted by

$F(t)$ then it has a corresponding density, obtained by differentiation, which we write as $f(t)$. The expression $y = F(t)$ is an increasing function of $t \geq 0$ taking on values between zero and one, with a unique inverse $F^{-1}(y) = t$. Therefore if one chooses a number y at random in the interval from zero to one (that is, according to a uniform distribution on the unit interval), then

$$F(t) = \text{prob}[y \leq F(t)] = \text{prob}[F^{-1}(y) \leq t]$$

so that $F^{-1}(y)$ is a number drawn from the distribution whose density is $f(t)$. For instance, in the case of the above Poisson truck arrivals, the interarrival function is given by $F(t) = 1 - e^{-72.45t}$. Therefore, if y is a random number (there are many ways of choosing random numbers on a computer, most of them variants of the idea of spinning a roulette wheel which is marked between 0 and 1 and reading off the number at the location where the pointer stops) one simply inverts $F(t)$ to obtain $t = -(1/72.45)\ln(1-y)$. In this way each y gives rise to a value of t which is typical of exponential interarrival times. Virtually the same idea applies to obtaining service times which obey a gamma distribution. As one sees from Appendix C, when $n = 2$ the gamma is obtained as the distribution corresponding to the sum of two exponentially distributed variables. Thus in the case of weighing times, since the mean is 16 sec, one first obtains two values of t from an exponential distribution whose mean is 8 sec (using the procedure just described) and then their sum is computed to give the desired gamma distributed weighing time (actually one adds a constant 35 sec to this sum to conform with the delays at weigh-in). Dumping times are generated in an analogous way.

TABLE 3.1

Truck interarrival time	Weighing time	Dumping time
0	41	105
50	48	135
68	72	113
79	65	111
44	37	126
70	59	120

Table 3.1 corresponds to six randomly generated times obtained in the manner just explained (rounded, for simplicity, to the nearest second). Suppose now that the disposal facility has only two dumping bins. Keeping in mind the schematic of an MTS which was displayed earlier in this section, one begins by letting the first truck arrive at the dump at time zero. Since there is no waiting line initially, it is immediately weighed and it then goes

TABLE 3.2

SIMULATION OF WAITING LINES AT A DUMPSITE

Truck	Accumulated arrival time	Waiting time to weigh	Accumulated end of weigh time	Waiting time to dump	Accumulated end of dump time		Total time in the facility
					Bin 1	Bin 2	
1	0	0	41	0	146	0	146
2	50	0	98	0	146	233	183
3	118	0	190	0	303	233	185
4	197	0	262	0	303	373	176
5	241	21	299	4	429	373	188

to one of the two empty bins. Reading Table 3.1, one sees that the truck spends a total of $41 + 105 = 146$ sec in the facility before leaving. The second truck arrives 50 sec after the first one. Again there is no waiting and, as the reader verifies, its total time in the system is $48 + 135 = 183$ sec. Note however that it must use the second dumping bin since the first one is already occupied by the first truck.

In order to keep track of what is happening it is convenient to order the events continuously in time starting at time zero, accumulating as we go along. The first five trucks would then be recorded as in Table 3.2. What happens to the sixth truck is left as an exercise to the reader. By the time the fifth truck arrives the weighing platform is occupied and so it must wait on line for 21 sec. Moreover, upon terminating the weigh-in it then finds that neither dumping bin is available and so there is a further delay of 4 sec until the first bin is again free for use. In each case the total time between departure and arrival is easily computed and is shown in Table 3.2. The total of these times is $146 + 183 + 185 + 176 + 188 = 876$ and so the estimated average time in the system is $\frac{876}{5}$ or about 176 sec. It is a characteristic property of sample means that with more and more samples or trials they become increasingly accurate estimates of the actual, but unknown average value. Because each truck cycle through the facility can be obtained very rapidly on a computer, a large number of samples can be generated until one has sufficient confidence in the estimates.

There is another point that should be made and it concerns the use of simulation to test certain transient effects that are hardly accessible to a steady state queuing analysis. For example, if the arrival rate of trucks is increased at an already congested disposal facility this has the effect of exacerbating the problem but perhaps it could be compensated for by having trucks at weigh-in rush through their procedure in response to the impatient backlog of waiting vehicles. This "horn-honking" effect, as a colleague of mine once referred to it, can be tested by shortening the mean weighing time in proportion to each increase in mean arrival times. The interesting thing to observe here is that as trucks move more quickly into the dumping area it is likely that the probability of finding all bins occupied will also increase and so after a time new arrivals are blocked from entering the area. Therefore there is no point in attempting to improve the service time of weighing beyond a certain level. This is illustrated in Fig. 3.7 which reproduces in rough outline the kind of results obtained in actual computer trials.

The same question could be raised about new arrivals which balk at joining an already long queue. This can be modeled by assuming that the arrival rate is dependent on the number of vehicles already on line. The truck which balks presumably goes to some other facility and one would like to determine average waiting times based on this assumption. Incidently, during the

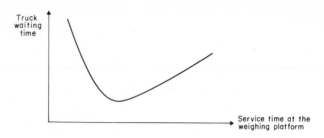

FIG. 3.7 Truck waiting time as a function of weighing time. Waiting time is assumed proportional to interarrival time.

gasoline shortages of early 1974 it would have been interesting to observe whether long lines encouraged quicker service and whether cars balked at entering such lines or, because of a concern of being deprived of another opportunity to fill up, long lines actually enhanced the arrival rate.

3.2 COST VERSUS SERVICE

Let us consider again an ambulance response system consisting of s primary vehicles, each of which services a call at an average service rate μ. We ignore dispatcher delay and so μ refers essentially to roundtrip travel time together with service time at the scene of an incident. Thus an ambulance is busy when it is out on call. Let us assume that if all s units are occupied then the call is lost in the sense that it is serviced by some secondary emergency unit or is serviced by a unit dispatched from a neighboring sector or district. Therefore as far as the s primary servers are concerned *no waiting line* is ever formed. In this case an appropriate measure of service (that is, of how well the ambulance system performs) is the *probability that all s units are occupied* because this then means that the call has to be serviced by a secondary unit.

This service level is affected by the value of s and of μ. The value of μ is determined principally by average speed of the vehicles and the area of the response sector for the s units. Before we examine the tradeoffs involved, we need to derive the steady state formulas for the probability that n out of the s units are busy. Since no line is allowed to form, this is the probability π_n of there being exactly n units in the system, $n \leq s$. Assume, to begin with, that the service times for each ambulance are exponential with mean $1/\mu$. Assume, also, Poisson arrivals with $\lambda_n = 0$ for $n > s$ and $\lambda_n \equiv \lambda$ for $n \leq s$. Then from Eq. [C.12] of Appendix C,

$$\pi_n = [(\lambda/\mu)^n/n!]\,\pi_0, \qquad n \leq s$$

However, $\sum_{n=0}^{s} \pi_n = 1$ in this case, and so π_0 is found to be

$$\pi_0 = \left(\sum_{n=0}^{s} \frac{(\lambda/\mu)^n}{n!} \right)^{-1}$$

Therefore,

$$\pi_n = \frac{(\lambda/\mu)^n/n!}{\sum_{n=0}^{s} (\lambda/\mu)^n/n!} \qquad\qquad [3.2.1]$$

which are known as the *Erlang loss formulas*. In particular, when $n = s$, the probability of all s units being busy is given by

$$\pi_s = \frac{(\lambda/\mu)^s/s!}{\sum_{n=0}^{s} (\lambda/\mu)^n/n!} \qquad\qquad [3.2.2]$$

It has been shown (see reference in the notes) that [3.2.1] continues to be true in the general case of an arbitrary service time distribution with mean $1/\mu$. Note that if s is very large or, equivalently, if λ is small compared to μ, then

$$\sum_{n=0}^{s} (\lambda/\mu)^n/n! \sim e^{\lambda/\mu}$$

in which case [3.2.1] becomes

$$\pi_n = \rho^n/n!\, e^{-\rho} \qquad\qquad [3.2.3]$$

which is the Poisson distribution, with mean $\rho = \lambda/\mu$. This shows that the average number of busy servers is roughly ρ and so $(\rho/s) = (\lambda/s\mu)$ is the average fraction of busy units. This is the *utilization rate* of the service capacity represented by s ambulances. However it is the parameter ρ itself rather than ρ/s that will be identified as the measure of system utilization in what follows since it represents the intensity of demand for service. The expression π_s represents the "cost" to a customer and $1 - \pi_s$ is designated as the *service level*. If one plots π_s versus ρ for different s, the Fig. 3.8 results.

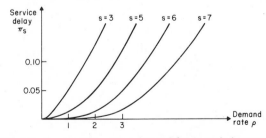

FIG. 3.8   Service delay versus demand for an ambulance system.

Note that in order to maintain a 95% service level (or probability of a delay equal to .05) at $\rho = 1$ requires three ambulances. If the arrival rate doubles so that $\rho = 2$ then one only needs five ambulances to achieve the same level of performance. At $\rho = 3$, six ambulances suffice. Once again, as in Section 3.1, this illustrates the dictum that a *doubling of demand does not have to be matched by a doubling of service effort* to meet a given performance goal but that something less will in fact be enough. This also suggests the general principle that *it is more efficient to provide service over a large sector than a small one* (that is, in response to a higher demand rate λ) since better utilization is achieved this way. In fact the utilization rates ρ/s for $\rho = 1, 2, 3$ are respectively $\frac{1}{3}, \frac{2}{5}, \frac{3}{6}$ which means that the cost per vehicle to the municipality decreases as the area of the service sector increases. This is a question of economy of scale. Thus, as λ increases it is generally better to increase the number of vehicles working that sector than to split the sector into smaller nonoverlapping areas with some vehicles assigned to each. To put it another way, the marginal return in terms of achieving a desired service level $1 - \pi_s$ is greater in large regions with high utilization rates than in smaller sectors with low demand rates. Notice, however, that when service levels are already close to one then small further improvements in service level require a disproportionate increase in vehicles required. This is shown in the Fig. 3.9, which is taken from Fig. 3.8.

Note, for example, that improving service from the 95% to 99% levels at $\rho = 3$, let us say, requires that we increase ambulances from six to eight— a $33\frac{1}{3}\%$ increase! This law of diminishing returns can also be read off of Fig. 3.8 by noticing that service level is concave as a function of the number of vehicles, for each ρ. That is, as the number of units increases, the marginal improvement in performance decreases.

If a call needs to wait for a secondary unit to service it (with probability π_s) then this has two effects. The first is that the caller will probably either

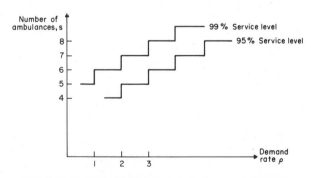

FIG. 3.9 Number of required ambulances versus demand.

experience some delay until a more distant ambulance arrives or will be inconvenienced by being handled by less experienced secondary units. From the point of view of the municipality which operates the ambulance service, secondary units cost more since they are paid on a per call basis which is usually higher than that of the primary units. The cost of the primary service is roughly proportional to the number of manned ambulances, cost $= sC_p$, where C_p is the cost per vehicle per hour. The secondary source gets paid C_s dollars per call. If $1/\mu$ is also the mean service time (in hours) of the secondary unit then $C_s' = \mu C_s$ is the expected cost of these extra vehicles. The expected secondary cost is therefore the expected number of calls per unit time multiplied by the expected cost per call. Now during a unit time of 1 hr, secondary units are needed a fraction of time equal to π_s. Since λ calls arrive per hour then $\lambda \pi_s$ is the expected number of calls answered by the secondary service. Therefore total cost is

$$\text{Cost} = sC_p + \lambda \pi_s C_s = sC_p + \lambda/\mu \, \pi_s C_s'$$

Now let $\gamma = C_s'/C_p$, the average ratio of secondary to primary cost per hour. Then

$$\text{Cost} = C_p(s + \gamma \rho \pi_s) \qquad\qquad [3.2.4]$$

It can be shown from [3.2.4] that if $\gamma < 1$ then it is more economical to operate without primary ambulances. When $\gamma > 1$ this is still true provided ρ is small enough. This is because for low service demands it tends to be too costly to keep an underutilized full-time staff on the payroll. A more expensive part-time service may be more worthwhile in such cases.

3.3   A SPATIAL "HYPERCUBE" MODEL

The queueing analysis used in the previous section can be extended considerably by asking not only for the number of vehicles required to provide a service but also for the deployment policy that permits these vehicles to be efficiently utilized. Although the analysis to be given presently was designed in the context of a police response system, similar considerations would be applicable in fire response work. The idea is this. A given area is broken down into a number of disjoint sectors or beats each of which is the responsibility of some response unit. If there are m sectors and s vehicles, one would like to determine which vehicle is assigned to what sector so as to minimize average response time and so that workload for each of the units is roughly the same. Indeed one could also ask what the size and shape of each beat should be in addition to knowing how to deploy the vehicles. These questions take on real significance in an urban environment where the alarm or call rate is high

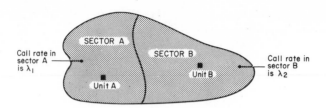

FIG. 3.10   A 2-sector response area.

because the probability that a unit is busy is then also high. This means that one needs to know which units to assign as backup vehicles for intersector dispatching. Consider a simple prototype situation in which there are two sectors, as shown in Fig. 3.10, with one response vehicle stationed at each of the marked locations. If a call arrives in area A and the unit A is free, it responds to the incident. If A is busy, then unit B is dispatched and if both are busy then the call is assumed lost or serviced elsewhere, as in Section 3.2. Similarly for an incident reported in sector B. Using this dispatch policy: what is the average response time to any call in sectors A or B and what is the workload of units A and B? What, in fact, is the fraction of time that each unit spends in responding to calls outside its own sector and what should be the boundary separating both sectors so as to improve these measures of performance? These are the questions we intend to look at.

Using the analysis of Section 3.2 it is possible, of course, to find the probability that none or one or both units are busy (and therefore that a call is "lost") by using the Erlang formulas [3.2.1] with $s = 2$. However now one asks a more subtle queueing question since the *calls distinguish between servers*! That is, the spatial configuration of the problem (we previously ignored spatial considerations) together with the dispatch policy dictates that a call arriving in A *prefers* server A over B whereas a call in B prefers service by B. This means that whereas for $s = 2$ there previously were three possibilities to consider defined by π_0, π_1, and π_2 one now has four possible outcomes defined by P_0, the probability that both units are free; P_1, the probability that unit A is busy, unit B is free; P_2, the probability that unit B is busy, unit A is free; and P_3, the probability that both units are busy and therefore that the call is lost. It is apparent that $P_0 = \pi_0$ and $P_3 = \pi_2$ and that $P_1 + P_2 = \pi_1$. It is also apparent that $P_0 + P_1 + P_2 + P_3 = 1$. It turns out that the key to evaluating the various performance measures listed above is to first determine values for the probabilities P_n. In the process of doing so one extends the Erlang formulas in a significant way.

Although the derivation of steady-state formulas can be carried out for arbitrary s we wish to make the discussion more specific by looking at a concrete example in which there are $s = 3$ vehicles and $m = 5$ sectors, as

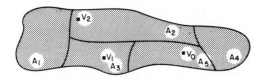

FIG. 3.11 Example with three vehicles stationed within five sectors.

displayed in Fig. 3.11. Here the sectors are labeled by $S_1, ..., S_5$ and the responding units by V_0, V_1, and V_2. The sector A_i is assumed to generate calls in a Poisson manner at average rate λ_i and service is taken to be exponential with a constant rate of μ for each vehicle (which by and large excludes most ambulance services). The dispatch policy, one of the many possible, is defined in Table 3.3. In order to keep track of the various possibilities let a triplet

TABLE 3.3

Call originates in sector	Responding unit		
	First choice	Second choice	Third choice
A_1	V_2	V_1	V_0
A_2	V_2	V_1	V_0
A_3	V_1	V_0	V_2
A_4	V_0	V_2	V_1
A_5	V_0	V_1	V_2

binary vector denote which units are busy or free. For example, $(0,0,0)$ means all are free; $(0,1,1)$ means units V_1 and V_2 are busy and V_0 is free; $(1,0,1)$ means units V_0 and V_2 are busy and V_1 is free; etc. Notice that there are $2^3 = 8$ possibilities in all. In general, with s vehicles there would be 2^s binary vectors representing the various "states" of the system in contrast to the $s+1$ states possible when servers are not distinguished (as in the classical Erlang formula case).

Returning to the dispatch policy we see for example, that if the system is in state $(0,1,0)$ then V_2 is sent to a call in A_1 or A_2 and V_0 to a call in V_3 or in A_4 or A_5 and when the system is in state $(0,1,1)$ then V_0 is sent to any call, where ever it originates. In order to derive steady-state equations of balance from these rules, the arguments employed in Appendix C need to be extended somewhat. To begin with, we assume as always, that *at most one departure or one arrival* can occur in any sufficiently small interval of time h. This means that during h the transitions from one binary state vector to another occur with at most one busy unit becoming free or one free unit

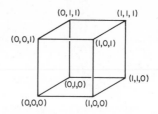

FIG. 3.12   Transition states for the case of three vehicles.

becoming busy. A pictorial view of what is happening can be obtained by drawing a cube with $2^3 = 8$ vertices (Fig. 3.12), each of which represent a possible state of the system. Instantaneous transitions (i.e., in very small time intervals) only can occur *from a given vertex to an adjacent one*. In the case of $s > 3$ vehicles, one correspondingly represents the 2^s states by a hypercube in s-dimensional space (unfortunately, no pictures can be drawn) in which transitions again occur to neighboring vertices only.

It will be convenient to label the vertices from zero to seven with the associated steady-state probability of being in that state denoted by π_n (instead of P_n) as shown in Fig. 3.13. There is some perversity in the choice of notation, since π_n meant something different in Section 3.2, but we are certain there will be no confusion.

Each state is linked to exactly three others by adjacency. To find the associated probabilities let us examine some cases. Thus, to go from state 3 to state 5 means that either calls arrive in A_1 or A_2, or that calls arrive in A_4 and are answered by V_2 since V_0 is busy. The probability of one or the other of these disjoint events during time h is

$$1 - e^{-\lambda_1 h} + (1 - e^{-\lambda_2 h}) + (1 - e^{-\lambda_4 h}) \sim (\lambda_1 + \lambda_2 + \lambda_4)h$$

To reach state 5 from vertex 7 requires simply that V_1 becomes free during h.

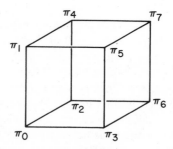

FIG. 3.13   Transition probabilities for the case of three vehicles.

This probability is μh. In order to go from vertex 1 to 5 means that V_0 becomes busy because of a call in A_4 or A_5. Ignoring higher order terms this probability is $(\lambda_4 + \lambda_5)h$. Finally, state 5 remains unchanged if V_0, V_2 do not become free and V_1 does not become busy which, to first order terms, is $1 - (2\mu h + \lambda h)$, where

$$\lambda = \lambda_1 + \lambda_2 + \lambda_3 + \lambda_4 + \lambda_5$$

Therefore,

$$\pi_5(t+h) = \pi_5(t)(1 - 2\mu h - \lambda h) + \pi_1(t)(\lambda_4 + \lambda_5)h \\ + \pi_3(t)(\lambda_1 + \lambda_2 + \lambda_4)h + \pi_7(t)\mu h$$

and so

$$[\pi_5(t+h) - \pi_5(t)]/h = -(2\mu + \lambda)\pi_5(t) + (\lambda_4 + \lambda_5)\pi_1(t) \\ + (\lambda_1 + \lambda_2 + \lambda_4)\pi_3(t) + \mu\pi_7(t)$$

Letting $h \to 0$ and then setting the derivative to zero (as in Appendix C) gives the steady state algebraic relation

$$(2\mu + \lambda)\pi_5 = (\lambda_1 + \lambda_2 + \lambda_4)\pi_3 + (\lambda_4 + \lambda_5)\pi_1 + \mu\pi_7 \qquad [3.3.1]$$

The remaining steady-state probabilities are derived in a similar manner by noting the transition rates as displayed in the diagram of Fig. 3.14. These rates are obtained by following the dispatching rules to determine those units which can possibly become busy or free in any given move from one

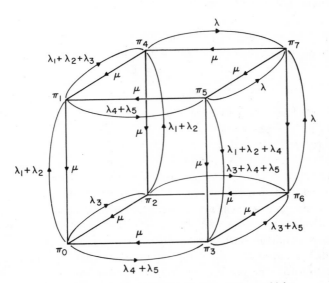

FIG. 3.14 Transition rates for the case of three vehicles.

vertex to an adjacent one. Following this prescription, the balance equations are found to be

$$\lambda \pi_0 = \mu(\pi_1 + \pi_2 + \pi_3)$$
$$(\lambda + \mu)\pi_1 = \mu(\pi_4 + \pi_5) + (\lambda_1 + \lambda_2)\pi_0$$
$$(\lambda + \mu)\pi_2 = \mu(\pi_4 + \pi_6) + \lambda_3 \pi_0$$
$$(\lambda + \mu)\pi_3 = \mu(\pi_5 + \pi_6) + (\lambda_4 + \lambda_5)\pi_0$$
$$(\lambda + 2\mu)\pi_4 = \mu\pi_7 + (\lambda_1 + \lambda_2 + \lambda_3)\pi_1 + (\lambda_1 + \lambda_2)\pi_2 \qquad [3.3.2]$$
$$(\lambda + 2\mu)\pi_5 = \mu\pi_7 + (\lambda_1 + \lambda_2 + \lambda_4)\pi_3 + (\lambda_4 + \lambda_5)\pi_1$$
$$(\lambda + 2\mu)\pi_6 = \mu\pi_7 + (\lambda_3 + \lambda_5)\pi_3 + (\lambda_3 + \lambda_4 + \lambda_5)\pi_2$$
$$3\mu\pi_7 = \lambda(\pi_4 + \pi_5 + \pi_6)$$

In addition, of course, one has

$$\pi_0 + \pi_1 + \cdots + \pi_7 = 1 \qquad [3.3.3]$$

More abstractly, [3.3.2] can be written as

$$\pi_n[\delta_n\lambda + \beta(n)\mu] = \mu \sum_{\substack{\text{all adjacent} \\ \text{higher states}}} \pi_j + \sum_{\substack{\text{all adjacent} \\ \text{lower states}}} \pi_j \sum \lambda_v, \qquad n = 0, \ldots, 7 \qquad [3.3.4]$$

where $\sum \lambda_v$ are the sums of the transition rates given in the cube diagram, $\delta_n = 1$ for all n (except for $\delta_7 = 0$), and $\beta(n)$ is the number of busy units in states n. Notice that if one does not distinguish between servers, then state 1, 2, and 3 coalesce into a single state and so do states 4, 5, and 6. In fact, if π_n' denotes the probabilities of n units being busy (without caring which) then

$$\pi_0' = \pi_0$$
$$\pi_1' = \pi + \pi_2 + \pi_3$$
$$\pi_2' = \pi_4 + \pi_5 + \pi_6 \qquad [3.3.5]$$
$$\pi_3' = \pi_7$$

We leave it to the reader to verify that, except for the prime, [3.3.5] are the same as [3.2.1] when $s = 3$.

The Eqs. [3.3.2], together with [3.3.3] are an algebraic system which can be solved to find the π_n. As s increases this becomes a burdensome problem, but for the purposes of our discussion, the significant fact is how these equations can be used to yield significant information about the emergency response system, and we will not concern ourselves with the computational aspects. However, a computer program which handles reasonably large problems is available. Reference to this package, as well as to some of the work which has been devoted to turning the hypercube model into a flexible planning tool for emergency operations, is given in the notes at the end of the chapter.

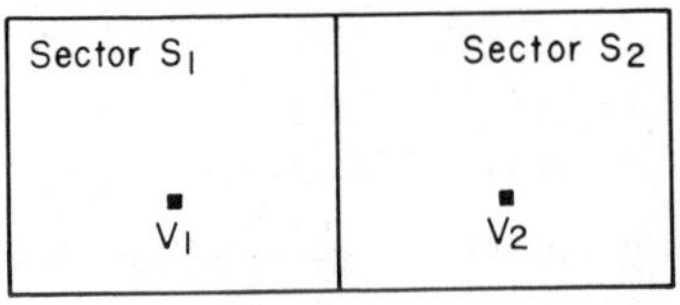

Sector S_1	Sector S_2
■ V_1	■ V_2

FIG. 3.15 A simple 2-sector example.

In order to illustrate more concretely the significance of the steady-state formulas, let us restrict our attention to the very special example of two rectangular sectors S_1 and S_2 in which two vehicles are located (Fig. 3.15). The call rates in S_1 and S_2 are λ_1, λ_2 (Poissonly generated) and the simple dispatch policy is the one given in Table 3.4. If neither vehicle is available

TABLE 3.4

Call originates in sector	First choice	Second choice
S_1	V_1	V_2
S_2	V_2	V_1

the call is lost. There are $2^2 = 4$ possible states now whose probabilities are denoted by π_n and defined pictorially in Fig. 3.16 (the zero–one notation is the same as before). We leave it to the reader to develop the appropriate steady-state probabilities, using the same type of argument given in the case of three vehicles. They are

$$\lambda \pi_0 = \mu(\pi_1 + \pi_2)$$
$$(\lambda + \mu)\pi_1 = \mu \pi_3 + \lambda_1 \pi_0$$
$$(\lambda + \mu)\pi_2 = \mu \pi_3 + \lambda_2 \pi_0$$
$$2\mu \pi_3 = \lambda(\pi_1 + \pi_2)$$

[3.3.6]

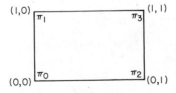

FIG. 3.16 Transition probabilities for the 2-vehicle case.

Using the fact that $\pi_0 + \pi_1 + \pi_2 + \pi_3 = 1$, one can solve [3.3.6] to obtain

$$\begin{aligned}
\pi_0 &= 1/(1 + \rho + \rho^2/2) \\
\pi_1 &= [(\rho_1 + \rho^2/2)/(1 + \rho)] \pi_0 \\
\pi_2 &= [(\rho_2 + \rho^2/2)/(1 + \rho)] \pi_0 \\
\pi_3 &= (\rho^2/2) \pi_0
\end{aligned} \qquad [3.3.7]$$

where $\rho_1 = \lambda_1/\mu$, $\rho_2 = \lambda_2/\mu$, $\rho = \lambda/\mu$, $\lambda = \lambda_1 + \lambda_2$.

The first measure of performance we look at is that of *workload*, for unit V_j $(j = 0, 1)$ which we denote by W_j. It is defined as the sum of the probabilities π_m of those states in which V_j is busy. Therefore

$$\begin{aligned}
W_1 &= \pi_1 + \pi_3 = \{(2\rho_1 + 2\rho^2 + \rho^3)/[2(1 + \rho)]\} \pi_0 \\
W_2 &= \pi_2 + \pi_3 = \{(2\rho_2 + 2\rho^2 + \rho^3)/[2(1 + \rho)]\} \pi_0
\end{aligned}$$

and so the *difference in workload* (workload imbalance) is computed as

$$\Delta W = |W_1 - W_2| = \pi_0/[\mu(1 + \rho)]|\lambda_1 - \lambda_2| \qquad [3.3.8]$$

Now let ρ_{ij} be the probability that a call from sector A_j is answered by unit V_i, conditional on the call not being lost due to having both units busy (the probability of this last event is clearly $1 - \pi_3$). Then, for example, ρ_{11} is $\pi_0 + \pi_2$ divided by $1 - \pi_3$, since a call in S_1 is serviced by V_1 when V_1 is free, or by V_2 when V_1 is busy (and V_2 free). One can therefore write the formulas

$$\begin{aligned}
\rho_{11} &= (\pi_0 + \pi_2)/(1 - \pi_3) \\
\rho_{21} &= (\pi_1)/(1 - \pi_3) \\
\rho_{12} &= (\pi_2)/(1 - \pi_3) \\
\rho_{22} &= (\pi_0 + \pi_1)/(1 - \pi_3)
\end{aligned} \qquad [3.3.9]$$

Note that $\rho_{11} + \rho_{21} = \rho_{12} + \rho_{22} = 1$. From [3.3.9] the probability q_i that vehicle V_i responds to a call from outside its own district is computed as

$$\begin{aligned}
q_1 &= \rho_{12}/(\rho_{11} + \rho_{12}) \\
q_2 &= \rho_{21}/(\rho_{21} + \rho_{22})
\end{aligned}$$

and the probability that any given dispatch is intersector (rather than intrasector) is therefore simply

$$\rho_{12} + \rho_{21} = (\pi_1 + \pi_2)/(1 - \pi_3)$$

Finally we would like an expression for average response time to any incident. To obtain this, let d_{ij} be the average travel time between a vehicle located in sector i and an incident in j. As one can readily demonstrate, the fraction of calls which occur in sector S_j is λ_j/λ and so if the travel time d_{ij} is made conditional on the call in j being answered by the vehicle stationed in i, given that indeed a call originates in j, one has that the overall average response time is given by

$$T = 1/\lambda \sum_{i=1}^{2} \sum_{j=1}^{2} \lambda_j \rho_{ij} d_{ij}$$

From [3.3.9], this can be written as

$$T = \frac{(\pi_0 + \pi_2)\lambda_1 d_{11} + \pi_2 \lambda_2 d_{12} + \pi_1 \lambda_1 d_{21} + (\pi_0 + \pi_1)\lambda_2 d_{22}}{\lambda(1 - \pi_3)}$$

[3.3.10]

Both λ_j and d_{ij} depend on the area (and shape) of the response sectors and so a redrawing of the sector boundary will alter these values. In order to be truly useful, the above performance measures, especially that of response time, should be expressed in terms of the sector design. Roughly, this can be done (at least in our 2-zone model) by writing λ_2 as $\lambda - \lambda_1$, with λ the fixed call rate for both sectors combined, and then noting that λ_1 is itself a function of the area A of the sector S_1. It follows that λ_2 is also dependent on A and therefore average response time and workload inequity can both be expressed as $T(A)$ and $\Delta W(A)$.

Now consider the simple 2-district configuration in which V_1, V_2 initially lie in symmetrically placed locations $-L$, L about the sector boundary which is taken to be the y-axis at $x = 0$ as displayed in Fig. 3.17. Suppose that initially the incident rates are such that $\lambda_2 > \lambda_1$. It is clear that as the dividing line is moved to the right, then the area of S_1 increases, and with it, λ_1. From [3.3.8] one also sees that at the same time $\Delta W(A)$ decreases and eventually reaches a minimum of zero when the area is such that $\lambda_1 = \lambda_2$. If A, A' are two areas of S_1 such that $\Delta W(A') \leq \Delta W(A)$ *and* $T(A') \leq T(A)$, with at least one of the inequalities being strict, then A' is said to *dominate* A. In a particular numerical example that has been worked out (see the references) the dividing line in the figure above was moved to the right to various positions and the corresponding values of ΔW and T were those displayed (roughly) in Fig. 3.18.

We see from this figure that if one moves the dividing line in Fig. 3.17 to

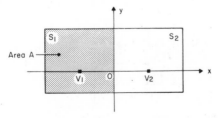

FIG. 3.17   A 2-sector configuration.

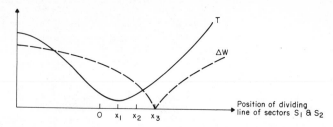

FIG. 3.18 Workload difference and response time as a function of sector boundary.

lie between the values of $x = 0$ and $x = x_2$, then the corresponding areas of sector S_1 all dominate the original area defined by $x = 0$. However between x_1 and x_3 the division gives rise to areas that are not dominated by any other. That is, neither T or ΔW has any advantage over the other between these two locations and for this reason the location of a sector boundary anywhere between the minimum response time area and the equal workload area is Pareto optimum in the sense discussed in Section 1.4. Indeed the *notion of dominancy as used here is but another version of the concept of inferiority which was introduced in Section* 1.4 in order to cope with multidimensional objectives. In the present, nondeterministic framework, one has the two conflicting goals of workload imbalance and response time to trade-off against each other, much as cost and the level of waste water treatment were put into contest earlier. There, a portion of the set of feasible alternatives was noninferior in the same sense that a portion of the set of possible boundaries is indominant (one boundary does not dominate another). The example above is therefore an interesting illustration of multidimensional optimization in the context of stochastic modeling.

The example above also shows that when intersector dispatching is permitted, the "optimum" district boundary need not be the one in which each possible incident is assigned to the closest responding unit. This conclusion is not a priori obvious and the fact that the configuration of Fig. 3.19 may be preferable to that of Fig. 3.17 requires some thought.

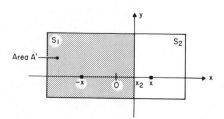

FIG. 3.19 Sector boundary moved to the right so that incident rate λ' in S_1 is greater than previous rate λ.

In summary we see then that the hypercube model allows one to design response sectors and to devise optimum dispatch policies from the point of view of both response time and workload. The significant features of the model are that it accounts for the probabilistic nature of demand and also allows for dispatching between sectors. All this contrasts sharply with the deterministic model discussed in Section 1.2 in which none of these features were present, as we already pointed out then. The unwary analyst might well presume to consider the plant location model given earlier as a plausible framework for the siting of urban fire stations. The present discussion serves to indicate just how inappropriate that would be even if at first glance there is a superficial resemblance between emergency and nonemergency location problems. This issue will be explored again in Section 5.1 in the context of deployment in rural areas, where yet another variant of the question of facility location and districting will appear.

3.4 PRIORITIES

In the previous section we encountered queues in which the arrivals distinguished· between servers. *We now consider the case in which the servers distinguish between arrivals* through the mechanism of priority classes. That is, all arrivals are separated into one of k mutually exclusive priority classes labeled by an index j, with $j = 1$ being the highest, as we see in the Fig. 3.20. In emergency work, calls are screened by the dispatcher and depending on the kind of call or where it came from, the dispatcher will assign preferential treatment to one type over another. The simple model which follows illustrates the effect of such distinctions on the average waiting times of units in each class. Let the arrivals also be Poisson with arrival rate λ_j for class j and grant a single exponential server with mean service rate μ. If one does not distinguish between arrivals, then the mean waiting time in line for an arbitrarily chosen arrival is still given by [3.1.1] where $\lambda = \sum_{j=1}^{k} \lambda_j$. However we now want to derive the mean waiting times W_j for each of the different classes and to compare them. The proof is heuristic.

There are two possibilities. One is that service is preemptive in that an arrival of priority p will displace a unit of priority $j > p$ which is already in

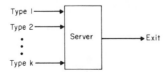

FIG. 3.20 Queue in which arrivals distinguish between K types of arrivals.

service. A nonpreemptive service discipline does not allow for that to happen and service is always completed. We deal here with the latter case. Incidentally, the assumption of constant service rate μ is not necessarily consistent with actual practice since high priority calls may require different service than low priority ones.

Suppose then that an item of priority p enters and that its waiting time prior to service is the random variable $T \geq 0$. There are n_j calls of priority $j \leq p$ ahead of it when it arrives (n_j could be 0) and we let T_j be the times required to flush out all these calls of type j. T_0 will denote the time necessary to complete the call already in service, if any. During T an additional n_j' items of priority $j \leq p-1$ enter and are also serviced before our randomly chosen call of type p. Let T_j' be the corresponding times required to flush out these additional calls. Then

$$T = T_0 + \sum_{j=1}^{p} T_j + \sum_{j=1}^{p-1} T_j'$$

Therefore the mean waiting time for the pth type is

$$W_p = E(T) = E(T_0) + \sum_{j=1}^{p} E(T_j) + \sum_{j=1}^{p-1} E(T_j') \qquad [3.4.1]$$

If the server is busy (with probability $\pi_0 = \lambda/\mu$, as we know) then the remaining service time of the unit in service is some quantity t, and if idle (with probability $1 - \lambda/\mu$) the service time is zero. Thus, $T_0 = t \cdot \lambda/\mu$ and so $E(T_0) = \lambda/\mu \cdot E(T) = \lambda/\mu^2$.

Now note that n_j, the number of units of type j that wait in line, is the product of the random variables u_j and v_j, where u_j is the number of arrivals of type j per unit time and v_j is the waiting time on line for a type j unit. It is reasonable to suppose that in a steady state u_j and v_j are independent so that

$$E(n_j) = \lambda_j W_j \qquad [3.4.2]$$

But $T_j = n_j$ times the service time for any call and therefore

$$E(T_j) = E(n_j) \cdot 1/\mu = \lambda_j W_j/\mu,$$

again under assumed independence. Similarly $E(T_j') = E(n_j') \cdot 1/\mu$. Now n_j' is the number of arrivals of type j per unit time multiplied by the time T, from which it follows that

$$E(n_j') = \lambda_j W_p \qquad [3.4.3]$$

Observe that both [3.4.2] and [3.4.3] are analogous to Eq. [C.18] of Appendix C.

By inserting [3.4.2] and [3.4.3] into [3.4.1] one therefore obtains

$$W_p = \frac{\lambda}{\mu^2} + \frac{W_p}{\mu} \sum_{j=1}^{p-1} \lambda_j + \frac{1}{\mu} \sum_{j=1}^{p} \lambda_j \cdot W_j \qquad [3.4.4]$$

Let $\sigma_j = \sum_{i=1}^{j} \lambda_i/\mu$, with $\sigma_0 = 0$. Then

$$W_p(1-\sigma_{p-1}) = \sum_{j=1}^{p} \frac{\lambda_j}{\mu} W_j + \frac{\lambda}{\mu^2}$$

and so inductively one obtains

$$W_p = \frac{\lambda/\mu^2}{(1-\sigma_{p-1})(1-\sigma_p)}, \qquad p = 1,...,k \qquad [3.4.5]$$

In order to ensure a steady-state limit assume, as usual, that $\lambda/\mu < 1$ where $\lambda = \lambda_1 + \cdots + \lambda_k$. Consider now the case $k = 2$. Then

$$\begin{aligned} W_1 &= \lambda/[\mu(\mu-\lambda_1)] \\ W_2 &= \lambda/[(\mu-\lambda_1)(\mu-\lambda)] \end{aligned} \qquad [3.4.6]$$

where $\lambda = \lambda_1 + \lambda_2$.

If one does not distinguish between arrivals, then the mean waiting time in line W_q is $W_1 \cdot \text{prob}(\text{type 1 arrival}) + W_2 \cdot \text{prob}(\text{type 2 arrival})$ which equals

$$W_1 \cdot \lambda_1/\lambda + W_2 \cdot \lambda_2/\lambda$$

and, as one easily shows, this results in the value

$$W_q = \lambda/[\mu(\mu-\lambda)] \qquad [3.4.7]$$

which we recognize as [3.1.1] all over again. Note that $W_1 < W_q < W_2$, as one would expect.

The proof that a type j arrival occurs with probability λ_j/λ is the following. The probability of a single arrival of type 1 in a time interval t is, as we know, $1-e^{-\lambda_i t}$. Similarily $1-e^{-\lambda t}$ is the probability of any arrival during t. Therefore the prob(type 1 arrival|some arrival occurs at t) is the unconditional probability of a type 1 arrival, divided by the probability of some arrival. This equals

$$(1-e^{-\lambda_i t})/(1-e^{-\lambda t})$$

which, ignoring other than linear terms in t, is λ_i/λ. In fact this value is exact as $t \to 0$.

The graphs of [3.4.6] are given in Fig. 3.21. One observes that as λ/μ approaches one (that is, as the combined arrivals begin to saturate the service

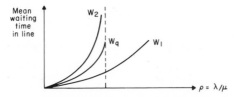

FIG. 3.21   Waiting time versus demand for different priority classes.

system) the waiting times W_q and W_2 become progressively unbounded; whereas W_1 approaches a finite limit. This characterizes a system in which low priority arrivals effectively never get serviced because of the backlog but in which high priority calls get serviced in a reasonable time.

3.5 EXERCISES

3.5.1 In the simulation example of Section 3.1 (garbage trucks waiting to unload), carry out one more computation of a simulated truck moving through the MTS. Follow the format of Table 3.2 and use the data given in Table 3.1. Recompute the mean time in the system.

3.5.2 Show that Eqs. [3.3.5] reduce to those of [3.2.1] when $s = 3$.

3.5.3 For a region involving ten sectors or beats and with an emergency vehicle located in four of these sectors, how many steady-state transition probabilities π_n need to be accounted for?

3.5.4 Derive Eqs. [3.3.6] of the text and draw the corresponding rate transition diagram. Using the fact that $\pi_0 + \pi_1 + \pi_2 + \pi_3 = 1$, compute the solutions presented as Eqs. [3.3.7].

3.5.5 Assume a region made up of k sectors in which calls arrive at a rate λ_j in sector j (each Poissonly) and for which the region-wide rate is $\lambda = \sum_{j=1}^{k} \lambda_j$. Show that the fraction of all calls which originate in sector j at any time is λ_j/λ (*hint*: compare the argument given in Section 3.4).

3.6 NOTES AND REMARKS

3.1 Examples of congestion and delay abound in the public sector. An overview of such problems in the area of fire services is given by

E. Blum, "Deployment Research of the New York City Fire Project," *Urban Anal.* **1** (1972), 63–94.

The example of a telemedical system was worked out in depth by

T. Willemain, "Approximate Analysis of Hierarchial Queue Network," *Operations Res.* **22** (1974), 522–544,

while the garbage truck delay at an MTS illustrates a problem that was worked on by L. Bodin, R. Agarwal, and the author in a study for the New York City Sanitation Department; sample data have been published by

R. Agarwal, MS thesis, Dept of Appl. Math., SUNY at Stony Brook (1972).

The mathematical treatment of steady-state queueing systems can be extended in a number of directions. Three illustrations of this are provided in Sections 3.2–3.4. Section 3.2 contains an example of a queue in which arrivals "balk" and do not wait on line (or are turned away) when all servers are busy; in Section 3.3 the queue is one in which the spatial as well as temporal nature of the arrivals is accounted for, while in Section 3.4 priority service disciplines were considered. Other cases one could have considered, among many, are those in which arrivals renege and leave the queue if waiting time is too long. In Section 3.1 we also briefly considered situations in which service rate depends on the number of waiting calls (service rate increases with backlog) or in which arrival rate decreases with increasing queue length (the limiting case of increased hesitation in joining a queue is, of course, that of balking). As for priority queues, they could also have been examined for the case of $s > 1$ servers and for service rates which depend on priority class. Note that the mean waiting time formulas we use, based on the results of Appendix C, do not depend on the service discipline that is applied. However it could well happen that the variance of waiting times is affected and that is why in the literature one specifies whether the queue discipline is "first come, first serve" (FCFS) or "last come, first service" (LCFS) or simply at random.

The fact that personnel need not be allocated in proportion to demand when calls for service are Poissonly distributed in time (since this leads to an overallocation during peak call periods!) shows that the manpower allocation ideas of Chapter 2 for deterministic systems would need to be modified when demand for service is uncertain. A study along these lines is that by

R. Larson, "Improving the Effectiveness of New York City's 911," in *Analysis of Public Systems* (A. Drake, R. Keeney, and P. Morse, eds.), MIT Press, Cambridge, Massachusetts, 1972.

The use of computer simulation in emergency services is illustrated by a study done a few years ago in New York during the administration of Mayor Lindsay. It consisted of an analysis of the adequacy of the ambulance response system with recommendations on ways to improve it. The study was implemented ("City Is Revising Emergency Ambulance Service," *New York Times*, July 3, 1969), and some details of the investigation are available in the paper by

E. Savas, "Simulation and Cost–Effectiveness Analysis of New York's Emergency Ambulance Service," *Management Sci.* **15** (1969), 608–627.

We would like to review here briefly one aspect of that work which is related to the fact that because of demographic shifts which occur over a period of years, a hospital may not now be ideally located in terms of demands for

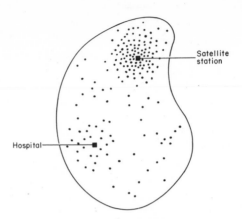

FIG. 3.22 A hypothetical district serviced by a hospital. Dots indicate demand locations.

service. Ambulances dispatched from the hospital to an incident will therefore have longer response times than may be desirable. In order to offset this
the suggestion was made that a satellite garage be placed in the vicinity of a
high demand location with ambulances stationed at both the hospital and
the satellite. Figure 3.22 shows a typical district serviced by a hospital with
the dots representing population clusters. It is apparent in this case that calls
are not spatially distributed in a uniform manner and so the location of a
satellite garage at the site shown would appear to be a reasonable choice in
terms of reducing overall response time (which is taken here to mean time
of travel until arrival at the scene). Several options were chosen as alternative
approaches to achieving this goal, but we only compare three of them here:
seven and ten ambulances located at the hospital, seven ambulances allocated
optimally between hospital and satellite, and similarly ten units allocated
between the two locations. Using data obtained from actual operational
conditions in the Kings County Hospital district of Brooklyn, a computer
simulation involving about 175,000 calls for service was run, with attention
focused on the peak load period (4 p.m.–midnight). The average interarrival
time between calls was found from actual observations to be 7.28 min. Costs
were based on the capital expense of new vehicles and of a garage for the
satellite station, and the operational expenses comprised personnel and
vehicle maintenance. As found by simulation, the incremental improvements
in response time (or, if one wishes, the incremental "benefits") over the case
of seven ambulances all stationed at the hospital, are given in Table 3.5 (in
minutes saved) together with the incremental costs for each new configuration (in dollars per minute). The optimal arrangement in terms of response
is seen to be the one with ten vehicles located at two stations (with six at the
satellite and four at the hospital, as the simulation showed). However, in

TABLE 3.5

	Average response time (min)	Incremental cost per month	Incremental improvement in response time (min)	Cost–effectiveness in dollars per minute saved
7 ambulances at the hospital	11.9	0	0	—
10 ambulances at the hospital	11.6	$6286	.3	$5.28
7 ambulances with a satellite	10.2	$7182	1.7	$1.16
10 ambulances with a satellite	9.3	$13,468	2.6	$1.42

terms of the cost–benefit ratio, seven ambulances with a satellite would be preferred. The configuration actually chosen would depend, of course, on exogenous factors such as how compelling the reduction in response delay is relative to cost. The reader should compare these remarks with our previous discussion of costs and benefits in Section 1.7.

We should point out that other performance measures could have been chosen in this study. An apparent one is total time until the patient reaches the hospital. A less common measure, however, would be to compute the probability that a call has to wait more than, let us say, 10 min before an ambulance arrives at the scene. If this probability is small then excessive delays are avoided a large fraction of the time. However, in all cases it is clear that we are dealing at best with surrogates for the goal of reducing patient risks.

It is also useful to recall here one other aspect of the study which is that ambulance utilization (the fraction of the time that a unit is on call; see also Section 3.2) is traded off against level of service. As the number of ambulances decreases, utilization is improved but service level is degraded. However, as the load increases (by increasing the size of the response sector, for example) then the same level of service can be achieved at a higher level of utilization. That is, a doubling of demand can be met by something less than a doubling of ambulances in order to attain the performance level as before. These conclusions are hardly a surprise to us by now, but they are worth reaffirming because of their significance in emergency work.

There is at least one other simulation study that we would like to draw attention to and that is the work of the New York Rand Institute's Fire Project which is discussed in several references, mostly recently by

G. Carter, E. Ignall, and W. Walker, "A Simulation Model of the New York City Fire Department: Its Use in Deployment Analysis," Rand Rep. P-5110-1 (July 1975).

This work played a core role in the analysis of fire department operations.

3.2   This section is based on work by

K. Stevenson, "Emergency Ambulance Transportation," in *Analysis of Public Systems* (A. Drake, R. Keeney, and P. Morse, eds.), MIT Press, Cambridge, Massachusetts, 1972,

K. Stevenson, "Operational Aspects of Emergency Ambulance Services," Tech. Rep 61, Operations Res. Center, MIT (May 1971).

Figures 3.8 and 3.9 are adapted from Stevenson's work. The loss formulas [3.2.1] were originally developed by A. Erlang in connection with telephone trunk link problems in 1918 and later established for arbitrary service time distributions (with constant service rate μ) by

B. Sevastyanov, *Theor. Probability Appl.* **2** (1957), 104–112.

3.3   The hypercube model was worked out by   ·

R. Larson, "A Hypercube Queueing Model for Facility Location and Redistricting in Urban Emergency Services," *Computers and Operations Res.* (1974), 67–95,

and by

G. Campbell, "A Spatially Distributed Queueing Model for Police Patrol Sector Design," Rep. 75, Operations Res. Center, MIT (June 1972).

The model has been experimented with in the Boston area and one report on this is that by

R. Larson, "Illustrative Police Sector Re-design in District 4 in Boston," *Urban Anal* **2** (1974), 51–92.

A computer code for implementing the model is available:

R. Larson, "Computer Program for Calculating the Performance of Urban Emergency Service Systems: User's Manual," Rep. TR-14-74, Operations Res. Center, MIT (Mar. 1975).

The concept of dominance as well as details on the two-sector case are provided by

G. Carter, J. Chaiken, and E. Ignall, "Response Areas for Two Emergency Units," *Operations Res.* **20** (1972), 571–594.

Rather than having to specify the dispatch rules a priori, as in Section 3.3, a more satisfactory procedure would be to determine the optimal dispatch policy (in terms of some measure of workload and response time) as part of the analysis. This has been worked out by

J. Jarvis, "Optimal Dispatch Policies for Urban Service Systems," Rep. 02-73, Operations Res. Center, MIT (Sept. 1973).

An alternate approach to the question of an optimal dispatch policy, in the context of fire response units, is given by

A. Swersey, "A Markovian Decision Model for Deciding How Many Units to Dispatch," N. Y. Rand. Inst. (1972), unpublished.

Since losses at serious fires depend on the response times of the first and second units to arrive, the problem is to determine how many units to dispatch (one or two) as a function of the number of busy units and the probability that an alarm represents a serious fire. An other than serious fire will require only one unit, but if only one is sent and two are actually required, then the delay in the second arrival increases the likelihood of loss. On the other hand, if two units are sent to an incident in which only one is needed, then one of these units is unavailable to respond elsewhere until it returns to its fire station. The optimum tradeoff between these possibilities is the basis of Swersey's analysis. In line with this fire problem is a question of the utility to a fire chief in adopting one response strategy over another. For example, does he prefer to have two units arrive with a delay of 1.5 min or one unit with a 1-min delay followed by a second unit a minute later? A quantification of such preferences has been carried out by

R. Keeney, "A Utility Function for the Response Times of Engines and Ladders to Fires," *Urban Anal.* 1 (1973), 209–222.

A simple illustration graphically portrays the reason why a sector design which assigns the closest available response unit is likely to be less than optimal whenever a mutual aid system is in operation. Consider, as in Section 3.3, the rectangular 2-zone region shown in Fig. 3.17. Suppose an alarm occurs in sector S_2 at point P (Fig. 3.23). It is answered by unit V_2, since sector S_2 is busier with calls than is S_1 (we assumed that λ_2 is greater than λ_1). Then the next call is liable to occur there again, say at Q. Since V_2 is occupied, V_1 responds. The overall travel time to the two incidents is greater however than if the sector design provided a boundary as in Fig. 3.19 since now the first call would have been answered by V_1 instead of V_2 (Fig. 3.23b).

3.4   Our reference for this section is the paper by

A. Cobham, "Priority Assignments in Waiting Line Problems," *Operations Res.* 2 (1964), 70–76.

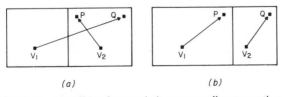

(a)   *(b)*

FIG. 3.23   The effect of sector design on overall response time.

4

Models for Deploying Emergency Services II: Allocation of Units

4.1 DEPLOYMENT OF FIREFIGHTERS

A typical ploy of the systems analyst is to reference all change in terms of some numerical *measure of effectiveness*. One of the attractions in modeling municipal services is that they appear susceptible to descriptions involving easily observable operational measures. But this can be deceiving for two reasons. First, when viewed closely, the social goals of a service system elude unequivocal description and simple numerical indices must be considered at best *proxy or surrogate measures* of the real thing. For example, missed refuse collections (in tons) only partly reflect how satisfactory garbage collection really is to the citizen, and average response time of an emergency vehicle to an accident (or, if one wishes, the probability that response delay exceeds a certain value) is only more or less correlated with the goal of saving lives. Second, there are often *multiple and sometimes conflicting objectives* in the delivery of a service and a choice of one or the other represents a decision on the part of the analyst which reflects the taste and judgment of only those people who happen to influence the modeling process. To cite an example, the deployment of fire companies can be judged in terms of *equity* of coverage (equal first unit response time to all areas of the city) or by *efficiency* of coverage (minimum average response to all alarms) which are not necessarily consistent operational goals.

Indeed in the later case one would put the more fire companies in the busy sectors of the city, thereby leading to longer travel times in the less busy areas. Such sectors are, in a sense, penalized for their lower incident rate. However in the first instance by insuring that no area had a worse average response time than any other, the result would be an overallocation of units in low incidence areas, thereby overburdening fire companies in the busy sectors. The conflict between these goals extends further. Since many urban residents live in crowded areas of low property value compared to certain low density–high property value zones, equity of coverage tends to coincide with insurance company standards which require that each property be guaranteed a minimum level of coverage. In fact, taken in dollar terms, equity favors the protection of valuable properties relative to those in slum areas whereas efficiency leans, for the same reason, toward protecting the greatest number of lives. For mathematical convenience, one proxy is chosen but it is not unusual to later find, in consultation with the municipal "client," that the choice was a poor one and has to be reevaluated. Our point in raising the issue here is that it reinforces our earlier comments on the hazards of modeling public sector activities without some sensitivity to how municipal services work in practice. Of course the problem could be treated as one with a multidimensional objective but, as we have seen, this complicates the analysis and it precludes the possibility of obtaining a uniquely defined optimum.

Let us consider briefly now some of the work of the New York City Rand Institute in the area of fire protection in light of the above comments. The standard deployment of units to an alarm consists of sending one or more engine companies and ladder companies, each consisting of a truck together with its compliment of fire fighters. The main question is that of how many units to allocate city wide into different sectors. This problem will be examined in Section 4.3 in terms of the inverse square root law. A problem of more tactical interest is how many and which units to dispatch to each alarm. This is a difficult question which depends on the probability that an alarm is serious (many calls for service are false), and the availability of units. The traditional response strategy has been to send the three closest engine companies and two ladder companies, if available. However, during peak alarm periods, certain high incidence areas find there are no fire engine or ladder units which can be dispatched since all are out on call. The traditional long term solution to the problem of how to relieve these hard-pressed units has been simply to hire new fire fighting companies. However, in such cases, the additional units only serve to increase the response coverage and may give little actual workload relief. Indeed, in at least one recorded instance, the addition of a unit to an existing one which was already responding to some 7000 alarms a year meant that now both units together responded annually to 14,000 alarms. What was accomplished, in fact, was to increase the availability of units to handle calls that previously were either serviced by less hard working peripheral fire companies or, when these were not available, by at most one local engine and ladder company. That is, the additional unit merely filled out a service gap by providing an often unneeded second or third unit.

In Chapter 3, we briefly discussed the question of an optimum dispatch policy as well as the issue of whether the dispatch of the closest unit is indeed the best tactic to use (see Section 3.3 in particular). Another problem, which we consider now, is to determine how many and which units to *temporarily reposition* in order to relieve hard pressed engine companies in high incidence areas. To do this we must first define a *response neighborhood* (or RN) as the locus of all possible alarm sites (say fire alarm box locations) which are serviced by the same three closest engine companies. A similar definition applies to the two closest ladder companies but we need not consider that here since the analysis in this case is similar to the one we are about to give. With this notion of RN, the city is partitioned into nonoverlapping zones. Note that a fire company can belong to (that is, respond to calls in) more than one such zone. A response neighborhood is said to be *uncovered* if none of the three assigned units is available to respond because they are all busy on other calls. In this case some other engine company is temporarily assigned to one of the empty fire houses in order to cover the previously uncovered neighborhood, as shown in Fig. 4.1. The black circles are busy (unavailable) units and white ones are candidates for relocation. An appropriate question now is to determine which empty houses to fill so that the number of relocated companies is minimal. A second problem, given the solution to the first one, is to determine *which* of the available companies should be moved and *not only how many*. However, this second question will be bypassed here and a mathematical formulation given to the first one only. To do this let

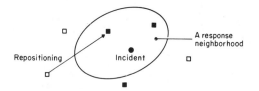

FIG. 4.1   An example of repositioning.

A be a matrix with entries a_{ij} defined by

$$a_{ij} = \begin{cases} 1, & \text{if the } j\text{th busy company "belongs" to the } i\text{th uncovered RN} \\ 0, & \text{otherwise} \end{cases}$$

and let

$$x_j = \begin{cases} 1, & \text{if the empty house of the } j\text{th busy company is to be filled by} \\ & \text{relocation} \\ 0, & \text{otherwise} \end{cases}$$

Here we assume L busy companies (empty fire houses) and M uncovered RNs. Then one wishes to

$$\text{minimize} \quad \sum_{j=1}^{L} x_j \qquad\qquad [4.1.1]$$

subject to

$$\sum_{j=1}^{L} a_{ij} x_{ij} \geqq 1, \qquad i = 1, ..., M \qquad\qquad [4.1.2]$$

by determining the zero or one decision variables x_j. The constraints [4.1.2] say that the relocation should be such that each of the M RNs will be covered by at least one unit. That is, no response neighborhood is to remain un-covered after the relocations. Note that the objective function [4.1.1] reflects the notion of equity of coverage that was mentioned earlier and it does not necessarily imply that after relocation the average response time will be less than before. The integer programming problem consisting of [4.1.1] to-gether with [4.1.2] is of course of the set covering type that we first encoun-tered in Chapter 2 (and that we will meet again in the next chapter). To illustrate the essential ideas let us consider an uncomplicated example of four RNs shown in Fig. 4.2 with four engine companies $V_1, ..., V_4$. We assume for simplicity, that each RN is defined in terms of the two closest units only, as

RN 1   units 1 and 2
RN 2   units 2 and 3
RN 3   units 1 and 3
RN 4   units 3 and 4

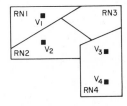

FIG. 4.2   An example of four response neighborhoods.

Now suppose that units 2 and 3 are both busy. Then RN 2 is uncovered. It is clear that either unit 1 or 4 must be relocated. In terms of [4.1.2] the A matrix is in this case simply the vector (a_{22}, a_{23}) and so the problem is to minimize $x_2 + x_3$ subject to $x_2 + x_3 \geqq 1$ (since $a_{22} = a_{23} = 1$) and this certainly requires either x_2 or x_3 to be nonzero, as we already knew. However, the more subtle question now is to decide which unit to move. If V_1 moves, then RN 1 is uncovered. If V_4 moves to replace V_2, then RN 4 is uncovered also. The only feasible solution therefore is to move V_4 into the house occupied by V_3. Similar considerations apply to more complicated examples.

After a digression concerning some topics involving geometric probabilities in the next section, we will return to a review of the Rand Fire Project in Section 4.3 by considering an allocation problem of even more strategic significance than the one treated here.

4.2 SOME GEOMETRIC MODELS

In the previous chapter we saw that in emergency vehicle dispatching the role of travel time looms large. In this section we want to examine some models that express average travel time as a function of the locations of an incident and the responding unit. The full significance of these models will be revealed in the next section. However, the reader who is not too experienced with probability arguments, particularly in the geometric context given here, can bypass this section since it may be considered useful, but not essential, to what follows later in the chapter.

In terms of allocating response vehicles, the core discussion of this chapter is contained in Sections 4.1 and 4.3 and, together with the hypercube model given earlier, they constitute the basic deployment models of an urban emergency service system. This is not to say that other models are not available but it does represent the extent to which we will discuss this topic in the present book. In Chapter 5 other deployment models are dealt with which appear to be more suited to a rural or suburban environment where the level of demand is not as intense.

Let us begin with the simplest case, that of a single stationary response unit (perhaps at a hospital or fire station) located at the center of a square of area d^2. A call occurs at random—that is, the x, y coordinates are uniformly and independently distributed—and one wishes to find the expected travel distance between the center of the square and the incident. Although we talk of distance, one can convert to average travel time by dividing by the appropriate average speed. Later a more accurate representation of time as a function of distance will be introduced.

It appears reasonable to suppose that travel occurs not "as the crow flies,"

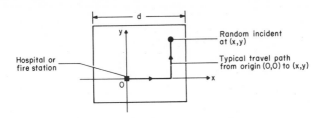

FIG. 4.3 A simple hospital response sector.

in the usual Euclidean metric, but according to the picturesquely named "taxi cab" or "Manhattan" metric which is defined by: distance between locations (x_1, y_1) and (x_2, y_2) is

$$|x_1 - x_2| + |y_1 - y_2| \qquad [4.2.1]$$

According to [4.2.1] travel is always parallel to one of the coordinate axis as we see in Fig. 4.3. The distance between the responding unit and the incident at (x, y) is therefore $|x| + |y| = D$ and we are interested in obtaining the probability distribution defined by

$$\text{prob}(D \leq l) \qquad [4.2.2]$$

From [4.2.2] one differentiates to obtain a density function and from that, the expected value and variance will follow. Now the locus of points which satisfies $D \leq l$ is, for $l \leq d/2$, given by the shaded area shown in Fig. 4.4 as the reader may convince himself. Certainly, then, for $l \leq d/2$, the $\text{prob}(D \leq l)$ is simply the ratio of the shaded area to the area of the square and so

$$\text{prob}(D \leq l) = (2l^2)/d^2, \qquad 0 \leq l \leq d/2 \qquad [4.2.3]$$

However, for $l \geq d/2$, the picture is somewhat more complicated since the probability we seek is the shaded area displayed in Fig. 4.5. In this case it is easier to compute $1 - \text{prob}(d > l)$ since the region $D > l$ is defined by the area of the four unshaded triangles in the corners of the figure. Elementary geometric considerations show that each triangle has an area of $\frac{1}{2}(d-l)^2$

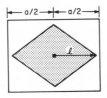

FIG. 4.4 Geometric computation for Eq. [4.2.4].

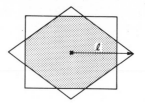

FIG. 4.5   Geometric computation for Eq. [4.2.4], continued.

and so $\text{prob}(D < l) = 1 - \text{prob}(D > l) = 1 - (4 \cdot \text{area of a corner triangle})/$ area of the square $= 1 - [2(d-l)^2]/d^2$. Thus, together with [4.2.3] one has

$$\text{prob}(D \leq l) = \begin{cases} (2l^2)/d^2, & 0 \leq l \leq d/2 \\ 1 - [2(d-l)^2]/d^2, & d/2 < l \leq d \end{cases} \qquad [4.2.4]$$

Differentiating with respect to l yields the density function

$$f(l) = \begin{cases} 4l/d^2, & 0 \leq l \leq d/2 \\ [4(d-l)]/d^2, & d/2 < l \leq d \end{cases} \qquad [4.2.5]$$

from which one readily computes the expected value $E(D)$ as $d/2$ and the variance $V(D) = d^2/24$. Incidently, if travel time is *roundtrip time* plus a fixed time T at the scene of an incident (as is approximately true in the case of an ambulance) then, assuming unit speed for simplicity, total time is $2D+T$ and its expected value and variance are, respectively, $d+T$ and $d^2/6$ (why?).

We now consider a more complicated example, which is that in which both the incident and the responding vehicle are randomly located in the square. This is the situation most typically encountered by a police car when a call arrives for dispatch during one of its patrols. We can generalize somewhat and consider the rectangular configuration in Fig. 4.6.

D is given by [4.2.1] in which the x and y locations of both vehicle and incident are assumed to be independent of each other. The expected value of D is the sum of the mean values of each component in [4.2.1] separately and this allows for a great simplification since one now may consider the

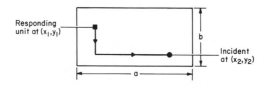

FIG. 4.6   A simple police response sector.

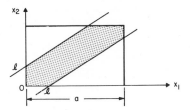

FIG. 4.7 Geometric computation for Eq. [4.2.6].

computation of the mean value of $D_1 = |x_1 - x_2|$ apart from that of $D_2 = |y_1 - y_2|$. Although the probability density function of the combined variable D is lost in this way, this fact will not cause us any discomfort. So, since x_1, x_2 are independent random variables identically and uniformly distributed on the interval $[0, a]$ the joint density function $f(x_1, x_2)$ equals $f(x_1)f(x_2) = 1/a^2$ for all x_1, x_2 in the square of area a^2. Within this region the locus of points which satisfy $D_1 \leq l$—that is, $|x_1 - x_2| \leq l$, is given by the shaded area of Fig. 4.7. Since the area of the two unshaded triangular pieces are easier to compute, one has, in the same spirit as before

$$\text{prob}(D_1 \leq l) = 1 - \text{prob}(D_1 > l) = 1 - (2 \cdot \text{area of each triangle})/a^2$$
$$= 1 - 2/a^2 \cdot (a-l)^2/2$$

and so

$$\text{prob}(|x_1 - x_2| \leq l) = 1 - (a-l)^2/a^2, \qquad 0 \leq l \leq a \qquad [4.2.6]$$

The corresponding density function is, after differentiating,

$$f(l) = 2(a-l)/a^2 \qquad [4.2.7]$$

from which one easily computes the expected value and variance of D_1 as $a/3$ and $a^2/18$. A similar argument applies to D_2 and its mean value is $b/3$. Therefore, the expected value of D itself is given by

$$E(D) = (a+b)/3 \qquad [4.2.8]$$

In particular, when $a = b$, this becomes $\frac{2}{3}b$. Another way of computing this result is indicated in the notes at the end of the chapter.

Let us now consider a slight extension of the result given by [4.2.8]. Suppose again that one is faced with a rectangle in which a barrier of length s impedes travel as shown in Fig. 4.8. For simplicity we take the barrier to be at the middle of the figure but the reader can easily generalize to an arbitrary location. The travel distance is now denoted by $D' = D + D_e$ where D is the distance in the case of no impediments and D_e is the added travel due to the presence of the barrier. If either y_1 or y_2 are greater than s in value, then D_e is certainly zero. In fact, $D_e > 0$ is conditioned on two disjoint events

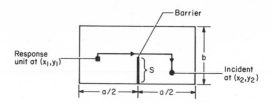

FIG. 4.8 A sector with half-barrier.

A_1 and A_2 defined by:

$$A_1: \quad x_1 < a/2, \quad y_1 < s \qquad \text{and} \quad x_2 > a/2, \quad y_2 < s$$
$$A_2: \quad x_1 > a/2, \quad y_1 < s \qquad \text{and} \quad x_2 < a/2, \quad y_2 > s$$

Since the locations of the s, y coordinates are assumed to be independent and uniformly distributed, the probability of $A = A_1 \cup A_2$ is easily computed to be $2(s/2b)^2$.

In order now to compute the value of D_e consider the extra travel distance that the response vehicle must travel to reach the incident. A glance at Fig. 4.8 shows that if one defines V_1, V_2 as

$$V_1 = s - y_1$$
$$V_2 = s - y_2 \qquad\qquad [4.2.9]$$

then

$$D_e = 2 \, \text{minimum}\,(V_1, V_2) \qquad\qquad [4.2.10]$$

The probability distribution of $D_e > 0$ is found by

$$\text{prob}(D_e < l) = 1 - \text{prob}(D_e > l) = 1 - \text{prob}[\min(V_1, V_2) > l/2]$$

But V_1, V_2 are independent random variables and, since the event $\min(V_1, V_2) > l/2$ is the same as $V_1 > l/2$ *and* $V_2 > l/2$, then $\text{prob}[\min(V_1, V_2) > l/2] = \text{prob}(V_1 > l/2) \cdot \text{prob}(V_2 > l/2)$. Now V_1, V_2 are each uniformly distributed on the interval $[0, s]$ and so

$$\text{prob}(V_1 > l/2) = 1 - \text{prob}(V_1 \le l/2) = 1 - l/2s$$

Prob$(V_2 > l/2)$ has the same value and therefore, combining all the pieces,

$$\text{prob}(D_e < l) = 1 - [1 - (l/2s)]^2, \qquad 0 \le l \le 2s \qquad [4.2.11]$$

with a density function of $1/s[1 - (l/2s)]$. From this the expected value of D_e is given in the usual way as

$$E(D_e) = E(D_e \mid D_e > 0) \, \text{prob}(D_e > 0) = E(D_e \mid D_e > 0) \, \text{prob}(A)$$

or

$$E(D_e) = (2s/s) \cdot \tfrac{1}{2}(s^2/b^2) = (s^3/3b^2) \qquad\qquad [4.2.12]$$

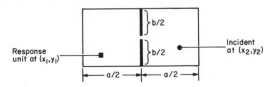

FIG. 4.9   A sector with full barrier.

Therefore one finally has that

$$E(D') = E(D) + E(D_e) = [(a+b)/3] + (s^3/3b^2) \qquad [4.2.13]$$

in which we use the relation [4.2.8]. In particular, if $s = b/2$ (a halfway barrier) then

$$E(D') = (a+b)/3 + b/24$$

Our interest in this calculation is twofold. First, note that even when $s = b/2$ the average travel distance is increased slightly. Indeed, without the barrier $E(D') = E(D) \sim .67a$ (in the simple case of $a = b$) whereas when $s = b/2$ one has $E(D') \sim .71a$. Our second purpose is to approximate the effect of a natural or man-made barrier such as a railroad or a river which can be crossed at only one point. For simplicity we choose the crossover point at a location at the center of the rectangle, as shown in Fig. 4.9. As before, $D' = D + D_e$ except that now $D_e > 0$ occurs as the union of two events A, B where $B = B_1 \cup B_2$ with

$$B_1: \quad x_1 < a/2, \quad y_2 > b/2 \quad \text{and} \quad x_2 > a/2, \quad y_2 > b/2$$
$$B_2: \quad x_1 > a/2, \quad y_2 > b/2 \quad \text{and} \quad x_2 < a/2, \quad y_2 > b/2$$

For reasons of symmetry, the distribution of the random variable $D_e > 0$ is given by

$$E(D_e) = E(D_e \mid D_e > 0)\,\text{prob}(A \cup B) = \tfrac{2}{3}(b/2) \cdot (b^2/4b^2) = (b/12)$$

and so

$$E(D') = (a+b)/3 + b/12$$

which, for $a = b$, yields the value $E(D') \sim .74a$, which is about 13% more than in the case of no barrier whatever. This insensitivity of travel distance to an impediment is perhaps surprising and not obvious at first glance. Another insensitivity result emerges by considering travel to be restricted along a rectangular grid in order to approximate an actual urban street network (Fig. 4.10). If each block is of unit length then $a = m$ and $b = n$ for some integers m, n. It can be shown in this case that the expected travel distance lies between the values $(m+n)/3$ and $(m+n+1)/3$ so that the additional travel caused by having to move along the grid pattern is at most $\tfrac{1}{3}$ of a block length!

FIG. 4.10   Grid structure imposed on a rectangular sector.

Incidently, for a rectangular sector of given area A (sides of length a, b) the optimum sector design, in terms of minimizing average response distance, is a square. We see this in the following way: minimize travel distance $(a+b)/3$ subject to the constraint $ab = A$ and find that $a = b = \sqrt{A}$ (why?). Note that we assumed here that the square is oriented so its sides are parallel to the coordinate axis. However by rotating the square 45° into a diamond-shaped configuration the average response is even less (Fig. 4.11). For example, the shaded area above represents the probability that $D \leq l$ for the special case treated earlier of a response unit located at the center. But now this probability is simply the ratio of the shaded area to the area a^2 for all l ranging between $l = 0$ and $l = a/\sqrt{2}$ and so $\text{prob}(D \leq l) = 2l^2/a^2$ with a density of $f(l) = 4l/a^2$. The expected value of D is then

$$4/a^2 \int_0^{a/\sqrt{2}} l^2 dl = 2/3a \sim .46a$$

which is close in value to the $.5a$ obtained when the square was not so rotated. This is the best improvement obtainable by rotation of the response sector and we see that it is but a marginal change. This is one more example of design insensitivity.

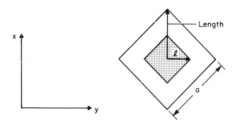

FIG. 4.11   The optimal configuration of a diamond-shaped sector.

4.3   THE INVERSE SQUARE ROOT LAW

Continuing in the spirit of the previous section let us now consider what the average travel distance (or time, if speed is constant) would be to a randomly occurring incident in some *arbitrary region* of area A when there are a number of randomly located response vehicles. More specifically one would ask for the expected distance between the incident and the nearest response unit, as shown in the Fig. 4.12. The significance of this question in urban emergency work will be clarified presently. In order to formulate the problem mathematically, suppose that incidents occur within the region at random in a spatially homogeneous manner, as in the previous section, and that response vehicles are Poissonly distributed at an average spatial density of γ so that the probability of no units within a subregion whose area is, let us say B, is simply

$$e^{-\gamma B} \qquad\qquad [4.3.1]$$

(see Appendix C for a definition of spatial Poisson processes). Let there in fact be N response units located at random within the region. Divide the area into m pieces each of area ΔA small enough so that within each there is none or at most one unit. Since the finding of a vehicle in each of the sub-areas constitutes independent events, one has m Bernoulli trials with a probability p of finding a vehicle in each ΔA which for large m is roughly equal to N/m. Therefore N is interpreted as the average number of vehicles within

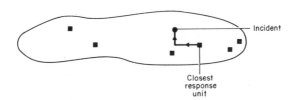

FIG. 4.12   Arbitrary response sector with randomly located response vehicle.

the area A as $m \to \infty$ and from this fact we see that $\gamma = N/A$. Now ΔA is some fixed sector size and so, since $m\Delta A = A$, the statement $m \to \infty$ is tantamount to $A \to \infty$. Thus the interpretation of γ as N/A is equated with $A \to \infty$. This means that in practice one assumes very large sectors in order for a Poisson fit with parameter N/A to be acceptable.

Now let us compute the probability that the *closest* unit is within an area B of an incident. This occurs if there is *at least one* unit within that area, which is one minus the probability of no unit there. From [4.3.1] this is

$$1 - e^{-(N/A)B} \qquad\qquad [4.3.2]$$

Using the same distance metric as in Section 4.2 the total area of all points a distance l from an incident location is given by $B = 2l^2$ as we see from Fig. 4.11. Therefore in terms of distance of an incident to the nearest responding vehicle the probability density function is found by differentiating [4.3.2] with respect to l to give

$$f(l) = (4Nl)/A\,e^{-(2Nl^2)/A}, \qquad l \geq 0$$

and the average response distance to the nearest vehicle is found by

$$4N/A \int_0^\infty l^2 e^{-(2Nl^2)/A} dl = \tfrac{1}{4}(2\pi A/N)^{1/2} \sim .63\gamma^{-1/2} \qquad [4.3.3]$$

Let us compare this result with one obtained from a dispatch policy that assigns each of the N units to its own diamond-shaped sector of area A/N within the given region of area A, each optimally positioned to minimize response distance to call. If we ignore the fact that diamond-shaped sectors cannot be constructed along the arbitrarily shaped boundaries of the original region (for large A these edge effects are insignificant) the sector design would look like that shown in Fig. 4.13. When an incident occurs, the vehicle in whose sector it occurs will respond and, as we know from the previous section, the average response distance is

$$(2^{1/2})/3 \cdot (A/N)^{1/2} \sim .46\gamma^{-1/2} \qquad [4.3.4]$$

since the length of any one side of a sector is the square root of its area. As vehicles are allowed to respond to the nearest call (regardless of whether the

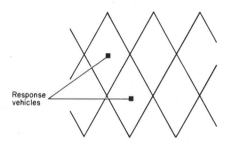

Response
vehicles

FIG. 4.13 Diamond-shaped sector design.

call is within the vehicles' sector or not) and are given the freedom to position themselves anywhere within their own sector, one begins to approach the situation of randomly located vehicles. However even though the deployment policy of prepositioned vehicles within specified sectors and intersector dispatching is the very opposite of random positioning with no sector boundary, a glance at [4.3.3] and [4.3.4] reveals a small difference in travel distances. This is a surprising result that again suggests that response time is relatively insensitive to sector design. It is also of interest to ask for the probability that the kth nearest unit responds to a given call. For $k = 1$, this is the probability that within an area if there are at least two units available (since this includes the first and the second closest ones) which is itself one minus the probability of none or one vehicle, within B. Since exactly k units occur with probability

$$(\gamma B)^k e^{-\gamma B}/k!$$

then our required probability, when area $B = 2l^2$, is given by

$$1 - e^{-2\gamma l^2} - 2\gamma l^2 e^{-2\gamma l^2}$$

Differentiating with respect to l gives the probability density of the second closest unit being at a distance l from a call for service:

$$f(l) = 8\gamma^3 l^3 e^{-2\gamma l^2}$$

A similar argument applies to higher order k. In fact if D_k denotes the response distance to the kth nearest unit then $\text{prob}(D_k > l)$ is the probability of none or $\cdots(k-1)$ units being within a distance l to the incident. That is,

$$\text{prob}(D_k \leq l) = 1 - \sum_{j=0}^{k-1} \frac{(2\gamma l^2)^j e^{-2\gamma l^2}}{j!}$$

If we now let $z = l^2$ then $\text{prob}(D_k \leq l) = \text{prob}(D_k^2 \leq z)$, which can be differentiated in z to yield a density function for D_k^2 defined by the gamma distribution (see Appendix C, Eqs. [C.8] and [C.9]). Hence the expected value of D_k^2 is given immediately by $E(D_k^2) = k/2\gamma$. In particular, when $k = 1$, $E(D_1^2) = 1/2\gamma$ and so one computes the variance of D_1, using [4.3.3], to be

$$\text{Variance } D_1 = E(D_1^2) - E^2(D_1) = (1/2\gamma) - [\tfrac{1}{4}(2\pi/8)^{1/2}]^2 = (8-2\pi)/16\gamma$$

which means that the variance of the response distance to the nearest unit is inversely proportional to the density γ. Note, incidentally, that if our distance metric had been Euclidean, found by drawing the straight line between incident and unit, then the area B equals πl^2 (why?). In this case, one recomputes the density as

$$f(l) = 2\pi l(N/A) e^{-\pi(N/A)l^2}, \qquad l \geq 0$$

and so the average travel distance to the nearest responding unit is now given by

$$2\pi\gamma \int_0^\infty l^2 e^{-\pi\gamma l^2} dl = .5\gamma^{-1/2} \qquad [4.3.5]$$

Since the Euclidean metric represents the shortest possible way of getting between two locations the value obtained in [4.3.5] can be considered as a lower bound on the actual travel distance one might expect.

It should be pointed out that in practice it is difficult to dispatch the closest unit unless one knows where all units are located. Without a car locater system in effect the usual procedure is to assign each unit to its own sector or beat allowing however for the possibility of intersector dispatching. What the analysis above shows is that there is not much difference between these several deployment possibilities in terms of mean response.

In all the geometric models worked out in this and the previous section we have seen that average response distance is always proportional to $\gamma^{-1/2}$ (with N vehicles in a large region of area A this means that each vehicle has a beat of area $A/N = 1/\gamma$). Mathematically this stipulates how response relates to the number of responding vehicles and the size of the response area. As it happens this relation has been tested against fire response data in New York City and elsewhere and it appears to be a remarkably robust indicator of how actual response depends on N and A. For this reason it is often referred to as the "*inverse square root law*" and it provides a useful rule of thumb in deciding how many units to allocate in a given region in order to achieve an acceptable level of service. In practice one would estimate the constant of proportionality for any given area by observing actual response times given that a certain number of vehicles are available to dispatch. This constant reflects local conditions such as the street configuration and fire house location.

Incidently, response time is more or less linearly related to distance in those sectors in which length of travel is not insignificant. In such cases the average *response time* can therefore itself be gauged by $\gamma^{-1/2}$.

There is, however, an important refinement that must be introduced in order to make the inverse square root law correspond more closely to actuality. Of the N vehicles some are already busy on other calls when a new alarm appears. For this reason one must work not with N but with the average number of response units which are free and therefore available. Assume for simplicity that N is reasonably large so that the event of no unit being available is an infrequent occurrence of low probability. Then, as we saw in Section 3.2, the probability π_n of n out of N units being busy is approximately given by the Poisson distribution with the average number of busy units determined by λ/μ where λ is the Poisson arrival rate of calls and μ is the average service rate (which is assumed to be the same for each vehicle). Now the average response distance (or, roughly, response time) as given by the inverse square root law is a convex function of N in the sense that if $f(n) = k\gamma^{-1/2} = k(A/n)^{1/2}$ for some constant k, then

$$f\left(\sum_{n=1}^{N} \alpha_n n\right) \leq \sum_{n=1}^{N} \alpha_n f(n) \qquad\qquad [4.3.6]$$

where $\alpha_1, ..., \alpha_N$ is any set of nonnegative constants that add up to one. In particular, if $\alpha_n = \pi_{N-n}$, which is the probability that n out of N units are not busy on call, then $\sum_{n=1}^{N} n\pi_{N-n} = N - \lambda/\mu$ is the average number that is available for dispatch and therefore

$$f(N - \lambda/\mu) = f(\textstyle\sum n\pi_{N-n}) \leq \sum_{n=1}^{N} \pi_{N-n} f(n)$$

The right-hand side is the average response distance when the number of available vehicles is a random variable. We denote this by $E(N)$. Therefore, the most conservative estimate for the value of $E(N)$ is $f(N - \lambda/\mu)$ and so by accepting a possible underestimate we can write

$$E(N) \sim k(A/[N - \lambda/\mu])^{1/2} \qquad [4.3.7]$$

A graph of $E(N)$ versus N is shown in Fig. 4.14.

Suppose now that one has a large region of area A (for example, one of the boroughs of New York City) which has been divided into m sectors and that one wishes to allocate N response vehicles to the sectors so as to minimize the region wide response distance (or time). If N_i units are deployed in sector i then clearly,

$$N = N_1 + N_2 + \cdots + N_m \qquad [4.3.8]$$

Our measure of overall response $R(N)$ is the sum of the individual sector responses, each weighted by the probability of a call arriving in a sector of area A_i:

$$R(N) = \sum_{i=1}^{m} \frac{\lambda i}{\lambda} k_i \left(\frac{A_i}{N_i - \lambda_i/\mu} \right)^{1/2} = \sum_{i=1}^{m} R_i(N_i) \qquad [4.3.9]$$

Here λ_i is the Poisson call rate in sector i (with $\lambda_1 + \cdots + \lambda_m = \lambda$) and k_i is the proportionality constant suitable to that area. From Exercise 3.5.5 we see why the weights are given by λ_i/λ.

Expression [4.3.9] appears to be a reasonable choice of what the region wide effectiveness would be for a given vehicle deployment strategy. One can safely assume that $N_i > \lambda_i/\mu$ in all zones if unbounded solutions are to be avoided. The optimal deployment strategy is found by minimizing $R(N)$ subject to [4.3.8]. This is a nonlinear programming problem of the type discussed in Appendix D except that here one wishes the solutions N_i to be nonnegative integers. However a simple algorithm exists in our case for obtaining the optimal N_i values. Since the objective function [4.3.9] is separable in each N_i variable a little reflection will convince the reader that the following iterative procedure will always guarantee an optimal solution.

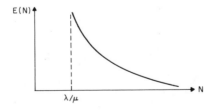

FIG. 4.14 Expected response distance as a function of the number of vehicles.

Begin by assigning the smallest possible integer values of N_i to each sector i. It is clear that these values are given by $\lambda_i/\mu + 1$. If the sum of the numbers equals N we are done. Otherwise assign one additional unit to that sector which yields the largest decrease in the value of $R_i(N_i)$. If the sum now equals N, the iteration stops. Otherwise one continues in this manner, adding a unit at a time until the total allocation does finally sum up to N.

If one ignores the integer requirement on the N_i then the multiplier rule of Appendix D offers a useful insight. Assume for simplicity that call rates are small in comparison to μ (which implies that intersector dispatching will occur infrequently) so that λ_i/μ can be taken to be zero. Since the optimal N_i are assumed to be positive, the rule [D.5] of Appendix D shows that there exists some constant α (to avoid confusion with the arrival rate of calls, the multiplier λ of [D.5] is replaced by an α) for which

$$- [\partial R_i(N_i)/\partial N_i] = \alpha \qquad [4.3.10]$$

at the optimum. The minus sign comes from the fact that we are minimizing and not maximizing. Letting $\beta_i = 2k_i/\lambda$ one finds from [4.3.10] that

$$\frac{\beta_i \lambda_i (A_i)^{1/2}}{N_i^{3/2}} = \alpha$$

and so the optimum N_i are found to be

$$N_i = \left(\frac{\beta_i \lambda_i}{\alpha}\right)^{2/3} A_i^{1/3} \qquad [4.3.11]$$

where the constant α can be determined from condition [4.3.8]. Therefore the ratio of vehicle deployment in two sectors i and j is, in the optimum case, given by

$$N_i/N_j = (\beta_i \lambda_i/\beta_j \lambda_j)^{2/3}(A_i/A_j)^{1/2} \qquad [4.3.12]$$

In the special case of a region divided into only two sectors and assuming equal call rates ($\lambda_i = \lambda_j$) and equal sector characteristics ($k_i = k_j$) one has

$$N_1/N_2 = (A_1/A_2)^{1/3} \qquad [4.3.13]$$

from which one obtains (using $N_1 + N_2 = N$) that the optimal allocation is given by

$$N_1 = \frac{N(A_1/A_2)^{1/3}}{1 + (A_1/A_2)^{1/3}}$$

$$N_2 = \frac{N}{1 + (A_1/A_2)^{1/3}}$$

It is immediately apparent, even in the simple case, that the units are not allocated in proportion to sector size nor, as an analogous argument based on [4.3.12] would show in the case $A_1 = A_2$ and $\lambda_1 \neq \lambda_2$, are they allocated in proportion to demand. Once again this demonstrates that a policy of allocating resources in proportion to apparent need is often wrong. The reason, of course, lies in the fact that the response function $E(N)$ is both nonlinear and convex. Increasing allocations give decreasing marginal returns (the law of diminishing returns). Another illustration of this fact will appear in the next section.

Note however that if one redefines the $\hat{\lambda}_i$ to be *call rates per unit area*—that is, if we let $\hat{\lambda}_i = \lambda_i/A_i$—then the optimal solution is indeed a linear function of sector size for in this case [4.3.11] becomes

$$N_i = \left(\frac{\beta_i \hat{\lambda}_i}{\alpha}\right)^{2/3} \cdot A_i \qquad [4.3.14]$$

The advantage of using $\hat{\lambda}_i$ instead of λ_i is that two sectors of widely different sizes can now be compared in terms of their effective demand without regard to area. There is also another interpretive advantage. Returning to the simple case of two sectors having equal characteristics k_i and equal values of λ_i one sees that the two zones can be coalesced into a single one of area $A = A_1 + A_2$. Indeed, since $N_i = cA_1$ and $N_2 = cA_2$ (where c is the constant $(\beta_1 \hat{\lambda}_1/\alpha)^{2/3}$), it follows that the allocation of units to A is simply the sum of the individual assignments

$$N = bA = bA_1 + bA_2 = N_1 + N_2$$

On the other hand if the sectors have unequal k_i and $\hat{\lambda}_i$ then it can be shown that combining the two is not an optimal thing to do. This is because a busy region, which benefits from economies of scale, is diluted when combined with a less busy one and, as a result, more vehicles are required. This shows that sectors should be formed as homogeneous as possible in terms of their internal characteristics and of their alarm rates per unit area.

It is also to be pointed out that the expression [4.3.9] for $R(N)$ can be generalized by defining a new objective function given by

$$R_\beta(N) = \sum_{i=1}^{m} \frac{\lambda_i}{\lambda} E_i(N_i)^\beta, \qquad \beta \geq 0$$

in which

$$E_i(N_i) = k_i \left(\frac{A_i}{N_i - \lambda_i/\mu}\right)^{1/2}$$

When $\beta = 1$, $R_\beta(N)$ reduces to [4.3.9] which is a measure of average response time, as we know. As $\beta \to 0$, $R_\beta(N)$ becomes less and less dependent on response time and the optimal allocation is therefore increasingly proportional to workload in each sector as described by λ_i/λ. As $\beta \to \infty$ the opposite occurs in that longer travel times begin to predominate in $R_\beta(N)$

and so the optimum in this case tends to reduce discrepancies in travel without regard to alarm rates. It follows, therefore, that as β moves from zero to unity and from there to unrestrictedly large values, the corresponding optimal solutions range from minimum workload imbalance in each zone, to minimal average response times region wide (efficiency of coverage), to minimal response time imbalance in each zone (equity of coverage). Thus, the tradeoff between the various conflicting performance measures can be achieved by varying the parameter β. It is interesting to note in this regard that in New York City in 1973 the actual fire unit allocations corresponded closely to a compromise value of this parameter given by $\beta = 3$.

4.4   RANDOM PATROLS

One of the many problems facing police administrators concerns the allocation of patrol units to different sectors of the region under their jurisdiction. The purpose of the patrols is to apprehend a crime while it is taking place or to serve as a deterrent. In order to maintain an element of surprise and so as not to develop predictable patrol patterns, it is assumed that the police vehicles move through their assigned routes in a random manner. The assumption of randomness is basic in what follows and what it means, simply, is that there is no fixed way in which the patrol units cover the allotted area of streets, parking lots, parks, and other public places. The occurrence of a crime can also be treated as a random event and the probability that a patrol detects a crime depends on the space–time coincidence of the police with a crime in progress. Some data is available to determine an average duration t during which the police have an opportunity to come into contact with a crime: it is the time during which the perpetrator can be observed or otherwise identified by the police. More thorough data analysis is necessary to determine t for different locales, but, generally speaking, it appears to be in the neighborhood of 2–3 min for most crimes.

Suppose that a police vehicle is assigned a sector or "beat" of area A in which there are c street miles which are accessible to patrol and that the average speed is v miles/hr. In a time t the patrol moves a distance vt. In general the movement is zig–zag, but for small enough time intervals t, it is unlikely that the randomly moving patrol will retrace or overlap any of its own path. The small distance vt is itself randomly located among the c miles of street network within the sector and the incident is also assumed to be uniformly distributed among the same c miles. Hence the probability that in time t the path of the patrol overlaps the location of the incident is simply

$$vt/c \qquad\qquad\qquad\qquad\qquad [4.4.1]$$

Equation [4.4.1] is the conditional probability of detecting a crime, given that a crime is in progress of duration t. As t increases so does the likelihood that the searcher will traverse his own path so this simple ratio is no longer an accurate description of detection probability. However one can argue as follows.

Let $P(t)$ be the probability of *no detection* during time t. Increase t by a small increment h. Then $P(t+h) = P(t)P(h)$ since nonoverlapping time intervals are presumed to yield independent events. From [4.4.1] we see that

$$P(h) = 1 - (vh/c)$$

and so $dP(t)/dt = -(v/c)P(t)$ is obtained as $h \to 0$, from which

$$P(t) = e^{-vt/c} \qquad [4.4.2]$$

In deriving [4.4.2] we used the evident fact that $P(O) = 1$. Hence the conditional probability of detection of a crime of duration t in progress is

$$1 - e^{-vt/c} \qquad [4.4.3]$$

Note, incidentally, that c/v is not the time it takes for our patrol to cover the entire street network once. This would be true if the vehicle moved through the streets in a regular pattern without retracing its steps (except for inevitable deadheading). But in a random patrol, some points may be covered several times and others not at all. It can be shown, in fact, that c has the interpretation as the average number of miles between successive passings of any given point, but this will not be demonstrated here.

Suppose now that N vehicles are assigned to the given region. There are two possibilities here. The first is that each is assigned a sector of c/N miles without overlap. Then, during t, the detection probability is

$$1 - e^{-vNt/c} \qquad [4.4.4]$$

On the other hand, if all N vehicles are assigned to the same sector of c miles with overlapping patrols then, for small enough t, the probability of contact, ignoring higher order terms, is

$$Nvt/c \qquad [4.4.5]$$

This follows since during t there are N independent and randomly located intervals of length vt located somewhere on the street network (with negligible probability of two such intervals overlapping) and so if the crime is located in a spatially homogeneous way, then the detection probability is given by [4.4.5]. For large t the same argument as before gives a probability which is again equal to [4.4.4].

Suppose calls arrive within the region in a Poisson manner at a rate λ and that each vehicle responds at a service rate μ (exponential service times).

Let b be the probability that a vehicle is busy on a call and is unavailable for patrol. Then a fraction $(1-b)N$ units are patroling at any time and [4.4.5] is modified to be $(1-b)Nvt/c$. Hence [4.4.4] is now

$$1 - e^{-(1-b)(vNt/c)} \qquad\qquad [4.4.6]$$

In the case of N disjoint patrol "beats" the call rate within each is λ/N in a spatially homogeneous call process. Since each is a single server queue, the probability of the patrol being unavailable is $b = \lambda/N\mu$ (see Appendix C, Eq. [C.14]).

However, in the case of overlapping patrols this is less clear. Let us examine the case of two vehicles. The probability of one busy unit is π_1 and of both being busy is $1-(\pi_0+\pi_1)$ and therefore the average number of busy units is $\pi_1 + 2(1-\pi_0-\pi_1)$. Referring to the multiserver formulas of Appendix C (Eqs. [C.12] and [C.22]) we see that $\pi_1 = \rho\pi_0$ and that $\pi_0 = (2-\rho)/(2+\rho)$ for $s = 2$ servers. Hence the average number of busy servers becomes, simply, $\rho = \lambda/\mu$. It follows that a fraction $\lambda/2\mu$ of the servers are busy at any time and so the probability b of a patrol being unavailable is $\lambda/2\mu$, which is identical to the value of b in the case of two nonoverlapping patrols, as we computed it above.

Note that if t is small enough (as it is for certain crimes) then one can assume that during the entire time period t a unit is either available or unavailable. Then the probability of detection, P_A, for two vehicles patroling in nonoverlapping sectors is simply

$$P_A = (1-b)(1-e^{-2vt/c})$$

whereas in the case of overlap one must account for the probabilities of one or two units being available which, in view of the fact that $\pi_1 = \rho\pi_0$ and $\pi_0 = (1-b)/(1+b)$ (with $b = \lambda/2\mu$ and $\rho = \lambda/\mu = 2b$), gives a combined probability of

$$P_B = [2b(1-b)/(1+b)](1-e^{-vt/c}) + [(1-b)/(1+b)](1-e^{-2vt/c})$$

It can be shown with some calculational effort (we leave the details to the reader) that for all t, $P_B > P_A$. Therefore an overlapping patrol policy is more effective in terms of detection probability than one in which each unit is assigned a disjoint beat. This is similar to the improvement in average waiting time one gets when two single server queues are merged into a 1-queue 2-server system.

Suppose now that a large region is divided into k areas (such as high density slum and low density residential). The probability of a crime of a certain type of duration t varies with each area and if we let q_i be the ratio of crimes reported in the ith area to the total reported crimes $\left(\sum_{i=1}^{k} q_i = 1\right)$ then the overall unconditional probability of detection during t given that N vehicles are assigned to each zone (with no overlap between them) is

$$P = \sum_{i=1}^{k} q_i(1 - e^{-[(1-b_i)N_i v_i t/c_i]}) \qquad [4.4.7]$$

An interesting problem now is to maximize the probability in [4.4.7] with respect to the allocations $N_i \geq 0$ subject to the restriction that the sum of the available vehicles is N:

$$N_1 + \cdots + N_k = N \qquad [4.4.8]$$

This is again a nonlinear programming problem which we examine in the special case of $k = 2$ ignoring the need for integer valued allocations. Letting $\alpha_i = (1-b_i)v_i t/c$ allows us to rewrite [4.4.7] in this case as

$$P = q_1(1 - e^{-\alpha_1 N_1}) + q_2(1 - e^{-\alpha_2 N_2}) \qquad [4.4.9]$$

The maximum of P subject to $N_1 + N_2 = N$ is a separable problem of the type treated in Appendix D and the multiplier rule [D.5] of that appendix shows that at the optimum there exists some constant (which we label as β to avoid confusing it with λ) such that

$$\begin{aligned} \partial P/\partial N_i - \beta &\leq 0 \qquad \text{if} \qquad N_i^0 = 0 \\ \partial P/\partial N_i - \beta &= 0 \qquad \text{if} \qquad N_i^0 > 0 \end{aligned} \qquad [4.4.10]$$

where N_i^0 denotes the optimum values of N_i. That is,

$$\begin{aligned} q_i \alpha_i e^{-\alpha_i N_i^0} &= \beta \qquad \text{if} \qquad N_i^0 > 0 \\ q_i \alpha_i &\leq \beta \qquad \text{if} \qquad N_i^0 = 0 \end{aligned}$$

from which we see that the optimal deployment strategy is

$$N_i^0 = \begin{cases} 0, & \text{if} \quad q_i \leq \beta/\alpha_i \\ (\ln \alpha_i q_i - \ln \beta)/\alpha_i, & \text{if} \quad q_i > \beta/\alpha_i \end{cases} \qquad [4.4.11]$$

What [4.4.11] tells us is that if the crime frequency is small enough, or equivalently, if β/α_i is large enough, then no vehicles are allocated at all to the ith zone. Incidentally, β/α_i will be large if t is small, which indicates that crimes of short duration are discounted in preference to searching for crimes of longer visability since the latter have a higher search payoff. One can also show, using the fact that $N_1^0 + N_2^0 = N$, that as N decreases β increases so that in order to maximize performance the search patrols are restricted to smaller and smaller areas as the supply of available vehicles becomes scarcer. The important fact for us is again that, as we have seen repeatedly, the optimal strategy requires that one does not allocate in proportion to demand (the crime intensity are the "demands" in our case) contrary to intuitive belief and to widespread practice among many municipal services.

There are a few objections to the analysis just given. The first is that crimes occur at random and so during a time interval t during which patrol is in progress, a crime may just be ending or initiating. The treatment we give implicitly assumes that crime and patrol are temporally coincident during the required t time units. But this need not be the case in practice. Also since a typical tour of duty lasts several hours, the probability of space–time coincidence during a brief fragment of the duty hours does not in itself tell us what the detection probability will be during the entire period. In fact, if successive crimes occur at random, then the probability of detection over time will satisfy a law of diminishing returns.

4.5 EXERCISES

4.5.1 In Section 4.2 we stated that the minimum of $(a+b)/3$ subject to $ab = A$, with A (the area) given, is found by $a = b = A^{1/2}$. Prove this.

4.5.2 Given two adjacent square sectors, each of area d^2, show that the average response distance for *inter*sector dispatching is twice the expected *intra*sector dispatch length. Incidents occur at random, uniformly within one of the two sectors, and the vehicle is randomly located within the adjacent zone.

4.5.3 Given sectors S_1 and S_2, find the optimal *integer valued* allocation of five vehicles in the two zones when the overall response time is given by

$$R(n_1, n_2) = 6/(n_1)^{1/2} + 5/(n_2)^{1/2}$$

Here n_i are the vehicles assigned to sector S_i with $n_1 + n_2 = 5$, $n_i \geq 0$.

Note: In the next two exercises one needs to be familar with the notions of convex and concave functions. A function f is convex if the graph of f between two point $f(x)$ and $f(y)$ lies on or below the chord connecting the two points. If the word "below" is replaced by "above," this defines a concave function. Mathematically what this means is that if α is any number which ranges from zero to one, then since $\alpha x + (1-\alpha) y$ represents the line segment between x and y, a function is convex when

$$f[\alpha x + (1-\alpha) y] \leq \alpha f(x) + (1-\alpha) f(y) \qquad [4.5.1]$$

As α varies, the right-hand side of [4.5.1] represents the straight line linking $f(x)$ to $f(y)$. When the inequality is reversed one obtains the definition of concavity. By plotting their graphs one can, for example, determine that $1/x^{1/2}$ is strictly convex and x^q strictly concave ($0 < q < 1$), for $x > 0$ (*strictly* means that [4.5.1] is a strict inequality).

4.5.4 Show that a convex function f has the property that if $\alpha_1, \ldots, \alpha_N$ is a set of positive numbers whose sum is unity, then

$$f\left(\sum_{n=1}^{N} \alpha_n x_n \right) \leq \sum_{n=1}^{N} \alpha_n f(x_n) \qquad [4.5.2]$$

Here the x_n represent any N positive quantities (*hint*: it suffices to establish [4.5.2] for $N = 3$; the same argument applies to arbitrary N by induction). Note that this exercise establishes that the function constant/$n^{1/2}$ is convex in the extended sense of Eq. [4.3.6] in the text.

4.5.5 If two sectors of areas A_1, A_2 are given in which the call rates per unit area are $\hat{\lambda}_1$, $\hat{\lambda}_2$, with $\hat{\lambda}_1 \neq \hat{\lambda}_2$, then the optimal allocation of units to the *combined* sector of area $A = A_1 + A_2$ is always greater than it would be if the units are allocated optimally to each sector separately. This was pointed out in Section 4.3 and it should now be shown. Use formula [4.3.14] assuming that the β_i are equal in the two zones. The combined call rate is given by the weighted sum $\hat{\lambda} = (A_1/A)\hat{\lambda}_1 + (A_2/A)\hat{\lambda}_2$.

4.6 NOTES AND REMARKS

4.1 The repositioning model was worked out by

P. Kolesar and W. Walker, "An Algorithm for the Dynamic Relocation of Fire Companies," *Operations Res.* **22** (1974), 249–274.

Much of the other work of the New York Rand Institute is summarized in the report by

E. Ignall, P. Kolesar, A. Swersey, W. Walker, E. Blum, G. Carter, and H. Bishop, "Improving the Deployment of New York City Companies," Rand Rep. P-5280 (July 1974).

as well as in several other Rand reports mentioned below (and in the notes to Chapter 3).

4.2 The use of geometric probability in urban modeling was illuminated by

R. Larson, *Urban Patrol Analysis*, MIT Press, Cambridge, Massachusetts, 1972,

where there are a number of examples of how such models can be put to use. Additional material of interest is given by

R. Larson, "Response of Emergency Units: The Effects of Barriers, Discrete Streets, and One-Way Streets," Rand Rep. R-675 (April 1971).

4.3 The basic reference to the work which centers around the inverse square root law is that by

P. Kolesar and E. Blum, "Square Root Law for Fire Engine Response Distances," *Management Sci.* **19** (1973), 1368–1378.

Additional work on making this law into a tool for deployment is given by

K. Rider, "A Parametric Model for the Allocation of Fire Companies," Rand Rep. R-1615 (April 1975).

An allocation policy based on the model discussed in this section influenced the Fire Department's decision in 1972 to eliminate six companies and permanently relocate seven others in high incidence areas. Despite the Fireman's Union opposition to the changes, expressed in a legal suit brought against the city (see *New York Times*, December 22, 1972, "Union Fights Fire Department Cuts"), the redeployment strategy became effective in 1973 at an annual savings to the municipality of over four million dollars. Since then the budget crisis in New York has resulted in further cuts in service.

The relation between travel distance and time is explored by

P. Kolesar, "A Model for Predicting Average Fire Company Travel Times," Rand Rep. R-1624 (June 1975).

In particular, for sectors in which distances are short, average response time is (roughly) proportional to $\gamma^{-1/4}$ rather than $\gamma^{-1/2}$. In regions which are spatially more extensive, the average time is essentially a linear function of $\gamma^{-1/2}$, as we assumed in Section 4.3.

4.4   The central reference here is Larson's book mentioned previously. Recent refinements are due to K. Chielst of MIT in as yet unpublished work (1974/75). The pioneering work in search theory was carried out by B. Koopman during the Second World War, in the context of searching for submarines. Incidently, there is a problem in geometric probability, which comes out of the analysis of patrols. One disputed question in police circles is whether it is better to assign two men or one to a patrol car. The first option tends to increase the safety of the officers (a debatable issue), but the second alternative increases efficiency in that two cars now patrol a sector formerly assigned to one. However, in responding to an incident there is a minor drawback. If the call is deemed a dangerous one, then two cars are sent (each with one officer) which then rendezvous at some safe location near the incident before proceeding together. The average response time to the incident is now the maximum of the individual response times of each car and so is never less than the response time of an individual car. For a square sector we computed the average response of an individual vehicles as proportional to $\frac{2}{3}A^{1/2}$ where A is the area. Let the actual time be the random variable denoted by T_i for vehicle i $(i = 1, 2)$, and consider the rendezvous response time given by $T = \max(T_1, T_2)$. Then the average $E(T)$ is never less than $E(T_i)$ for either i. Note that $\text{prob}(T \leq l) = \text{prob}(T_1 \leq l \ and \ T_2 \leq l) = [\text{prob}(T_1 \leq l)]^2$ if one assumes the T_i to be identically and independently distributed. From this one can then compute the corresponding density function and the value of $E(T)$.

CHAPTER

5

Network Optimization

5.1 WHERE DO WE PUT THE FIRE STATION?

Consider a problem faced by three cities. In Glasgow

large central areas are scheduled to be virtually completely redeveloped by the late 1980s. Provision for emergency services, such as the Fire Brigade, must be incorporated at the planning stage. Perhaps the most important decision facing the Firemaster is how many fire stations to have and on which sites to build them ... the criterion for optimization is that which minimizes the total journey time of all pumping appliances attending fires.

East Lansing, Michigan, is a town dominated by the Michigan State University. In a comprehensive development plan for the year 1980, the town determined that the existing fire station in the city center would be inadequate by 1980 and that new stations would be needed. This gave rise to the question: How many fire stations should East Lansing have and where should they be? The criterion adopted in this case was essentially the same as that used in Glasgow except that that the travel time from fire stations to incidents should

131

not exceed certain maximum response times as recommended by the American Insurance Association. In Denver, the City Council and the Mayor asked for a way of providing the then-current level of fire suppression service (which was generally considered acceptable) at a reduced cost. The measure of performance for a fire station configuration was the maximum permissible response time for the engine closest to each of 240 "focal points" throughout the city (a focal point is a location at which all fires in the vicinity are assumed to occur). Thus response time relates to specifying the maximum permissible response time to focal points.

How does one go about solving such problems? We will adopt here a more simplistic approach than the one used in the preceding chapters by ignoring the stochastic nature of demand and by assuming that fire house locations, as well as the incidents, are located at only a finite number of sites. These assumptions are introduced to ease the analysis and in order to avail ourselves of graph–theoretic (or, if one prefers, "network") techniques. There is an extensive literature concerning such methods, some of which are to be reviewed in this chapter (a brief background is provided in Appendix E). Although these limitations may be unduly restrictive in the dense confines of an urban area where high alarm rates are endemic, it appears that they are less critical in rural or suburban areas. We will assume then that an actual street network can be abstractly modeled by a graph whose nodes represent areas of the city to be serviced by a fire station (for example, the focal points) and that two nodes have an edge or link between them if the corresponding areas are directly connected or adjacent to one another. There are many

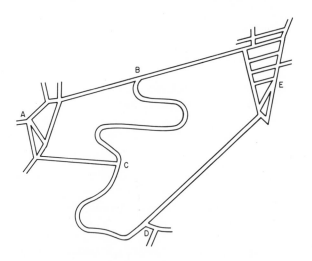

FIG. 5.1   Fragment of a street network in a rural community.

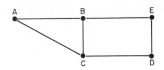

FIG. 5.2   Graph representation of Fig. 5.1.

ways of doing this depending on the level of aggregation or disaggregation that is desired but in all cases both the areas which demand service and the fire stations themselves will be located at one of the nodes.

Given a model of the street network, *one first determines the shortest travel time between any two nodes*. To pick a concrete case consider the fragment of a rural street network given in Fig. 5.1. Its representation as a graph is then shown in Fig. 5.2, in which nodes A, D, and E denote the focal points of the neighborhoods in which they are located.

Travel times (in minutes) between adjacent nodes is given in Table 5.1. The reader then easily verifies the shortest travel times between any two pairs of

TABLE 5.1

	A	B	C	D	E
A	0	1	1.5		
B	1	0	2.5		2
C	1.5	2.5	0	1.5	
D			1.5	0	1.5
E		2		1.5	0

nodes using the method discussed in Appendix E (or, more directly in this simple case, by "eyeballing"). Table 5.2 summarizes this information.

TABLE 5.2

	A	B	C	D	E
A	0	1	1.5	3	3
B	1	0	2.5	3.5	2
C	1.5	2.5	0	1.5	3
D	3	3.5	1.5	0	1.5
E	3	2	3	1.5	0

Referring to the Fig. 5.2 suppose now that fire stations can be potentially located at any of the nodes except for B and C and that fire insurance standards specify that no demand point shall be more than 1.5 min away from such a station. It is quite clear that a single facility cannot cover all the nodes with this restriction on maximum response time. If two facilities are to be used, then one possibility is to locate them at nodes A and D. The maximum response time in this case is exactly 1.5 min. and the two districts served by them are either (A, B) and (C, D, E) or (A, B, C) and (D, E) or, if one allows for overlapping service, (A, B, C) and (C, D, E).

Now travel time in itself is not the sole basis for judging between alternate configurations of facilities. It may cost more to establish a station at one location rather than elsewhere and, what is perhaps more significant, the workload implied by each node can vary considerably. Let us weight each node by the population serviced within the area determined by the node, or weight by a combination of both population and anticipated average frequency of fires (as determined for example by past data on the occurrence of serious incidents). Then the sum of the weights in each zone determined by a station is a measure of the demand, or, if one wishes, of the workload in that area. For the sake of argument, suppose that the weights in our five node problem are, respectively, 4, 1, 1, 2, 6. Then the configuration which minimizes the maximum sum of weights in any district is clearly (A, B, C) and (D, E). The choice of weights can also reflect other criteria for optimal siting. In contrast to population there is the possible conflicting objective of property value. Consider, for example, that the principal employer of the region is a costly chemical plant located at B, but with few people living there during nonworking hours. Or, again, contrast the frequency of fires in an area of low hazard against the possibility of a low probability but dangerous fire elsewhere. An explosion at the chemical plant, for instance, is an unlikely event but its occurrence would cause considerable concern. In view of these observations it is clear that the weights must be chosen with care if they are to denote something more than workload alone. Perhaps the appropriate approach would be to utilize a multidimensional objective function, as in Section 1.4, but in the interest of simplicity we stick to the idea of letting the weights reflect the significance of each objective at a given site.

Let us now abstract this procedure somewhat and give it a more elegant framework. Using the same illustrative five-node example (with all weights equal to unity) form all subsets N_i of the graph defined by the set of nodes j which are at a travel time not exceeding 1.5 min. when going from j to node i. Letting the first five integers denote A–E, one sees that

$$N_1 = (1, 2, 3)$$
$$N_2 = (1, 2)$$
$$N_3 = (1, 3, 4)$$
$$N_4 = (3, 4, 5)$$
$$N_5 = (4, 5)$$

Further, let x_j be one or zero according to whether or not a fire station is located at node j. From the assumptions in our problem $x_2 = x_3 = 0$. We then want to find the *least number of facilities* that are necessary to cover all nodes. That is to say, one wants to minimize $x_1 + x_2 + x_3 + x_4 + x_5$ subject to the restriction that each node is covered by at least one facility. This means that at node 1, $x_1 + x_2 + x_3$ must be greater than or equal to one or, since x_2 and x_3 are zero, that $x_1 \geqq 1$. Similarly, for nodes 2–5 one has

$$x_1 \geqq 1$$
$$x_1 + x_4 \geqq 1$$
$$x_4 + x_5 \geqq 1$$
$$x_4 + x_5 \geqq 1$$

It is apparent that what confronts us here is a simple example of a set-covering problem in which the solutions must be either of the integers zero or one. In general, the solution to such an integer-valued optimization problem is quite ornery to obtain but fortunately in our case the answer is particularly simple. In fact since x_1 has to be greater than or equal to one and since each x_j can be either zero or one, then $x_1 = 1$. But then the remaining inequalities are immediately satisfied even if $x_5 = 0$. Therefore one optimal solution is $x_j = 0$ except for $x_1 = x_4 = 1$, which is the same result as obtained earlier by visual inspection.

In general the set covering approach to this problem for an n-node network involves the minimization of a cost function

$$\sum_{j=1}^{n} x_j \qquad\qquad [5.1.1]$$

using

$$x_j = \begin{cases} 1, & \text{if a facility is located at } j \\ 0, & \text{otherwise} \end{cases} \qquad [5.1.2]$$

If one defines N_i as the set of nodes j for which the distance from j to i is less than or equal to s, where s is the maximum acceptable response delay, then the minimization [5.1.1] is carried out with respect to the following constraints for each $i = 1, \ldots, n$:

$$\sum_{j \text{ in } N_i} x_j \geqq 1 \qquad\qquad [5.1.3]$$

When a facility definitely will not be placed at node j, then x_j is set to zero; if a facility is definitely to be located at j (often existing facilities will not be demolished or abandoned because of the costs involved), then x_j is set to one.

The previous optimization problem has a duel interpretation. Instead of asking for the minimum number of facilities to provide a cover of all nodes so as not to exceed a maximum response time one can seek the location of a fixed number of facilities so as to minimize the maximum response time. This version of the problem is solved using the following idea. Given a fixed number k of facilities to locate, first cluster (partition) all nodes into k distinct (nonoverlapping) subsets according to the rule that the ith node belongs to the jth cluster if it is closer to the jth facility node than any other one. Then find that node within each cluster which minimizes the maximum travel time between it and all other nodes within that partition. This is easily found by considering the matrix of all shortest distances between nodes within the partition. Simply select the maximum entry in each row of this matrix. The node associated with the row which yields the minimum of these maxima is the one desired. This gives us k new "center" nodes and the process is then repeated until no further improvement is possible. If the maximum time for the k node centers is some number $s(k) > s$, then one repeats the process with $k+1, k+2, \ldots$ "centers" until the maximum response time at last satisfies $s(l) \leq s$ for some $l \geq k \geq 1$. This then is the minimum number of facilities (and their location) necessary to ensure that response is not more than s. The essential difference between this approach and the set-covering method is that set covering leads to possibly overlapping sectors or response districts. However, although we will not show it here, the just described "*k-center method*" does not always lead to the optimum answer and is in fact dependent on the initial choice of center nodes.

To illustrate the approach consider again our 5-node problem. If we let $k = 1$, then it is possible to find the best center node by starting, say, at node A. Since the entire graph forms a single cluster in this case one has to simply locate that node which minimizes the maximum distance between it and all other nodes. The maximum distance from node 1 to the others is 3, and it is 3.5, 3, 3.5, 3 for the others. Therefore, node A is a best choice of a facility for $k = 1$. But, of course, since $s(1) = 3$ in this case, a single facility does not suffice. Let then k equal 2. Choose nodes A and E as initial center nodes. The corresponding clusters are then (A, B, C) and (D, E) and the new center nodes are therefore A and D (although this choice is not unique). The new clusters therefore coincide with the old ones and we obtain the same result as before since $s(2)$ is now 1.5.

An alternate approach to "k centers" is by a return to a formulation similar to the set covering one given earlier. Suppose one defines y_i variables as

$$y_i = \begin{cases} 1, & \text{if node } i \text{ is within } s \text{ minutes of a fire house} \\ 0, & \text{otherwise} \end{cases}$$

Then one wants to maximize the covered area, which is given by $\sum_{i=1}^{n} y_i$

summed over all nodes in the network. The condition of having a fixed number of facilities is expressed as

$$\sum_{j=1}^{n} x_j = k \qquad [5.1.4]$$

where the x_j are defined as in [5.1.2]. It is clear that if demand node i is "covered" by some facility then [5.1.3] holds for that i but that otherwise the sum in [5.1.3] is merely nonnegative. Therefore one can write

$$\sum_{j \text{ in } N_i} x_j \geq y_i \qquad [5.1.5]$$

The maximum of $\sum y_i$ subject to [5.1.4] and [5.1.5] is an integer program whose solution is a set of zero–one variables y_i, x_j. If the graph has n nodes and if the sum $\sum y_i$ is less than n then one simply increases the value of k until the solution covers all nodes. A reexamination of our previous example shows that the maximum of $y_1 + y_2 + y_3 + y_4 + y_5$ can be accomplished by letting all $y_i = 1$ provided k equals 2. Indeed one solution is to let $x_1 = x_4 = 1$ with all other $x_j = 0$, as before. When $k = 1$ the only possible solution is $x_1 = 1$ and the sum of y_i values is then only three.

Notice that the last two approaches to siting also answer the question of what is the best coverage possible if only k facilities are available and no more. Cost considerations sometimes dictate that only a limited set of fire stations can be built and operated. One at least has available a way of determining the best protection for the price.

It is also of interest to compare the models discussed here with those discussed in Section 1.2. The objective function considered there could be interpreted as the sum of the travel times from the fire houses to all the "demand" nodes, weighted by fraction of time facility j is utilized to satisfy demand node i. We leave it to the reader to make the analogy more precise between plant location as considered there and emergency siting. In some contexts such a model could well be an appropriate one and indeed the stated goals of the Glasgow study cited at the beginning of this section would appear to be consistent with an objective function of this type. From a solution viewpoint, however, one is still faced with a (mixed) integer program, a virtually inescapable fact in modeling studies of this kind (the method of k centers is an exception but, as already noted, in practice it can offer convergence difficulties).

Before we make a more critical appraisal of these ideas it should be remarked that essentially the same approach can be used in a variety of contexts in both the public and private sector and that the methods discussed here not only give the minimum number of facilities but they also show where to locate them in addition to determining the district boundaries between them.

With so many desirable features, are there any objections to these clustering or covering methods? Well, regretably there are. Let us focus on two of them, even though they were encountered before.

First of all, there is the problem of workload imbalance. Consider a city in which there is a sparsely populated area with littler calls for service and another densely occupied area with intense demands for fire protection. If our sole criteria is that travel time be less or equal to s ("equity of coverage"), then some of the firehouse districts (located according to the methods proposed earlier) would have many more nodes to service than in sparser aress. The problem of maintaining equal workload is highly regarded by labor negotiators and must be given serious consideration along with response times.

One attempt to resolve this difficulty was given earlier in which all competing solutions are compared in order to select that one which minimizes the sum of the weights. But this is an ad hoc procedure whose success depends after the fact on the number of solutions that happened to be generated by the set-covering approach. Another possible way of bypassing this difficulty is to cluster according to a distance measure between two nodes i and j which is the actual travel time from i to j multiplied by the weight at node j. This "distorted" measure of distance tends to disperse nodes in dense areas of high incidence and to coalesce nodes in rural area thereby leading to partitions that tend to be more equal in the number of nodes contained within them. Or, again, one can decide to cover high incidence nodes with more than one fire station. If i is such a node, then this means that in the set-covering approach, the condition that the sum of x_j for j in N_i be greater or equal to unity is replaced by the sum being greater or equal to l where l is some suitable integer larger than one. Finally, if all else fails, a station in a high workload area is allocated more resources (men and equipment) than for less busy areas. However, the uncertain nature of the demand precludes knowing in a simple way how much to allocate to a high workload district—the intuitively plausible idea of doubling the service resources for a doubling of average demand is often wrong, as we have repeatedly seen.

A second objection is that in practice a fire station in a heavy demand area occasionally must rely on units that are dispatched from outside its own area of jurisdiction. This would occur when all available vehicles (ladder and engine units) are busy on other calls and cannot respond to a new incident. In urban areas, interdistrict cooperation is commonplace and yet the analysis given earlier ignores this fact by implicitly assuming that a fire station can respond to all calls within its own service area. The effect of this interdistrict "mutual aid" is less critical in rural areas.

A more sophisticated approach to facility location and districting for emergency units was suggested in Chapter 3 through the "hypercube model."

By contrast, the set-covering and k-center approaches discussed here have the virtue of comparative simplicity even though they tend to obscure some significant features of the response system. In particular they do not accurately reflect urban demand patterns which can vary both spatially and temporally in an unpredictable way. Above all, it should be stressed that a successful analysis of the fire-siting problem requires that one incorporates the intuitive understanding of a city manager or fire chief and their staffs in addition to the skills of an analyst. First-hand experience with the areas being served by the proposed facilities is essential in terms of being able to appraise a "solution" vis-à-vis political, social, and fiscal constraints. The models proposed here are at best only a framework for discussing various alternatives in participation with those officials who will have to live with the results.

Similar in character to the districting questions considered above is that of *political districting*. This is the process by which an area (such as a state) is partitioned into smaller areas, or districts, each of which satisfies the constitutional ruling of nearly equal population. Each district should also be compact (that is, not elongated and straggly) and contiguous (that is, not fragmented into disjoint pieces). Now if the original area is defined in terms of a discrete number of population centers—these could be census tract areas—then it may be represented as a graph in which the nodes are the population centers and in which an edge is inserted between two nodes if they designate geographically adjacent locations.

It is possible to formulate this problem mathematically in a manner that is analogous to that of the fire-siting model. To do this enumerate all the census tracts (let us agree to use this population unit as a basic indivisible geographic area) and then form a collection of districts, labeled by the index j, each of which consists of one or more tracts clustered in a reasonably compact and contiguous way. It is supposed that a large number M of such partitions have been formed out of the n tracts. If M is too small the optimization problem to be posed presently will result in simple but uninspired solutions, whereas a large M increases the difficulty of obtaining solutions.

Let N_j denote the set of all tracts i lying within the jth district and define a_{ij} by

$$a_{ij} = \begin{cases} 1, & \text{if tract } i \text{ lies in district } j \\ 0, & \text{otherwise} \end{cases}$$

Also define x_j by

$$x_j = \begin{cases} 1, & \text{if } j\text{th district is chosen} \\ 0, & \text{otherwise} \end{cases}$$

and let p_j be the population residing in j. If $\bar{p}$ is the "average" population obtained by dividing the total population by M then an optimal districting plan is one which minimizes the sum

$$\sum_{j=1}^{M} |p_j - \bar{p}|$$ [5.1.6]

subject to having each tract i belong to one and only one political district j

$$\sum_{j=1}^{M} a_{ij} x_j = 1$$ [5.1.7]

for $i = 1, ..., n$. Suppose that a constitutionally acceptable plan involves k districts. Then one also requires

$$\sum_{j=1}^{M} x_j = k$$ [5.1.8]

The solution to the problem of minimizing the sum of "costs" given by [5.1.6] subject to [5.1.7] and [5.1.8] is reducible to an integer program. This may be accomplished by using the device that was discussed in Section 2.1 for converting objective functions of the form $|w - \bar{w}|$ into a linear format. Such nonlinear functions were also encountered implicitly in Section 3.3, in connection with the deployment of fire fighter's units (the workload imbalance ΔW) and in Section 1.4 (equity of water use which is the absolute difference between average water use on a national basis and the allocations to individual regions within the country).

The fire location method of k centers given earlier, as well as the set-covering approach, both result in compact sectors. The reason is that they implicitly minimize the maximum response distance between the fire station and the demand sites (which are nodes in a graph) and so it is apparent that such districts will tend to be globular clusters and not at all straggly. For the same reason they will also be contiguous although in the set-covering approach the districts generally overlap each other. Therefore the design of fire districts and of political districts, as obtained from the models of this section, will tend to yield the same kind of partitions. If the method of k centers is used for political districting then there still remains the problem of equipopulation which is analogous to equiworkload treated earlier. The analogy can be made precise by attaching to each node the population at that site and using that value as a weight, much in the same manner as we did in the fire station case. There are a number of formulations of the political districting problem but most are variants of the above mentioned ideas.

5.2 HEURISTIC TECHNIQUES FOR VEHICLE ROUTING

In the previous section our optimization was on a graph, or network. It is characteristic of problems posed on networks that some readily admit easy solutions while others resist all attempts at resolution. For example, given a graph with n nodes or vertices the problem of determining the tree of shortest length linking thees nodes can be determined by a simple algorithm. Indeed, one such procedure is given in Appendix E. The computation is straightforward, as is the one for determining the shortest path from a given node to any other node, as is also discussed in the same appendix. However if one now considers the problem of finding a closed path of minimal length from a given node which returns to itself after passing through each of the other nodes exactly once (the "*traveling salesman*" problem) then one is faced with a formidable task. Although it can be resolved in principle there is no known computationally feasible algorithm for problems of more than a few hundred nodes. This is surprising in view of the apparent simplicity of the problem statement which at first glance is no more demanding than that of the minimal tree problem. Notice that since graphs are finite structures it is always theoretically possible to explicitly enumerate all possibilities for a particular problem and then to choose the optimum one. However in practice this is virtually impossible except for very small structures. For instance there are $(n-1)!/2$ possible closed cycles through a graph of n nodes, one of which is of shortest length and therefore a solution of the traveling salesman problem. But if n is even of moderate value the number of possible candidates for optimality is enormous and the work involved in their enumeration would be prohibitive. Fortunately, when exact solutions are precluded it may still be possible to employ *heuristic techniques*. That is, formal reasoning is combined with intuitive but plausible arguments in order to circumvent unresolved mathematical difficulties. The use of such methods can have a dampening effect on those people who are mainly attracted to mathematical elegance. Nonetheless some of the best solution techniques used in the analysis of public sector models are of this type and, together with computer simulation, form a basic arsenal of methods for the practitioner. As it happens, computer simulation is well-documented in the literature of operations research but heuristic optimization methods are not and so, even though solution techniques are not a goal of these lectures, we will give a discussion of two such heuristic devices in the context of municipal services.

Before doing so let us briefly mention a study concerning an optimal pipeline network which was carried out several years ago for the Federal Power Commission. Gas reserves are located in the Gulf of Mexico and other offshore regions and must be carried through pipelines to onshore plants where it is processed and than transported to its markets. The cost of the underwater pipeline network is a substantial part of the total gas utilization. The problem was to select pipe sizes and a network configuration to minimize the sum of operating and investment costs, given gas field locations and flow requirements. The pipeline itself can cost up to several hundred thousand dollars per mile to buy and install, depending on pipe diameter.

At first glance the problem is one of forming a shortest length tree linking the gas wells with the onshore processing plant. However this first glance obscures several facts. To begin with it is true, although perhaps not obvious, that letting each branch of the tree be a straight pipeline between two nodes is not the optimal way to proceed. In fact, by adding certain additional juncture nodes the overall length of the network can be reduced. This point will be raised again in the notes at the end of the chapter. Secondly, as a practical matter there are constraints on the maximum pressure that can be applied at any point in the system and on the minimum pressure at which gas can be delivered ashore, based on safety factors and the limitations of onshore processing plants. The problem is to select a set of pipe diameters that minimizes total costs (with seven pipe choices, there are 7^{26} possible diameter combinations for 26 nodes, which is a typical number). Also, depending on the configuration of the tree one needs varying amounts of compression (at a cost) in order to meet the minimum required delivery pressure. If pipe cost were the only significant factor, one could of course find a minimal length tree but the requirements of pipe diameter and compressors precludes the possibility of such straightforward design. Of necessity, therefore, heuristic arguments had to be utilized in the actual study. Even so this resulted in a reduction in pipe layout costs in the Gulf of Mexico from initial design estimates of more than 200 million dollars to something between 100 and 150 million.

Let us now consider a different problem. Most refuse collection activities in New York City center around the pickup of household refuse in small bins. However, large institutional sites such as schools, hospitals, and apartment complexes have their refuse stored in large 6–12 cubic yard metal containers (equivalent to 40–80 normal garbage cans). Eventually a substantial number of such sites will need to be serviced by using large capacity trucks which depend on mechanical fork lifts to load the bins into the chassis where it is then compacted (these are called hoist–compactor trucks). Each truck can service several such sites before going to a dump to unload.

The problem we considered at one time was how to route the hoist–compactor trucks to minimize the total travel time of the vehicles and to determine the minimum number of trucks needed each day. The last condition is important from the point of view of minimizing the capital expenditure needed to outfit a fleet of trucks.

There is also a dual problem to the one just mentioned. That is, for a given number of trucks one seeks the maximum number of locations that can be serviced. We have found several organizations who have either purchased or leased a fleet of trucks interested in this question since they want to know how far they can expand their operations without additional capital expenditure. Both issues will be explored in this and in the following sections of the chapter.

The problem is not a simple one because of a number of complicating factors. First, one must be mindful of the limited capacity of the truck. This restriction requires it to make a number of roundtrips to the dump with at best only a few sites serviced on each tour. Second, the tour time cannot exceed the length of one work shift. Typically several roundtrips to the dump (landfill or incinerator or marine transfer station) are possible during one shift and so truck capacity is usually the binding constraint in such problems. *Each roundtrip will be called a tour* and the possibility of forming minimum time tours is what will occupy us in this section. Although a workshift begins and ends at a vehicle garage or depot the heuristic optimization to be described below is limited to the individual tours themselves. It is clear from what was just said that the problem is not simply one of finding a shortest path through all the nodes of a graph, with each node representing a pickup site, since vehicle capacity will force several interruptions of this path in order to unload. Note also that each site can have a different amount of refuse available for pickup and so it is not a priori clear how many demand points can be serviced on any given tour. Finally, some locations require daily service while others do not. Since there are typically many points to service, the problem is not only to arrange the routes feasibly but to assign each pickup point to days of the week to minimize the number of trucks needed. This last problem is treated later.

An analysis is based on a modification of a heuristic idea known as the *Clarke and Wright method*. The basic concept, quite simply, is this: assume, to begin with, that a tour consists of visiting one containerized location and then returning to the depot or a dumpsite. If now two locations are joined together to form one tour then the *savings in total travel time* is illustrated in Fig. 5.3. The savings S_{ij} between pickup points i and j is $S_{ij} = t_{Di} + t_{Dj} - t_{ij}$ where t_{ij} is the time to go between point i to j and t_{Di} (or t_{Dj}) is the time to go from dumpsite D to pickup point i (point j). One calculates the "savings" associated with all pairs of locations to be serviced and then sorts in decreasing order the list of pairs with positive savings. Starting at the top of the

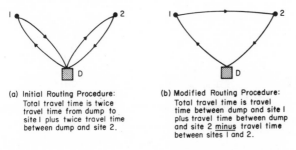

(a) Initial Routing Procedure:
Total travel time is twice
travel time from dump to
site l plus twice travel time
between dump and site 2.

(b) Modified Routing Procedure:
Total travel time is travel
time between dump and site l
plus travel time between dump
and site 2 minus travel time
between sites l and 2.

FIG. 5.3 Forming a tour by the Clarke and Wright procedure.

list, sites are combined provided that the resulting tour is feasible from the point of view of time and capacity. In this way increasingly longer and presumable better tours are formed until the list is exhausted.

In Fig. 5.4 we illustrate the procedure on a simple problem. Each of the sites is to be serviced every day, the demand at each location is one unit, the capacity of the vehicle is three units, and there is no time constraint.

The edges of the graph represent the shortest paths between adjacent pickup locations (namely those that can be reached without passing through

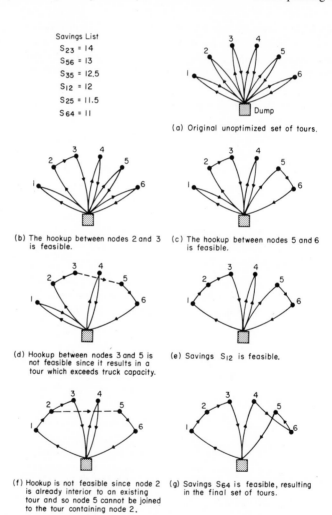

Savings List
$S_{23} = 14$
$S_{56} = 13$
$S_{35} = 12.5$
$S_{12} = 12$
$S_{25} = 11.5$
$S_{64} = 11$

(a) Original unoptimized set of tours.

(b) The hookup between nodes 2 and 3 is feasible.

(c) The hookup between nodes 5 and 6 is feasible.

(d) Hookup between nodes 3 and 5 is not feasible since it results in a tour which exceeds truck capacity.

(e) Savings S_{12} is feasible.

(f) Hookup is not feasible since node 2 is already interior to an existing tour and so node 5 cannot be joined to the tour containing node 2.

(g) Savings S_{64} is feasible, resulting in the final set of tours.

FIG. 5.4   Illustration of the heuristic routing problem.

another demand point) and the length of an edge is the associated travel time. It is assumed that a travel time matrix of shortest paths between all nodes (including the dump) has been determined from empirical data derived from actual street conditions. The tours which result from the heuristic procedure are now constructed step by step. Let S_{ij} be the savings derived by joining sites i and j together. We consider the street network to be undirected, and the savings to be defined over those sites which are adjacent. The savings list is a purely hypothetical one, designed only for the purpose of illustrating the method.

In order to coax this algorithm into finding better local optima it is possible to perturb the ordering of node pairs in the savings list. This is accomplished by increasing the distance from the depot or dump to one or more of the nodes and then resolving the problem subject to the original constraints. If the resulting solution is better we restore the perturbed distance to its original value and then compute the resulting payoff. It may appear strange that this procedure can be at all effective but sometimes it may be used to advantage as is illustrated by the following example.

Consider a 6-node problem in which $d_{i,D} = 6$ for $i = 1, ..., 6$ and for which each node has a unit demand. Vehicle capacity is three units and there is no time restriction. The distances between nodes is given by

$$d_{1,2} = 2$$
$$d_{3,4} = 2.3$$
$$d_{5,6} = 2.6$$
$$d_{2,3} = 3$$
$$d_{4,5} = 3.5$$

In this case the savings list and the resulting Clarke and Wright tours are

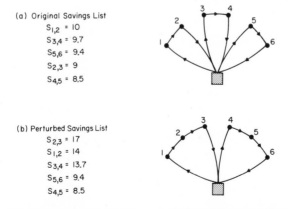

(a) Original Savings List
$S_{1,2} = 10$
$S_{3,4} = 9.7$
$S_{5,6} = 9.4$
$S_{2,3} = 9$
$S_{4,5} = 8.5$

(b) Perturbed Savings List
$S_{2,3} = 17$
$S_{1,2} = 14$
$S_{3,4} = 13.7$
$S_{5,6} = 9.4$
$S_{4,5} = 8.5$

FIG. 5.5   Improving tours by perturbation of the savings list.

exhibited in the Fig. 5.5a for a total travel distance of 42.9 units. We now let $d_{2,D} = d_{3,D} = 10$. The savings list is then reordered. The new list and the resulting tours are displayed in Fig. 5.5b. If we now reassign the value of 6 to $d_{2,D}$ and $d_{3,D}$ the total tour time is 35.1, a considerable improvement over the previous set of tours. In fact, 35.1 is the global optimum in this case.

It should be remarked at this point that several other possibilities exist for forming "optimal" tours but only extensive computational experience can vindicate the preference of one method over another. The procedure outlined above has been used in a study performed for New York City and was demonstrably an improvement over tours obtained by more straightforward methods. In particular the method is generally better than the "nearest neighbor" rule which forms a path by moving from a given site to the one closest to it.

An additional refinement of the Clarke and Wright procedure has to do with multiple dumps. If there are several disposal locations we preassign each collection node to the dump closest to it. The savings in combining two sites assigned to the same dump is computed as before. However if two points are combined when each is assigned to different dumps D, D' then the savings is now taken to be $S_{ij} = t_{D,i} + t_{D',j} - t_{ij}$.

A further refinement of the routing scheme allows us to introduce another heuristic optimization idea. Each of the tours obtained above are closed paths beginning and ending at a dumpsite D and passing through a subset S of nodes which include D. But, as we know, the optimum closed path through S is given by the solution to the traveling salesman problem (TSP) and so the heuristic device to be described presently can be used to "solve" the TSP. Note that a *traveling salesman tour* through S is one in which there are *no closed subpaths* (subcycles) *and for which every node is linked to precisely two other nodes*. The idea we use is one of a family of *branch interchange* methods, and is best described by an example. Consider the complete graph in Fig. 5.6 with "distances" as shown (these can represent any nonnegative measure of separation between nodes and not just geographic length). Label the nodes as n_i for $i = 1, ..., 5$ ($D = 5$) and let $d(n_i, n_j)$ be the distance between

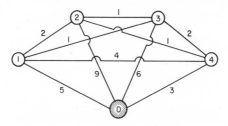

FIG. 5.6   Example of a complete graph.

n_i and n_j—that is, the value of the edge linking n_i and n_j. The edge is denoted by (n_i, n_j). Suppose now that one has obtained somehow an initial feasible tour through all the required nodes (using the Clarke and Wright procedure, for example). A local interchange is a replacing of two edges or branches by two others. If this effects an improvement in the sense of reducing the total tour length then the interchange is favorable and is said to be 2-*optimum*. The algorithm begins at the node with the lowest label and by asking whether either of the two branches incident to it can be removed and replaced by another incident edge of lower length. If not, one proceeds to the next highest node and repeats the question. Otherwise one explores the possibilities inherent in carrying out such a deletion and insertion. Assume, in our case, that the initial selection for a closed tour is given by Fig. 5.7, of total length 13.

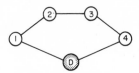

FIG. 5.7   A closed tour.

Then, starting at node 1, either (n_1, n_2) or (n_1, n_D) could be removed and replaced by (n_1, n_3). Since (n_1, n_D) has a higher value, delete it and insert (n_1, n_3) as in Fig. 5.8. The trouble with this interchange is that it leads to a

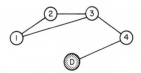

FIG. 5.8   Delete and add a branch.

closed subpath, which is inadmissable. So edge (n_2, n_3) is removed and, since a single closed tour is desired, the edge (n_1, n_D) must be inserted to complete the cycle (Fig. 5.9). Unfortunately, the added edges have a value

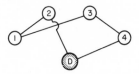

FIG. 5.9   Branch interchange forms a cycle.

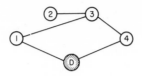

FIG. 5.10   Delete and add a branch again.

of $1+9$, which exceeds the deleted ones of $5+2$, and so this interchange is not acceptable. Another possibility at node 1 is to begin by deleting (n_1, n_2) while inserting (n_1, n_3), as in Fig. 5.10. But now node 3 is incident to too many branches and so, since we do not wish to isolate node 2, the edge (n_3, n_4) is deleted. But in order to form a closed tour through all nodes, (n_2, n_4) must be added (Fig. 5.11). In this case the added links have a total value of 2 which is less than the deleted branches and so the interchange is indeed 2-optimum. One now begins again at node 1 of this new tour and tries for local improvements. However removing (n_1, n_D) and adding (n_1, n_2)

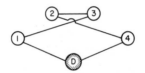

FIG. 5.11   Another cycle is formed.

or removing (n_1, n_D) and adding (n_1, n_4) does not lead to any improvement. For example the first option results in a local interchange (obtained in the same manner as before) as shown by Fig. 5.12. This does not result in an improvement, as one verifies. Similarly for the other possibilities at node 1. At nodes 2 and 3, moreover, the incident branches all have the value of unity which precludes any possibility of interchange since there are no other incident edges of lower value which are substitutable. At node 4 the only possibilities [such as delete (n_4, n_D) and add (n_3, n_4)] also do not lead to improvements and so the 2-optimum tour (of total length 11) is given by that shown in Fig. 5.13. The basic idea in the heuristic methods discussed above is to

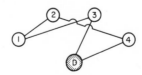

FIG. 5.12   Branch interchange gives still another cycle.

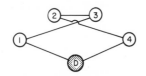

FIG. 5.13   Final 2-optimum tour.

improve on a given network configuration by local interchanges of nodes and branches until no further improvement is possible. In this sense the final improvement is *a local optimum* and a better procedure would possibly give a better value. Inherent in the notion of heuristic is that one sacrifices the evasive goal of a global optimum in return for a computationally feasible approach to a local one. The better the heuristic the higher is the "probability" that the local solution is close or even equal in value to the global one, but it is hard to make this notion precise.

Before closing this section let us review what we learned so far about vehicle routing. Given a finite set of service sites (pickup or delivery points, depending on the context) the heuristic algorithms given above enable us to find a set of reasonably optimum *roundtrip tours* between some depot location (a dump, in the case of garbage trucks) and the given sites. Each tour is feasible in the sense that it does not violate the capacity of the vehicle nor the time restriction imposed by the length of a work shift. The amount to be picked up (or unloaded) at a site may be a variable amount and each tour is then optimum in the sense of requiring the *least time per roundtrip*. Presumably this allows a truck to maximize the number of sites it can visit within one work shift. In the next section we then pursue the question of taking the set of tours and forming a collection of truck schedules which are now optimal in the somewhat different sense of requiring the *least number of vehicles*. That is, *vehicle scheduling* will be studied in contrast to vehicle routing.

In addition to refuse collection, public sector vehicle-routing problems can occur in other contexts, such as in the delivery of goods in sparsely populated areas (where travel time is significant) and in the routing of school busses. We have also been able to apply such ideas to the movement of barges which move refuse between marine transfer points and an offshore landfill site (see Section 1.1 for the setting of this problem).

5.3   SOME QUESTIONS OF SCHEDULING

What follows is a sequel to the previous section on vehicle routing. So far we have been able to construct efficient roundtrip tours which together cover the required service points. These tours can be assigned to a single vehicle which makes a number of back and forth trips or they can be assigned to several vehicles each of which completes one tour. If the linking together of tours to form a daily work schedule for a single vehicle exceeds the allotted time for one shift then clearly more than a single vehicle is required to service all clients on a single day. Therefore tours in themselves are not enough. What one wants is to be able to concatenate roundtrips to a dump to form a *daily and weekly schedule for each truck* in such a way that the *number of required vehicles is minimized.* There are many ways of hooking tours into daily routes which are feasible in the sense of not exceeding the time available in a work shift, and the optimal selection of such schedules can itself be posed as a set-covering problem. In order to show this assume, to begin with, that the weekly and daily schedules are identical. That is, the same number of demand sites are serviced each day and so the number of vehicles needed each week is simply equal to those required daily. It is also implicit in what follows that each tour requires less time for completion than that available in a shift. This conforms to the usual situation in which time is the binding constraint in forming daily routes out of tours, whereas vehicle capacity is the limiting factor in the formation of the tours themselves.

Let us then agree that a large number M of feasible daily routing schedules have been put together out of some available set of tours. Let

$$a_{ij} = \begin{cases} 1, & \text{if tour } i \text{ belongs to daily route } j \\ 0, & \text{otherwise} \end{cases}$$

and let x_j be defined as one if route j is selected and zero otherwise. Then in the by now usual way one wishes to minimize the sum

$$\sum_{j=1}^{M} x_j \qquad\qquad [5.3.1]$$

subject to the condition that each tour lies on some route or other

$$\sum_{j=1}^{M} a_{ij} x_j = 1 \qquad\qquad [5.3.2]$$

The optimum value of [5.3.1] is then the (least) number of trucks required to service all demand points.

There is an alternate way of looking at this problem, which is to assign each tour of duration t_i to a set of boxes, each of capacity Q, where each box represents a daily route for a single vehicle. The quantity Q is the total time available for one work shift (incidently, if a work day consists of more than one shift then the number of required vehicles is of course equal to the number needed in a day divided by the number of shifts since presumably the same truck can be used in consecutive shifts). What has been termed as a *loading problem* is to find the assignment of tours which minimizes the number of boxes needed. As it happens this problem can also be posed as an integer program but we forego the details (see reference in the notes at the end of this chapter). In general there is an intimate relation between this scheduling question and the problem of forming efficient tours which is not captured by the available models. We mean by this that the solution to the loading problem (as well as that of the problem posed by [5.3.1] and [5.3.2]) depends on being able to pack the boxes tightly so as to minimize the amount of dead (that is, unused) time in each shift. Therefore it may be worthwhile to form some tours which do not saturate vehicle capacity, in order to have available shorter roundtrips which can act as "fillers." For example, if a work shift is 6 hrs it is better to have four tours of 3 hrs each (for a total requirement of two trucks) than three tours of 4 hrs each (for a total now of three trucks) even if the 4-hr tours saturate vehicle capacity and the others do not. We encountered this question of constructing efficient routes (that is, routes with high truck utilization) in a study we completed in 1973 for the sanitation department of Milan, Italy, in which the interaction between routing and scheduling was worked out by heuristic arguments rather than by a formal optimization scheme.

A somewhat different set of scheduling problems arise from the fact that in practice not all sites are serviced the same number of times each week. As is typical in some areas, for example, a set of clients have their refuse removed on Monday, Wednesday, and Fridays (MWF), others on Tuesday, Thursday, Saturday (TTS), while the remainder are serviced every day (except Sunday). It is clear that in this context the formation of a weekly schedule is decoupled from that of finding daily schedules. In fact if one assumes that three times a week customers are indifferent to whether pickup is MWF or TTS then the problem is to assign tours to days of the week so as to minimize the number of required vehicles. This question will emerge with greater clarity as we continue this exposition.

We begin by modifying the Clarke and Wright procedure of Section 5.2 by forming a replica of each six times a week demand node and then constructing tours as before with the proviso that each such node and its replica image must appear on separate roundtrips. In this way each tour can be used to represent service on either MWF (let us call these "green" tours) or TTS (we call these "red" tours) and the six times a week sites will then be capable of appearing on both a red and a green tour (that is, these sites would be serviced on MWF and TTS, as required). The modifications of the basic algorithm need not be reviewed here except to note that if there are k six times a week nodes in a graph of n service nodes total, then the augmented graph (nodes plus their images) consists of $n+k$ nodes. It may sometimes happen that site $n+i$ (the "image" of site i) can be linked to site j even when

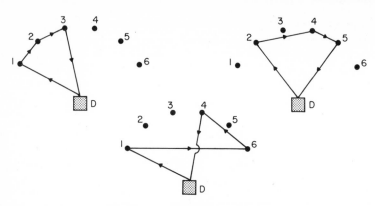

FIG. 5.14   An infeasible set of tours.

i cannot be joined to j. This can occur because i and its replica $n+i$ will necessarily lie on different tour segments as the algorithm progresses. Note however that the savings $S_{i,j}$ and $S_{n+i,j}$ will always be the same.

After forming the tours the next question is whether to label them as "green" or "red." This can pose a difficulty. Consider, for example, the three tours of Fig. 5.14 in which sites $1, 2, 4$ are serviced six times weekly and the others three times. Let tour 1 be red. Then, tour 2 should be green if site 2 is to be serviced every day (except Sunday, of course). But then tour 3 must again be a red one since tours 2 and 3 have site 4 in common. This now leads to an impasse since site 1 belongs to both red tours 1 and 3! Thus the set of tours of Fig. 5.14 is infeasible in the sense of not satisfying the *service frequency requirement* (note that the same difficulty arises even if tour 1 is labeled as green). In the process of circumventing this feasibility problem we will encounter an interesting question in graph theory.

So far we have constructed a bunch of tours which we have labeled, for pictorial effect, as red and green. Six times a week points are to appear on exactly two tours of distinctly different colors. Let us form a new graph T, call it a *tour graph*, where the vertices are the tours themselves and in which an edge is inserted between two vertices whenever the corresponding tours have a six day a week point in common. The least number of colors necessary to paint the vertices of any graph so that no adjacent vertex has the same color is called its *chromatic number*. In order for the collection of tours to form a feasible weekly schedule it is apparent that the chromatic number of T must be two. Otherwise some six times a week sites will be serviced twice on some days and not at all on the others. Thus, for instance, the set of tours in Fig. 5.14 can be represented by the tour graph of Fig. 5.15 and it is evident that this graph cannot be colored with red and green without adjacent nodes having the same color.

FIG. 5.15   Tour graph representation for the tours of Fig. 5.14.

The same difficulty can arise with other service frequency requirements. Consider, as an example, sites which are serviced Monday and Thursday (MT) or Tuesday and Friday (TF) or Wednesday and Saturday (WS) or every day. In the same manner as before one forms a set of tours by allowing each six times a week point to have two images and by insisting that each such point and its images must appear on different tours. Label all tours so found as Red (MT), Green (TF), and Blue (WS). The problem now is to paint the corresponding tour graph with exactly these three colors without adjacent vertices being identical. That is, we now want the tour graph to have a chromatic number of three. However the example of Fig. 5.16 shows that this is not always possible.

A *clique* in a graph is a set of mutually adjacent vertices. What goes wrong with the examples above is that each represents a clique of order one greater than the requisite chromatic number C (Figs. 5.15 and 5.16). In general, with a mix of service frequencies one wishes C not to exceed six. If L is the size of the largest clique, then graphs in which $L = C$ are of particular interest and a noteworthy exemplar is the class of graphs in which $L = C = 2$. A necessary and sufficient condition for this to be true is given in the theorem below but when C is greater than two, the conditions are more complicated and will be discussed later.

Theorem   A tour graph T is two colorable if and only if it has no cycles of odd order.

PROOF   Suppose that the graph has no cycles of odd order. Pick an arbitrary vertex and paint it with one of the two colors, say red. We then touch the

FIG. 5.16   Another infeasible set of tours.

vertices adjacent to the red vertex with the other color. Repeat this procedure until all vertices are painted. In this way no vertex is ever painted with both colors since this will happen only when there are two paths between two vertices, one of the paths having even length and the other odd. However this implies the existence of a circuit of odd length. Conversely, if T can be colored with only two colors then these pigments must alternate when a cycle is traversed. Hence the length of the cycle must necessarily be even. ∎

It is clear from this theorem that the graph of Fig. 5.15 is not two colorable since it consists of a single cycle of order three. We now have at hand a simple way of bypassing the obstacle posed in the formation of tours. As tours are constructed, the corresponding tour graph is built up along with them. As soon as an odd order cycle is about to be formed that tour is prevented from being considered further (that is to say, discarded) and the algorithm continues on with the formation of other tours. Incidently graphs which satisfy the theorem above are known as *bipartite* since all nodes in them can be assigned one of two colors in such a way that edges occur only between differently colored nodes.

When C is greater than two simple to apply tests which can be used to block the formation of an infeasible set of tours are unfortunately not known at present. However one heuristic is to make sure that there are no cliques of order $C+1$ in T whenever the service frequencies require C colors. A more formal way to determine C is by solving yet another set covering problem. To show how this is done one first defines an *independent set* in a graph as a subset of nodes no two of which are adjacent. Let us index all *maximally independent sets* in T by $j = 1, ..., M$, and label them as I_j. Form a matrix A whose entries a_{ij} are given by

$$a_{ij} = \begin{cases} 1, & \text{if vertex } i \text{ belongs to } I_j \\ 0, & \text{otherwise} \end{cases}$$

Then one wishes to solve the integer program

$$\text{minimize} \quad \sum_{j=1}^{M} x_j$$

subject to

$$\sum_{j=1}^{M} a_{ij} x_j \geq 1, \quad \text{for all nodes}$$

where x_j is one when I_j is chosen and zero otherwise. The constraint indicates that each vertex belongs to some independent set or other, which is to say that the independent sets cover the graph completely but with possible overlap. The objective is to obtain a covering using the least number of such

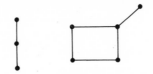

FIG. 5.17   A typical tour graph.

sets. Now each I_j can be painted with a single color since it has no adjacent vertices. Therefore the optimum value of the integer program provides the minimum number of colors necessary to paint the graph, which is therefore the value of the chromatic number C. It follows that the solution to this mathematical problem allows one to determine whether the collection of given tours is feasible in terms of service frequency.

The reader may have noticed that the service frequency problem could have been simply bypassed by preassigning demand sites to particular days of the week in conformity with their service requirements. Then one would carry out the formation of tours once for each day of the week with the optimization based solely on those nodes which happened to be assigned to that day. The disadvantage of this approach, of course, is that the resulting schedules need not be at all optimal from the point of view of vehicle utilization.

A simple example illustrates the loss of efficiency resulting from poor scheduling. Consider the tour graph shown in Fig. 5.17. Note, incidently, that such graphs need not be connected in general. Suppose that one requires two service frequencies, MWF and TTS. There are two ways of coloring the graph with red and green, as we see from Figs. 5.18a and 5.18b. Suppose that a days' shift is constituted by two tours in tandem. Then the first option requires three trucks on MWF and two of them on TTS, with one of the trucks only partially utilized every day. The other option provides for full utilization with only two trucks required at any time.

One last example of scheduling should by now convince the reader of the care necessary to achieve an efficient routing scheme. Suppose that three customers each require daily service, the first and third in the afternoon and the other one in the morning. Travel times between dump and the service

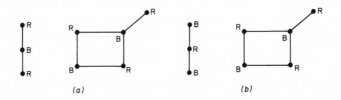

FIG. 5.18   Two scheduling options based on the tour graph of Fig. 5.17.

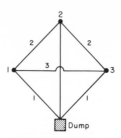

FIG. 5.19   Scheduling for a.m.–p.m. service.

sites is shown in Fig. 5.19 where we see that within a 6-hr shift a single truck does not suffice unless one of the p.m. clients is shifted to the morning. We remark parenthetically that this problem of a.m. versus p.m. pickup is itself a two coloring problem if the tours now represent either morning or afternoon service. A client which is to be handled twice daily would appear on two such tours.

5.4   CLEANER STREETS

Consider now the case of street sweeping. In New York City, as in a number of other places, this service is performed by trucks moving along the street curbs, with mechanically rotating brooms attached to the fronts of each vehicle. The goal of sweeping is an elusive and hard to quantify measure of cleanliness and so a surrogate is adopted of finding minimum time tours through the street network and, if more than one vehicle is required, of finding routes which require the least number of vehicles. Presumably these goals allow for the greatest number of streets to be swept in a given time period and with a given number of trucks.

The task of sweeping and, for that matter, of flushing the streets with water sprinkling trucks, requires that the vehicles move along the entire street network in a continuous roundtrip. Clearly if each street is covered exactly once without overlap this is necessarily the minimum time path. Unfortunately and in practice it is generally true that some streets need to be traversed more than once if the network is to be fully covered. Streets which are traversed but not swept are said to be *deadheaded*. A simple illustration is provided by Fig. 5.20 in which the reader sees that a single cycle covering the network (in solid lines) is not possible without some overlap. The necessary deadheading is shown in dotted lines.

A version of this problem was first mentioned by the mathematician L. Euler in 1736 in a celebrated paper in which he shows that each street in the network can be covered exactly once provided that the degree of each node in

FIG. 5.20   A simple cycle requiring deadheading (dotted lines).

the corresponding graph representing the network is even. That is, each intersection has an even number of streets incident to it. It is apparent that what is wrong with the network in Fig. 5.20 is that all the nodes, except one, are odd. Since this condition is rarely satisfied an optimization problem can then be posed which is to find a cycle that minimizes the amount of necessary deadheading. We will explore this question in the context of an urban street network in which the corresponding graph is a *directed* one. The reason the graph is directed is that some, if not most, streets are one-way and because in the process of sweeping or flushing each side of a street needs to be covered separately and in the direction of traffic. In the one-way case this means that each side is to be swept once but in the same direction. Figure 5.21a shows the graphical version of this fact using two edges to represent the sides of a street which terminates at the intersections denoted by the two nodes. Otherwise, for a two-way street, each side is swept in opposite directions (Fig. 5.21b).

For directed networks, Euler's condition is replaced by the statement that a necessary and sufficient condition for the graph to be covered once without deadheading is for each node to have the property that the number of branches leading into it equal the number of branches which leave. We assume here that the graph is connected. A proof of this assertion will be given next. When this condition is not met, as is usually the case, deadheading is necessary in order to complete a cycle.

Theorem   A directed graph possesses a cycle through all its edges, called an *Euler tour*, if and only if it is connected and if the following *Euler condition* is satisfied: *for every node the number of incoming edges equals the number of outgoing ones.*

(a)   (b)

FIG. 5.21   Directed edges to represent the two sides of a street for one-way (a) and two-way (b) streets.

PROOF   If an Euler tour exists it is evident that the graph is connected and that each edge entering a node must also leave. This implies that there are as many incoming as outgoing edges. Conversely if the condition is met then it is possible at each node to pair off incident edges in any way we please and to tie them together (clearly there must be an even number of such edges). This procedure, repeated at each node, results in a bunch of cycles which together cover the entire graph. Since the graph is connected each cycle is linked to some other one by at least one common node, and therefore all such cycles can be combined into a single one. This is the required Euler tour. ∎

The problem of obtaining a minimum time tour through the network is to *find a set of deadheaded links of shortest possible total length which, when added to the original graph, results in an augmented network in which the Euler condition is satisfied.* When a truck completes a cycle through the enlarged network the roundtrip is optimum in the sense that even though some edges are duplicated the total added travel time is as small as possible. We assume, incidently, a constant vehicle speed so that time and distance are commensurable quantities.

Note that in contrast with the refuse collection problem of Sections 5.2 and 5.3, which was to find a minimum time path through all the vertices of a graph, the present situation stipulates that the vehicle find a minimum time path through all the edges. There are also other differences. A significant one is that now there is no restriction on how much a vehicle can sweep and therefore capacity constraints are not needed. Moreover, as we will see, the previous restriction of worktime available on a shift is replaced by worktime available during those periods in which sweeping is actually possible. In urban areas the sweeper or flusher has access to the curbside only when no cars are parked there. Therefore these activities are carried out where and when alternate side of the street parking regulations (or some similar restrictions) are in effect. In New York City, for example, it is a legal violation to park on certain sides of a number of designated streets between 8 a.m. and 11 a.m. This ban is used by the sanitation department to schedule their cleaning and flushing operations along those streets.

There is a way of obtaining a solution to the minimum deadheading problem which will be discussed in the context of a specific street sweeping example. An explicit assumption is that the road network can be modeled by directed edges as in Fig. 5.21. Before we embark on the details let us note that essentially the same approach is valid in a number of other municipal contexts whenever the network is representable as a directed graph. For instance, the spreading of salt or sand on icy roads involves a routing along each edge exactly once (except for deadheading). Another case is that of household refuse collection

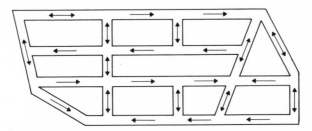

FIG. 5.22   Fragment of a street network. Arrows indicate one- and two-way streets.

which differs from the node routing example of Section 5.2 in that the "customers" are now sufficiently many on any given street that one can safely assume that their aggregate demand is spread continuously along the roadside. A garbage truck that services one container on a given street will of course service all of them on that street in a single pass. Alternate sides of the street parking rules play no role in these instances since the vehicles need only to traverse the center of the road and not each curb. Nor is deadheading itself a problem since the vehicles work quickly when not actually collecting. However there are other complications. The sand spreader must return to depot to refill its load, and the garbage truck must unload at a dump. Fortunately these restrictions can be handled as simple variants of the procedure to be discussed presently.

Consider, then, a sample fragment of an urban street network as shown in Fig. 5.22 in which arrows indicate whether the street is one-way or not. Assume that no parking regulations are in effect from 8 a.m.–9 a.m. on cer-

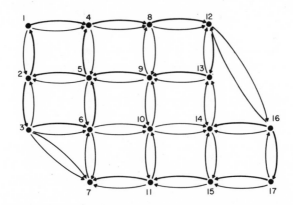

FIG. 5.23   Graphical representation of the street sweeping problem posed by the network of Fig. 5.22. Dark lines indicate no parking 8–9 a.m. Lighter lines indicate that parking restrictions are not in effect during that period.

tain sides of several streets. This is indicated on Fig. 5.23, which is a directed graph representation of the network, by using heavy dark lines to signal those curbsides that can be swept during this period. The lighter lines denote street segments which are not available for sweeping but which can however be used for deadheading.

If we extract from this graph the subset of edges which are to be covered by an Euler tour the directed graph of Fig. 5.24 results. This is a routing problem involving 16 nodes and 17 edges in which we immediately note that some of the nodes are unbalanced in terms of difference in edges which enter and leave. It follows therefore that some deadheading will be necessary and the linear program to be formulated next is designed to find a set of duplicate edges of shortest total length.

In order to do this we define the *polarity of a node* as the difference between the number of incident edges which enter and those that leave. For a Euler tour all nodes must have polarity zero, as we know, but after an appropriate number of deadheading links are inserted in the graph of Fig. 5.24, each node of the augmented graph will also satisfy this condition. All the nodes in Fig. 5.24 having nonzero polar values are:

Node number:	4	7	14	2	16
Polarity:	1	1	1	−1	−2

Let us agree to denote all nodes with positive polarity as *supply nodes* since they have an excess of incoming edges and therefore are in a position to donate some outgoing ones. Similarly we designate as *demand nodes* those with negative polarity since they are in a position to be edge recipients. This terminology was not chosen capriciously since what we have in mind is to solve a linear program in the transportation format (see Appendix A for terminology) in which supply nodes i are to be linked to demand nodes j in a

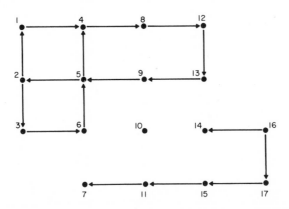

FIG. 5.24   Subgraph of Fig. 5.23 indicating streets that can be swept 8–9 a.m.

least cost way, where cost is the travel time c_{ij} between them. The interpretation of the solution is discussed later but we first pause to remark that for any graph this transportation problem is balanced in the sense that the total demand summed over all nodes equals the summed total of the supply, where supply or demand is taken to be the absolute value of the polarity value of a node. A proof of this assertion, which is not very difficult, is left as an exercise. In the particular example just discussed we verify that total demand = total supply = 3.

List the three supply nodes of our problem as s_1, s_2, s_3 and the demands by d_1, d_2 (these are the nodes 4, 7, 14, 2, 16, respectively). In order to set up the optimization program we need to compute the travel times c_{ij} along the shortest path which links s_i to d_j. It is important to recognize that this path may be taken *along any street in the original network*. The algorithm discussed in Appendix E would be used at this point for computing the shortest distance but in our case the paths are easily determined by visual inspection. Assume, for simplicity, that crosstown travel times are 8 min per block and are 5 min for each street up- or downtown. Two exceptions are the links $12 \rightarrow 16$ (10 min) and $3 \rightarrow 7$ (8 min). For these values we see that the shortest path from s_2 to d_1, the quantity c_{21}, is given by node $7 \rightarrow$ node $6 \rightarrow$ node $5 \rightarrow$ node 2 for a total of 18 min. Similarly for the other linkages. The following distance matrix summarizes the results for all the relevant nodes:

	d_1	d_2
s_1	13	26
s_2	18	41
s_3	29	20

We now pose the following transportation problem, which is to minimize total time between all supply and demand nodes. Each supply and demand requirement is to be met, as specified by the constraints:

$$\min\{13x_{11} + 26x_{12} + 18x_{21} + 41x_{22} + 29x_{31} + 20x_{32}\} \qquad [5.4.1]$$

subject to

$$
\begin{aligned}
x_{11} + x_{12} &= 1 \\
x_{21} + x_{22} &= 1 \\
x_{31} + x_{32} &= 1 \qquad [5.4.2] \\
x_{11} \quad\quad x_{21} \quad\quad + x_{31} &= 1 \\
x_{12} \quad\quad + x_{22} \quad\quad + x_{32} &= 2
\end{aligned}
$$

where each $x_{ij} \geqq 0$ is the number of times that supply node i is to be linked to demand node j along the shortest path. As is readily verified the optimum

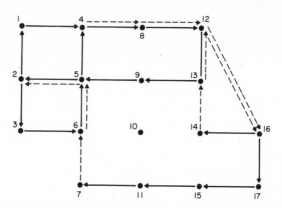

FIG. 5.25 Euler tour for street sweeping 8–9 a.m. Dotted lines indicate deadheading.

values of the assignments x_{ij} are $x_{11} = x_{22} = x_{31} = 0$, $x_{12} = x_{21} = x_{32} = 1$. This means that s_1 is to be joined to d_2, s_2 to d_1, and s_3 to d_2, each once. By adding these additional paths to the graph of Fig. 5.24, we obtain the augmented graph of Fig. 5.25 in which the supplementary links are denoted by dotted lines. These new edges represent streets which must be deadheaded. The optimization above assures us moreover that this is the least amount of extra travel that one can get away with. It is important to observe that the graph of Fig. 5.25 is such that all nodes have zero polarity and therefore a Euler tour can now be constructed. Simply begin anywhere and traverse a single closed loop. For example, the following cycle is a Euler tour:

$$1 \to 4 \to 8 \to 12 \to 13 \to 9 \to 5 \to 4 \to 8 \to 12 \to 16 \to 14 \to 13 \to 12$$
$$\to 16 \to 17 \to 15 \to 11 \to 7 \to 6 \to 5 \to 2 \to 3 \to 6 \to 5 \to 2 \to 1$$

We are not yet through. Since the parking regulations last 1 hr it is not possible for a single truck to cover the entire network and so the path must be partitioned into segments, each of which is less than an hour's length. But here an opportunity presents itself to reduce deadheading even further, as we shall see. It is typical of problems of this type that the time required for sweeping lies well within the duration of a workshift and therefore the time to travel from the truck depot to the starting point of a tour can be treated as incidental and as something which can be ignored. One may assume that each sweeper (or "mechanical broom," as they are sometimes referred to) is available to begin its route anywhere along the street network at the beginning of the time period (8 a.m. in our case). As a consequence it is possible to remove certain deadheaded segments which belong to either the front or tail end of a truck route. The driver simply begins at that intersection where actual sweeping is required.

We illustrate this idea by breaking the Euler tour constructed above into three truck routes with the elimination of 44 min of unnecessary travel:

Route 1: $1 \to 4 \to 8 \to 12 \to 13 \to 9 \to 5 \to 4$ (50 min)

Route 2: $16 \to 14 \to 13 \to 12 \to 16 \to 17 \to 15 \to 11 \to 7$ (57 min)

Route 3: $2 \to 3 \to 6 \to 5 \to 2 \to 1$ (31 min)

The final set of tours covers the entire network using 20 min of deadheading whereas total sweeptime is 118 min. Indeed only route 2 requires any overlap of its own path.

This example serves as a demonstration of how edge-routing problems can be handled in general. We summarize its salient features by listing the main ingredients used in the analysis. First, construct a directed graph G to represent the street network and extract a subgraph G_1 to denote those streets which, because of parking regulations, are available to be swept during a given period. Then isolate all nodes in G_1 which have nonzero polarity and label them either as "supplies" s_i or "demands" d_j. Compute the shortest path in G (that is, using any edge in the original graph) between all s_i and d_j and then solve a balanced transportation problem for determining the smallest total travel between supply and demand nodes:

$$\text{minimize} \quad \sum_i \sum_j c_{ij} x_{ij}$$

subject to

$$\sum_j x_{ij} = s_i$$

$$\sum_i x_{ij} = d_j$$ [5.4.3]

with $x_{ij} \geq 0$. The values of x_{ij} indicate the number of deadheading links to insert between s_i and d_j. Augment G_1 to a graph G_1' in which all nodes have zero polarity by adding in these extra links and form an Euler tour through it. Finally break the Euler tour into individual truck routes, each satisfying a restriction on the time available for sweeping, keeping in mind (as illustrated earlier) that it may be possible to eliminate certain deadheading links.

There are a number of refinements to this basic algorithm that we do not go into here (further references are given in the notes). However we do want to comment briefly on the question of scheduling. First of all observe that although alternate side of the street parking bans effectively reduce the size of the graph that needs to be considered (and thereby simplifies the construction of a tour) it also raises an interesting issue with regard to forming daily routes for the sweepers or flushers. Suppose, for instance, that between

9 a.m. and 11 a.m. the parking rules changed in such a way that the remaining set of curbsides could now be approached. One can of course form minimum deadheading tours for the 9–11 period, as we did above for 8–9, but then it is necessary to assign vehicles used in the preceding period to the newly generated routes in this later time slot. There are many ways of making this assignment, each of which requires some deadheading from the end of one tour to the beginning of the next. The optimum one is that which reduces this extra travel to a minimum. The resulting concatenation of tours then results in a set of schedules for each vehicle from 8–11 a.m. A similar argument applies to any time period within a work shift and indeed this is one of the basic questions in the routing of school buses. In that case the buses pickup and deliver children to several schools (subject to constraints on seating capacity), each of which have different starting and closing times. Indeed the staggering of the times at which schools open and close is often designed in accordance with the need to use the least number of buses. Incidentally, although in this section we have concentrated on travel time as a goal it is more or less true that an optimal routing scheme with regard to time is also optimal in terms of requiring the least number of vehicles. The relation between the two is essentially that discussed in Section 5.3 in terms of "the loading problem."

The problem takes on added significance if one stipulates that certain streets can be swept anytime during the 8 a.m.–11 a.m. period. Vehicles which complete a tour early can fill in any slack time available by sweeping such additional arteries as are available. What is not obvious is whether to assign a given 8–11 street to the 8–9 or the 9–11 period. In each case the graph G_1 is augmented by these additional edges and the question of minimum deadheading (and hence minimum vehicles) is now roughly analogous to that of assigning tours to either MWF or TTS so as to minimize the number of necessary trucks (see Section 5.3).

In closing it is important to observe that the routes formed by the mathematical schemes outlined above may not be implementable. The reason is that sweeper trucks usually find it inconvenient to maneuver from one side of a street to another since the driver must sit on the side facing the curb. Awkward turns, such as U-turns, or frequent changes from sweeping to deadheading and back, may foul up drivers who in general prefer long straight segments of the network whenever possible. This again illustrates the pitfall of not doing analysis in the context of an operating environment. One should also regard with caution recommended changes which may in fact cost more to implement than they are designed to save. For example, better routes could be obtained by altering the directions of certain streets or by altering the parking regulations. But the expense of sign changes as well as the disruption in traffic patterns would tend to preclude such "solutions."

5.5 EXERCISES

5.1 Suppose a network in a certain rural region can be modeled abstractly by the following graph (Fig. 5.26) in which the numbers on the edges represent travel time in minutes. Using the set-covering approach discussed in Section 5.1 find the least number of facilities necessary to ensure that each demand node is located no more than 2 min away from a fire station. Assume that a facility already exists at G and that none can be located at site B. The problem should first be formulated mathematically.

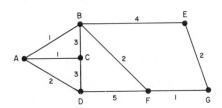

FIG. 5.26 Street network modeled by a graph.

5.2 Consider the complete graph of Fig. 5.6 with travel times given there. Suppose a truck has a capacity of four bins and that sites 1–4 have 1, 2, 1, 3 bins to pick up, respectively. Form tours using the Clarke and Wright heuristic and compare against the nearest neighbor rule, which is to go from the dump to the nearest node and from there to the next nearest node at which total load does not exceed vehicle capacity . . . and so on.

5.3 Find the maximally independent sets of the graph below (Fig. 5.27) and compute its chromatic number by solving an appropriate integer program, as in the text. Exhibit a specific coloring of the graph.

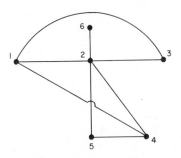

FIG. 5.27 An illustrative graph.

5.4 Show that in a directed graph the sum of the supplies over all supply nodes equals the sum of the demands over all demand nodes.

5.5 Working from the graph of Fig. 5.23 form the subgraph of streets which can be swept between 9 and 11 a.m. Assume all streets are handled sometime between 8 and 11 a.m. Determine the supply and demand nodes together with their polarity and verify the condition of Exercise 5.4 for this graph. Finally, find the shortest path from node 3 to node 17 using any part of the street network and show that it is not unique.

5.6 NOTES AND REMARKS

5.1 The study for the Glasgow Firemaster and Scottish Home and Health Department was prepared by

J. Hogg, "Planning for Fire Stations in Glasgow in 1980," Rep. 1/68, Scientific Advisors Branch of Home Office (1968).

The East Lansing study was prepared by the National Bureau of Standards in conjunction with the International City Managers Association:

L. Santone and G. Berlin, "Location of Fire Stations," in *Systems Analysis for Social Problems*, Washington Operations Res. Council, 1970.

The Denver study was funded by HUD:

T. Hendrick and D. Plane, "An Analysis of the Deployment of Fire-Fighting Resources in Denver, Colorado," Rep. WN-8949-HUD (Jan. 1975).

The set-covering formulation given here is due to

C. Toregas, R. Swain, C. ReVelle, and L. Bergman, "The Location of Emergency Service Facilities," *Operations Res.* **19** (1971), 1363–1373.

The method of k centers is given by

S. Hakimi, "Optimum Locations of Switching Centers and the Absolute Centers and Medians in a Graph," *Operations Res.* **12** (1964), 450–459.

As for political districting, a useful reference is the paper by

R. Garfinkle and G. Nemhauser, "Optimal Political Districting by Implicit Enumeration Techniques," *Management Sci.* **16** (1970), 495–508.

5.2 The study on gas pipeline networks is due to a multitude of authors:

"Design of Economical Offshore Natural Gas Pipeline Systems," Rep. R-1, Office of Emergency Planning (Oct. 1968).

This and a number of other basic papers on network optimization are also available in

Large Scale Networks: Theory and Design, IEEE Press, New York, 1976.

The heuristic truck routing scheme is fully discussed by

E. Beltrami and L. Bodin, "Networks and Vehicle Routing for Municipal Waste Collection," *Networks* **4** (1974), 65–94.

Other references include:

G. Clarke and J. Wright, "Scheduling of Vehicles from a Central Depot to a Number of Delivery Points," *Operations Res.* **12** (1964), 568–581;

S. Eilon, C. Watson-Gandy, and N. Christofides, *Distribution Management*, Hafner, New York, 1971.

A discussion of heuristic algorithms for traveling salesman problems is to be found in the paper by

S. Lin and B. Kernighan, "An Effective Heuristic Algorithm for the Traveling Salesman Problem," *Operations Res.* **21** (1973), 498–516.

It is useful to illustrate here the assertion made in the text that a minimal tree through a set of nodes can perhaps be improved by the addition of other nodes. Consider, for instance, the simple case of three nodes A, B, C placed at the vertices of an equilateral triangle. The minimal tree linking them is shown in Fig. 5.28a. However by inserting an additional node at the juncture point labeled as D in Fig. 5.28b, a tree of even smaller total length is possible. We leave it to the reader to verify this when edge length is the usual Euclidean distance. The added node D is called a *Steiner point* and it can be shown that for a graph of n nodes at most $n-2$ Steiner points can be added in order to improve the tree. In general, however, it is a nontrivial task to produce graphs with Steiner nodes although it is clear from the gas pipeline example that the significance of such constructions may be considerable in terms of overall savings.

The basic vehicles routing heuristics discussed in this section consisted of first clustering or partitioning all demand sites into a bunch of feasible tours, and then to improve each tour by reducing travel time as much as possible.

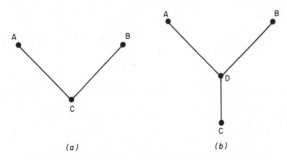

FIG. 5.28 Improving a tree by adding a Steiner point.

An alternate approach would have reversed this procedure by first forming a single time optimal cycle through all the nodes using the traveling salesman heuristic and then to bust this single cycle into a set of feasible tours. This last is easily accomplished by following the cycle until vehicle capacity (or shift time) is about to be saturated. At this node the trip is interrupted for a detour to the dump. From there the truck moves back to next node on the cycle and the process repeated until all sites are serviced. If the demand points are all reasonably close to the dump so that back and forth travel time for unloading is not too significant, then this approach to routing may be a useful one as, for example, in urban school bus routing where the pickup points are bus stops in the neighborhood of a school (the "dump"). A detailed comparison of both schemes is beyond the scope of this book. However we do wish to mention a theoretically useful way of measuring the performance of the traveling salesman heuristic. One can pose the question of finding a time optimal cycle as an Assignment Problem (see Appendix A) by minimizing the objective function

$$\sum_{i=1}^{n} \sum_{j=1}^{n} c_{ij} x_{ij}$$

where c_{ij} is travel time between nodes i and j. The x_{ij} are chosen to be one if i and j are linked together as part of a path and zero otherwise. A natural constraint is that every node lie on the path exactly once as both a predecessor and a successor to every other node on that same path:

$$\sum_{j=1}^{n} x_{ij} = 1$$

$$\sum_{i=1}^{n} x_{ij} = 1$$

The solution to the linear program gives an assignment of each node to every other node. If the result consists of a single cycle then this is in fact the optimal traveling salesman path. However, in general the path will consist of several disjoint cycles. One can preclude these subcycles from forming by imposing a large number of additional constraints but if this is not done then the resulting solution at least provides a lower bound for the optimum. That is, imposing additional constraints can only reduce the range of choices for an optimum value. Since a solution to the original assignment problem is relatively straightforward to obtain for reasonably small networks one has available a way of comparing any heuristic solution against the theoretically best one.

5.3 The "loading problem" is treated fully in Chapter 10 of the book by Eilon, Watson-Gandy, and Christofides quoted above in 5.2. The paper by

Beltrami and Bodin, also referenced in 5.2, discusses scheduling for node routing as well as the issue of service frequency. The first reference to the two-color problem in the context of garbage collection is in a paper by

S. Altman, N. Bhagat, and L. Bodin, "Algorithm for Routing Garbage Trucks over Multiple Planning Periods," presented at 8th TIMS meeting, Washington, D.C. (Mar. 1971).

The graph theoretic consequences of these coloring questions are explored by

A. Tucker, "Perfect Graphs and an Application to Optimizing Municipal Services," *SIAM Rev.* **15** (1973), 585–590.

Note, by the way, that since the tour graphs need not be planar graphs in general there is no connection here with the celebrated four color problem of graph theory.

We have refrained in this chapter from discussing the coding of routing problems for computer solution. This is in keeping with our aim to present only the basic modeling concepts. However this is not to deny that the development of algorithms for the numerical solution of such problems is of paramount importance and that it is an area of considerably subtlety and sophistication. Some of the issues involved here are treated by

L. Bodin, "A Taxonomic Structure for Vehicle Routing and Scheduling Problems," *Computers and Urban Soc.* **1** (1975), 11–29.

Finally, let us note two small details regarding node routing which are important in applications. First, travel time between nodes needs to be augmented by a fixed amount to account for loading at each site. Usually this is a constant quantity of perhaps a few minutes. In addition there is an unloading time of somewhat longer duration at the dumpsite for each tour. Second, in computing daily routes one needs to add on an initial travel time from the truck depot (or garage) to the first pickup point and then some time at the end of the shift to account for travel from the dump back to the depot. Neither of these additions affects the algorithms discussed in Sections 5.2 and 5.3. The principal restrictions, as we have seen, are truck capacity, length of a shift, service frequencies, number and location of the dumps and the number, location, and refuse bin sizes of each customer.

5.4 The problem of finding a single Euler tour through a network, with minimal deadheading, is sometimes picturesquely referred to as the *Chinese Postman problem*. In addition to the paper by Beltrami and Bodin referenced in the notes to 5.2 there are a few others which extend the basic ideas in several directions. One such is by

L. Bodin and S. Kursh, "A Computerized System for the Routing and Scheduling of Street Sweepers," *Operations Res.* (1977).

Of more theoretical interest is the paper by

J. Edmonds and E. Johnson, "Matching Euler Tours, and the Chinese Postman Problem,"
    Math. Programming **5** (1973), 88–124.

These routing ideas have been applied not only in New York City but also in
Washington, D.C. (Department of Environmental Services) and, in a different
context, in Zurich; see the paper by

T. Leibling, "Routing Problems for Street Cleaning and Snow Removal," in *Models for
    Environmental Pollution Control* (R. Deininger, ed.), Ann Arbor Sci. Publ., Ann Arbor,
    Michigan, 1973.

In the notes to 5.3 we observed that the node routing schemes were based
on first partitioning all demand sites into tours and then to reduce travel
time by optimizing over each of these cycles. In the case of edge routing we
follow the opposite procedure of first constructing a single time optimal
cycle which is then broken into individual tours. One disadvantage of this
approach is that it generally leads to a bunch of overlapping tours which
are somewhat undesirable from an administrative point of view in that they
tend to complicate the task of assigning responsibility for malfeasance of
service. Administrators would prefer individual truck routes to reside in
sectors having easily identifiable boundaries. This therefore suggests the
alternate and indeed opposite approach to routing, which is first to decom-
pose the entire street network into disjoint but contiguous regions, each of
which is serviced by a single vehicle during a given time period. Then a minimum deadheading Euler tour is found within each of the partitions. Of
course it is not a priori clear whether the sector is too large or too small for
a single vehicle during the given period but a rough guess can be made. The
main drawback is that now total deadheading over the entire network is
never less than in the first approach and may be considerably more. The
reason, of course, is that by stipulating beforehand the region to be swept
removes a degree of freedom in the choice of optimal route. This constraint
is not present in the procedure given in the text and therefore the resulting
optima are necessarily better (or no worse). The tradeoff is between efficiency
and administrative control. An interesting question in graph theory is to
find a decomposition of the graph into compact, contiguous subgraphs in
such a way that *total deadheading* is minimized and such that workload
along each subgraph corresponds (roughly) to a route for one vehicle. This
problem is not too dissimilar to that of political districting, which we considered in Section 5.1, except that workload now plays the role of population. This is a nontrivial stratification problem, especially when coupled
with the requirement that some streets must, because of parking regulations,
be swept in a given period whereas other streets can be assigned quite arbitrarily to different periods.

We have considered directed graphs. It is of interest to observe that in the undirected case Euler tours can still be obtained provided all nodes of odd degree are paired off with one another in such a way that the extra links introduced are of minimal length. If one augments the original graph with these added links, then all nodes now have even degree and, as we noted in the text, a single tour can then be constructed which overlaps itself the least amount possible. Although we do not wish to review the algorithm for pairing odd nodes it should be said that what makes such a pairing feasible is the easily proven fact that there is always an even number of odd degree nodes in the graph.

Incidently, the original paper of Euler is available in translation as

"The Seven Bridges of Konigsberg," in *The World of Mathematics* (J. Newman, ed.), Volume 1, Simon and Schuster, New York, 1956.

Urban Growth Models

Perhaps the most widely known models of public sector interest are the two by Jay Forrester ("Urban Dynamics") and Ira Lowry ("A Model of Metropolis"). I do not intend to discuss any details here except to bring them to the readers attention (further references are given at the end of this section) and to indicate in very loose terms how they differ from the conceptual tools developed so far in this book.

Both models purport to follow the growth (and the eventual possible stagnation and even decay) of an urban region based on given assumptions about how people, jobs, markets, and housing all interact with each other. They each begin with a spatially closed region in which there are initially a few pockets of people and jobs and lots of vacant land. A number of factors restrain and shape how that growth takes place. For example, tax rates play a role in urban dynamics while zoning regulations appear in the Lowry model. Eventually the available land begins to dwindle and growth is increasingly controlled by changes in land use which are designed to compensate for this saturation. The Forrester model evolves over time and spatial factors enter only implicitly. By contrast the Lowry model is spatially explicit but now it is time which enters only indirectly. Both are designed to be run on computers until the region reaches some level of equilibrium.

Unlike most of the models of this book, neither is concerned with optimization except that growth can be influenced by deliberate and exogenously chosen policies which act as mechanisms for controlling the future. For example, federal tax incentives and job programs will influence the outcome of the Forrester model while changes in the choice of basic industries and in zoning will affect the ultimate behavior of the Lowry model.

All the mathematical frameworks of this book are static in the sense of not reflecting either spatial or temporal changes explicitly. Exceptions are the time-dependent energy distribution model considered in Section 1.5 and the brief treatment of queues through simulation in Section 3.1. The two urban growth models are however dynamic in that they follow the evolution of a region beginning with some given configuration of people and jobs. This is done through the use of computer simulation (but not stochastically, as in our queuing study). The internal logic of these models is constituted by a number of coupled (that is, interacting) constraint equations designed to reflect what actual growth would be like under real world conditions. At every step of the simulation these linkages determine how each of the basic variables depend on the other variables and on their own previous values. The result is, to all appearances, that of a self-regulating system.

It is apparent that these models are inherently more complex and considerably more ambitious than anything considered by us previously. Indeed this complexity is the basis of much of their appeal, not only because it gratifies the intuition by feigning reality but also due to the fact that the simulated growth patterns often cannot be anticipated from the initial configurations and therefore sometimes result in an element of surprise (Forrester plays on this appeal by referring to the "counterintuitive" nature of the results generated by his model).

There has been much criticism of this work but there is no doubt that they have been of considerable influence on the thinking of a number of scientists concerned with public affairs. These provocative models cannot be ignored by serious analysts and an appreciation of their basic tenets should be part of the background of any professional whose interests include the contents of this book.

REFERENCES

There are several extensions of the basic urban growth models, but in the first instance the reader should turn to the original sources:

J. Forrester, *Urban Dynamics*, MIT Press, Cambridge, Massachusetts, 1969;

I. Lowry, "A Model of Metropolis," Rand Rep. RM-4035-RC (1964).

A brief overview of both these works, together with a discussion of a number of related topics (including a treatment of some of the municipal service models developed in the present book) is given by

W. Helly, *Urban Systems Models*, Academic Press, New York, 1975.

Two of the many critiques available are the informative report by

H. Garn and R. Wilson, "A Critical Look at Urban Dynamics: The Forrester Model and Public Policy," Rep. 113-39, Urban Inst., Washington, D.C. (1970),

and the paper by

W. Goldner, "The Lowry Model Heritage," *Amer. Inst. Planners J.* (1971), 100–110.

APPENDIX

A

Linear Programming

Our goal here and in Appendix B is a quick review of linear and integer programming. We want to give the reader sufficient orientation to make him or her an intelligent user of the various computer packages now available for general use. In order to simplify the discussion, a simple example is chosen to illustrate the general theory. The example is well-behaved, but in practice some pathologies can occasionally occur. However, most computer codes will signal the various difficulties as they happen.

LINEAR PROGRAMS

The general linear programming (LP) problem is to maximize a linear objective function $\sum_{j=1}^{n} c_j x_j$ subject to m inequality constraints of the form

$$\sum_{j=1}^{n} a_{ij} x_j \leq b_i, \qquad i = 1, ..., m \qquad [\text{A.1}]$$

together with $x_j \geq 0$; $j = 1, ..., n$.

More succinctly, the problem is to maximize $c^T x$ subject to $Ax \leq b$ and $x \geq 0$, where x is the column vector with components $x_1, ..., x_n$; A is the m

by n matrix whose entries are the a_{ij}, and T denotes vector transpose. The row vector $(c_1, \ldots, c_n)$ is denoted by c, and b is the corresponding column vector with entries b_i.

Although a linear optimization problem can occur in various other guises, it can always be reduced to above standard form by an appropriate use of negative signs. For example, the minimum of $c^T x$ is the same as the maximum of $-c^T x$ and $Ax \geqq b$ is the same as $-Ax \leqq -b$.

Generally speaking, the x_j denote activity levels of some kind, and the c_j are dollar profits per unit of activity j (in a minimization problem these would be dollar costs per activity). The b_i denote levels of available resources used in the various activities and the a_{ij} are amounts of resources i used in a unit of activity j. The inequality constraints indicate that the resources that can be used are strictly limited. To illustrate, consider a plant which produces two products A, B, measured in tons per day and that the unit profits of A, B are \$40 and \$60, respectively. Three scarce resources C, D, and E are used to produce A, B in the ratios given in Table A.1, where the rightmost

TABLE A.1

	A	B	
C	2	1	70
D	1	1	40
E	1	3	90

column is the maximum of each resource which is available each day (also measured in tons). Let x_1, x_2 be the activity levels of A, B. Clearly x_1 and x_2 are nonnegative and we want to

$$\text{maximize} \quad 40x_1 + 60x_2$$

$$\begin{aligned} \text{subject to} \quad 2x_1 + x_2 &\leqq 70 \\ x_1 + x_2 &\leqq 40 \\ x_1 + 3x_2 &\leqq 90 \end{aligned} \qquad [\text{A.2}]$$

FEASIBLE SETS AND OPTIMIZATION

Each of the inequalities [A.1] defines a half space in R^n with a boundary (a bounding hyperplane) defined by making the inequality a strict equality. The set of points in R^n which satisfy the constraints [A.1] taken together is called the feasible set. For $n = 2$, as in our illustration [A.2], the half spaces reduce to half planes and the hyperplanes are lines in the plane. The feasible set, being the intersection of convex sets, is itself convex and, if bounded,

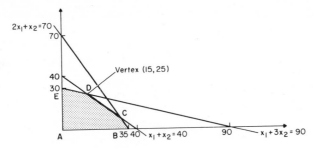

FIG. A.1   Feasible set corresponding to Eqs. [A.2].

is a convex polyhedron (a polygon for $n = 2$). In a well-posed problem the feasible set is nonempty (the case in which it is empty is one of the possible pathologies alluded to above), and it can be bounded or unbounded. In the latter case, an optimal solution may not exist for certain objective functions (this is another possible pathology). For example, the objective $x_1 + x_2$ does not possess a maximum in the feasible set $x_1 \geqq 0$, $x_2 \geqq 0$ (why?).

In our special case, [A.2], the feasible set is the polygonal region exhibited as a shaded area (Fig. A.1) with five corner points (or, as they are also called, *extreme points or vertices*). In general, the feasible set of [A.1] only has a finite number of extreme points.

Consider now a graphical solution to the problem [A.2]. For every constant value v, the points x_1, x_2 which satisfy $40x_1 + 60x_2 = v$ define a straight line. The greater the value of v, the larger the value of the objective function. Clearly then, one wishes to choose the largest v so that x_1 and x_2 still lie within the feasible set (that is, so as to satisfy the constraints). As v increases, the line $40x_1 + 60x_2$ moves parallel to itself until any further increase forces

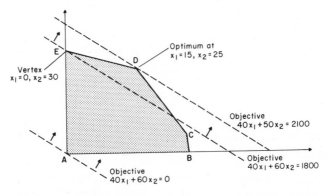

FIG. A.2   Graphical solution to the problem posed by Eqs. [A.2].

it out of the feasible region. As the reader will see from Fig. (A.2), this occurs at the corner point where $x_1 = 15$, $x_2 = 25$.

It is always true, in general, that if the optimum exists it can be found at a vertex, and so the search for the optimum reduces to a search at the (finite set of) extreme points. In principle this can be done as follows. Each vertex is the intersection of n bounding hyperplanes defined by the constraints—that is, as the solution of a system of equations in n unknowns. In our special case each vertex is the intersection of two lines or as the solution of two equations in two unknowns. Since there are $m+n$ constraint hyperplanes one has $\binom{m+n}{n}$ possible ways of finding extreme points. Some of these solutions may not define feasible points but those that do are labeled as extreme points. One then compares the value of the objective function at these finite number of points and chooses the maximum. However, $\binom{m+n}{n}$ can be a very large quantity (in our special case it is $\binom{5}{2} = 10$, of which half, or five, of these solutions defines extreme points) and one would like a more efficient procedure. The graphical technique used above is limited to two dimensions, but fortunately an algebraic equivalent of this idea does work in general and is called the *simplex method* (a convex polyhedron is sometimes referred to as a simplex).

THE SIMPLEX METHOD

We illustrate the method on our special problem [A.2]. To begin with, convert all inequality constraints into equalities by introducing *slack variables* x_3, x_4, x_5 so that

$$
\begin{aligned}
2x_1 + x_2 + x_3 \quad\quad\quad &= 70 \\
x_1 + x_2 \quad\quad + x_4 \quad\quad &= 40 \\
x_1 + 3x_2 \quad\quad\quad\quad + x_5 &= 90
\end{aligned}
\qquad [A.3]
$$

with $x_j \geqq 0$, $j = 1, \ldots, 5$.

A *basic variable* is defined to be any original or slack variable which is nonzero. Otherwise it is termed nonbasic. A solution to [A.3] with three basic and two nonbasic variables is called a basis or a *basic feasible solution*. In general, one introduces m slack variables for the m inequality constraints of [A.1] and then a basis consists of m basic and n nonbasic variables. There are $\binom{5}{2} = 10$ ways of choosing two nonbasic variables out of five and each of these ways leads to a solution of the equality constraints in [A.3.] However, only five of these define feasible solutions (in the sense of also satisfying $x_j \geqq 0$ for $j = 1, \ldots, 5$) and, as one might conjecture from the discussion, such feasible solutions correspond to extreme points. In fact, corner points and basic feasible solutions are in unique correspondence with each other in the general case as well. Table A.2 establishes this fact for this illustrative problem of Fig. A.1. Any other choice of basic and nonbasic variables is unfeasible. For example, letting $x_1 = x_4 = 0$ leads to the solution $x_2 = 40$, $x_3 = 30$, $x_5 = -30$ for [A.3], which is inadmissible. Therefore, one in particular sees that an optimal solution is basic feasible.

TABLE A.2

Vertex	Basis				
	x_1	x_2	x_3	x_4	x_5
A	0	0	70	40	90
B	35	0	0	5	55
C	30	10	0	0	30
D	15	25	15	0	0
E	0	30	40	10	0

The graphical procedure began by choosing a value of the constant v so that $40x_1 + 60x_2 = v$ would lie in the feasible set and then increasing v until the maximum is attained. The algebraic counterpart of this is to let x_1 and x_2 be nonbasic initially, as a starting guess. The corresponding basic feasible solution in [A.3] corresponds to the corner point A which, as one easily verifies, is where $x_3 = 70$, $x_4 = 40$, $x_5 = 90$. The objective function at A is 0. Can this be improved? If either x_1 or x_2 are increased beyond zero, then the objective also increases and it would appear that since x_2 has the largest coefficient, the greatest benefit accrues by increasing that variable. However, how far can x_2 be augmented and still obtain a feasible solution to [A.3]? Keeping $x_1 = 0$ we see from [A.3] that as soon as $x_2 = 30$, then $x_5 = 0$ and any further increase in x_2 renders x_5 negative. Therefore a new basic feasible solution can be obtained by letting $x_1 = 0$, $x_2 = 30$ in which case, as one easily verifies, $x_3 = 40$, $x_4 = 10$, $x_5 = 0$. This corresponds to the vertex E and so algebraically we moved the objective function parallel to itself from its intersection with A until it touches E (see Fig. A.2), where it has the value 1800. Can this be improved? Since x_1 is still zero, try a unit increase in that variable. Since $x_5 = 0$, the third constraint in [A.3] shows that x_2 must decrease by $\frac{1}{3}$. But then the objective has a value of 2120 and so it is clear that one should try to increase x_1 as much as possible, always preserving feasibility. From [A.3] one obtains (keeping $x_5 = 0$) that

$$x_2 = (90 - x_1)/3$$
$$x_3 = 40 - (5x_1/3)$$
$$x_4 = 10 - \tfrac{2}{3}x_1$$

from which we see that x_1 cannot increase beyond 15, after which x_4 becomes negative. Thus the new basic feasible set, corresponding to vertex D, is $x_1 = 15$, $x_2 = 25$, $x_3 = 15$, $x_4 = x_5 = 0$. Here the objective function has the value 2100 and since there are no further ways of increasing either x_1 or x_2 without diminishing the value of 2100, we are at the optimum. Thus the simplex method algebraically maneuvered us from A to E to the optimum at D. This is the essence of the method in general.

ARTIFICIAL VARIABLES

Suppose we add a constraint of opposite orientation to our sample problem; such as $x_1 + x_2 \geqq 10$ or equivalently,

$$-x_1 - x_2 \leqq -10 \qquad\qquad [A.4]$$

The modified feasible set is pictured in Fig. A.3, in which we see that the optimum still occurs at E, but we can no longer start with an initial basis in which $x_1 = x_2 = 0$, since this is not feasible.

In what follows we show how to handle this defect. Begin by introducing slack variables x_3, x_4, x_5, x_6 as before so that one has

$$
\begin{aligned}
2x_1 + x_2 + x_3 \qquad\qquad\quad &= 70 \\
x_1 + x_2 \qquad + x_4 \qquad\quad &= 40 \\
x_1 + 3x_2 \qquad\quad + x_5 \qquad &= 90 \\
x_1 + x_2 \qquad\qquad\quad - x_6 &= 10
\end{aligned}
\qquad [A.5]
$$

Notice that x_6 has a coefficient of -1 since this is a reducing slack variable. Note also, that if $x_1 = x_2 = 0$ then x_6 is negative, which is unacceptable. Remedy this by introducing yet another variable $\bar{x}_6$, called an *artificial variable*, in the last constraint so that

$$x_1 + x_2 - x_6 + \bar{x}_6 = 10$$

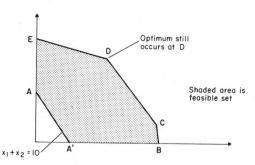

FIG. A.3   Problem modified so that it requires artificial variables.

Then, if we choose the initial nonbasic set by letting $x_1 = x_2 = x_6 = 0$, the initial basic feasible set is, as one readily verifies, $x_1 = x_2 = x_6 = 0$ and $x_3 = 70$, $x_4 = 40$, $x_5 = 90$, $\bar{x}_6 = 10$. This device gets us started except that $\bar{x}_6$ has no real significance as a variable (as we will show, the slacks however *do* have a concrete interpretation) and we would like to drive it to zero before reaching the optimum. To do this, add $\bar{x}_6$ to the objective function with a large negative coefficient, say -10^3, so that it now reads as

$$40x_1 + 60x_2 - 10^3\bar{x}_6 \qquad\qquad [\text{A.6}]$$

Since an increase in $\bar{x}_6$ contributes adversely to the increase of the total profit, it will eventually be eliminated. In fact, once $\bar{x}_6$ becomes nonbasic in the simplex algorithm, it never reappears as a basic variable because to do so would drag the value of [A.6] down beyond the value it previously would have held with $\bar{x}_6$ nonbasic. In our case, proceeding as before, we let x_1 remain zero and x_2 is increased as far as it can be. But as soon as x_2 is 10, then $\bar{x}_6$ is zero and so the second basic feasible solution occurs at $x_1 = x_6 = \bar{x}_6 = 0$ and $x_2 = 10$, $x_3 = 60$, $x_4 = 30$, and $x_5 = 60$. This corresponds to vertex A. One then continues to the next vertex except that $\bar{x}_0$ is henceforth ignored.

In some computer codes one is asked to determine if, and how many, artificial variables are needed. In general one adds as many artificial variables as there are constraints of the type in which they are either an equality or in which the inequality is $\geqq 0$.

DUALITY

If we call our original problem [A.2] the *primal*, then one can consider an associated *dual problem* given by

$$\text{minimize} \quad 70y_1 + 40y_2 + 90y_3$$

$$\text{subject to} \quad 2y_1 + y_2 + y_3 \geqq 40 \qquad\qquad [\text{A.7}]$$
$$y_1 + y_2 + 3y_3 \geqq 60$$
$$y_i \geqq 0 \qquad (i = 1, 2, 3)$$

More generally, using vector and matrix notation, since the primal in n variables is given by

$$\text{maximize} \quad c^T x$$
$$\text{subject to} \quad Ax \leqq b, \qquad x \geqq 0$$

(with A the m by n matrix of coefficients a_{ij}, c the n-vector of profits, x the *n*-activity vector, and b the m-vector of resources) then the dual is defined by

$$\text{minimize} \quad b^{\mathrm{T}}y$$
$$\text{subject to} \quad A^{\mathrm{T}}y \geq c, \quad y \geq 0$$

of which [A.7] is a special instance. The significance of the dual will now be explained.

Consider the illustrative example above. As it happens, [A.7] has the solution $y_1^0 = 0$, $y_2^0 = 30$, $y_3^0 = 10$ in which superscript zero indicates the optimal value. Thus the objective function has the value $40y_2^0 + 90y_3^0 = 2100$ which the same value of the primal objective at its optimum (where $x_1^0 = 15$, $x_2^0 = 25$). This illustrates the first general fact that if the primal or dual possesses an optimal, so does the other and their values are equal— that is, at an optimum one has $c^{\mathrm{T}}x = b^{\mathrm{T}}y$.

However, from the point of view of this book, a more significant fact lies in the interpretation of y_i^0 or, as they often are called, the *dual multipliers* (see Appendix D for an explanation for this terminology). Recall that x_j represent activity levels with c_j profits per unit activity and that b_i is a bound on the availability of the ith resource. Suppose we increase the resource levels by one unit. Begin with b_1 which we increase from 70 to 71 in the constraints [A.2]. What effect does this have on the optimum? By examining the graphical solution of the perturbed problem (we leave this pictorial detail to the reader) the optimum still occurs at $x_1^0 = 15$, $x_2^0 = 25$, and so a unit increase in the availability of the first resource has a null effect on total profit. However this is not unexpected since the slack variable x_3 at the optimum had a positive value $x_3^0 = 15$, which means that this re-source was *overallocated* to begin with, and so the marginal return in profit due to a further increase in b_1 is zero. This will be true in general for any constraint in which the final value of the slack is nonzero since that value indicates the extent to which the corresponding resource was overallocated. In such cases, the dual variable corresponding to that resource will be zero. Indeed, in our example $y_1^0 = 0$. Now increase the second resource level b_2 from 40 to 41 (with b_1, b_3 unaltered). If one again carries out a graphical solution for this perturbed problem, the optimum now occurs at $x_1^0 = 16.5$, $x_2^0 = 24.5$, and so the objective is 2130, which is an increase of 30 for a unit increase in b_2. Note that y_2^0 also has the value of 30. Consider, finally, a unit increase of b_3 from 90 to 91. The optimal solution now is $x_1^0 = 14.5$, $x_2^0 = 25.5$, with an objective function of 2110 and so a unit increase in b_3 give an increased return of ten, which is also the value of y_3^0. This illustrates the general fact that the *dual multipliers y_i^0 are the marginal increase in return due to a unit increase in the availability of the ith resource*, and so is an ex-pression of how much it is worth to increase the use of a scarce resource. In economic terms, these multipliers are known as *shadow prices*. Similarly, a unit decrease in b_i results in the same marginal decrease in profit. Note, in particular, that y_i^0 is zero whenever the corresponding slack variable in the ith constraint of the primal problem is nonzero (in economics, the corresponding resource is called a free good). This can be written as

$$y_i^0 \left(\sum_{j=1}^{n} a_{ij} x_j^0 - b_i \right) = 0 \qquad \text{for} \qquad i = 1, \dots, m \qquad [\text{A.8}]$$

As it happens, the dual of the dual can be shown to be the primal, and so analogous considerations indicate that the x_j^0 are shadow prices for the dual, from which one obtains

$$x_j^0 \left(\sum_{i=1}^{m} a_{ij} y_i^0 - c_j \right) = 0 \qquad \text{for} \qquad j = 1, \dots, n \qquad [\text{A.9}]$$

Taken together, relations [A.8] and [A.9] are known as the theorem on *complementary slackness.*

In some computer codes for linear programming, the dual multipliers are computed along with the optimal values of the primal variables.

Because of the interpretation of the y_i^0 the constraint equations

$$\sum_{j=1}^{m} a_{ij} y_i^0 \geqq c_j$$

mean that the total contribution to profit by using all available resources for any unit of activity j, must be at least as great as the profit c_j attributed to this activity. Otherwise one is not making the best possible use of the resources. Also, the y_i must be nonnegative otherwise it does not pay to use the ith resource since it contributes negatively to profit.

TRANSPORTATION PROBLEMS

There are some optimization problems that occur so often that they have been given intensive individual treatment. The two we will mention are examples of special kinds of linear programs. The first is to *minimize* the double sum

$$\sum_{i=1}^{n} \sum_{j=1}^{m} c_{ij} x_{ij} \qquad [\text{A.10}]$$

subject to the restrictions $x_{ij} \geqq 0$ and

$$\sum_{j=1}^{m} x_{ij} = a_i, \qquad i = 1, \dots, n$$
$$\sum_{i=1}^{n} x_{ij} = b_j, \qquad j = 1, \dots, m \qquad [\text{A.11}]$$

The waste collection problem given in Section 1.1, as well as several others (such as the idle classroom exercise) fall within this framework and in general such problems occur when one wants to ship or transport some items from an *origin* (*source*) i *to a destination* (*sink*) j at a minimum cost. The costs from

i to j are given by the c_{ij}, a_i is the amount of goods that must be shipped from i to b_j is maximum amount of goods that j can possibly accept (in some variants of this problem the capacity constraints on j are written as $\sum_{i=1}^{n} x_{ij} \leq b_j$, rather than as an equality). Such problems are called *transportation problems* and a specially tailored version of the simplex algorithm has been devised to solve them efficiently.

Generally speaking, the origins i can be thought of in economic terms as providing a *supply* and the destinations j as posing a *demand* for the transported items. An even further special case occurs when one takes $m = n$ in the transportation problem, with $a_i = 1$ for all i and $b_j = 1$ for all j. Such problems are known as *assignment problems* and it turns out that the solution is to allocate precisely one j location to each i location so that x_{ij} are either zero or one.

It is usually assumed in transportation problems that the supplies and demands are balanced in the sense that $\sum_{i=1}^{n} a_i = \sum_{j=1}^{m} b_j$. If this is not the case, then the procedure is to introduce either a dummy supply or demand location so as to make the problem balanced. An example of this procedure was noted in Section 1.1 in connection with the waste collection problem.

Note that if the problem is in balance, then the $m+n$ equality constraints in [A.10] are redundant in that one of them is linearly dependent on the others (we leave this to the reader to verify) and so [A.11] reduces to a system of $m+n-1$ independent constraint equations. Therefore in applying the simplex procedures, a basic feasible solution will have $m+n-1$ basic variables. However, even though no slack variables are required in principle, one would need $m+n$ artificial variables, one for each constraint. In practice one circumvents this nuisance by the simple expedient of finding an initial basic feasible solution in which the need for artificial variables no longer exists. A simple procedure (but not necessarily the most efficient) for doing this is known as the *northwest corner rule*. In the exercise of Chapter 1, in connection with the waste collection problem, the reader is asked to use this method in a specific instance. It is illustrated as follows.

Consider the following situation. There are two origins $i = 1$, 2 and three destinations $j = 1$, 2, 3 and we want to minimize a cost function given by

$$\text{cost} = \sum_{i=1}^{2} \sum_{j=1}^{3} c_{ij} x_{ij}$$

subject to $x_{ij} \geq 0$ and

$$\sum_{j=1}^{3} x_{ij} = a_i \qquad \text{(the supplies)}$$

and

$$\sum_{i=1}^{2} x_{ij} = b_j \qquad \text{(the demands)}$$

Assume the problem is balanced in that $a_1 + a_2 = b_1 + b_2 + b_3$ (total supply equals total demand). Specific coefficient values are indicated in Table A.3.

TABLE A.3

Origins (sources)	Destinations (sinks)			Supplies
	1	2	4	
1	$c_{11} = 30$	$c_{12} = 20$	$c_{13} = 10$	$a_1 = 500$
2	$c_{21} = 5$	$c_{22} = 15$	$c_{23} = 25$	$a_2 = 500$
Demands	$b_1 = 300$	$b_2 = 300$	$b_3 = 400$	

There are $3 + 2 = 5$ constraint equations. But one of them is redundant since it is linearly dependent on the rest. To see this, note that

$$\sum_{j=1}^{3} x_{ij} = a_1$$

whereas

$$\sum_{i=1}^{2} \sum_{j=1}^{3} x_{ij} = a_1 + a_2 = b_1 + b_2 + b_3$$

and so

$$\sum_{j=1}^{3} x_{2j} = b_1 + b_2 + b_3 - a_1$$

Therefore, given four out of the five constraint equations involving b_1, b_2, b_3, and a_1, the last relation is automatically determined. Thus, in effect, there are only four independent constraints and so one expects a basis to have only four basic variables. In general, with m supply and n demand constraints, one gets $m + n - 1$ basic variables, as we already noted.

We would like to generate an initial basis without introducing artificial variables—that is, to find a basic feasible solution in which there are $m + n - 1$ basic *real* variables. This would provide a shortcut through the simplex algorithm. A simple but effective way of doing this is to begin at the north-west corner of Table A.3 and assign as much as possible of source 1 to sink 1, followed by sink 2, and then sink 3. Since sink 1 can only absorb 300 units and source 1 has 500 to give we assign 300 to it (i.e., $x_{11} = 300$). The remaining 200 units can safely be assigned to sink 2 ($x_{12} = 200$). Then sink 3 has nothing to receive ($x_{13} = 0$). Now begin with the second row. Source 2 would like to give 300 units to sink 1, but that destination is already saturated. Therefore $x_{21} = 0$. However, sink 2 is capable of receiving 100 units and so $x_{22} = 100$. Finally sink 3 receives the rest: $x_{23} = 400$. All sinks and sources are thus satisfied and the solution is clearly feasible. Is it optimal? Not quite. The cost function is 24,500 and similar to the usual simplex procedure, we find that a unit increase in a current nonbasic variable, say x_{13}, may produce a lower cost value. However, to maintain feasibility, a unit increase in x_{13} needs to be compensated by a unit decrease in x_{23} (otherwise sink 3 is over-supplied) but this in turn requires that x_{22} be increased by one (in order that source 2 not be under utilized) which finally requires that x_{12} decrease by one. Carrying this argument as far as possible and still preserving feasibility (that is, no constraint violation including $x_{ij} \geqq 0$) we see that x_{13} can be increased to 200. Thus, one generates a new feasible solution with basic $x_{11} = 300$, $x_{12} = x_{21} = 0$, $x_{13} = 200$, $x_{22} = 300$, and $x_{23} = 200$. The cost function is now 20,500. Repeating this argument beginning with nonbasic variable x_{12} gives a new cost of 14,500. A final iteration with (nonbasic) x_{22} gives 10,500. Since it is no longer possible to alter a nonbasic variable and still effect a lowering of cost, we are done. The sequence of steps is illustrated in Table A.4. Note that at every iterate there are four basic variables.

TABLE A.4

Start			
	$x_{11} = 300$	$x_{12} = 200$	$x_{13} = 0$
	$x_{21} = 0$	$x_{22} = 100$	$x_{23} = 400$
		$\downarrow$	
	$x_{11} = 300$	$x_{12} = 0$	$x_{13} = 200$
	$x_{21} = 0$	$x_{22} = 300$	$x_{23} = 200$
		$\downarrow$	
	$x_{11} = 0$	$x_{12} = 300$	$x_{13} = 200$
	$x_{21} = 300$	$x_{22} = 0$	$x_{23} = 200$
Optimum		$\downarrow$	
	$x_{11} = 0$	$x_{12} = 100$	$x_{13} = 400$
	$x_{21} = 300$	$x_{22} = 200$	$x_{23} = 0$

We now ask how to handle un unbalanced problem. Suppose, to be specific, that source 1 has 700 units to supply. Then, to keep total supply equal to total balance, allow a dummy sink to be created with a demand of exactly 200. Thus j runs up to four and the new problem is a balanced one. Following the prescription given in Table A.4, the initial feasible solution (with $2 + 4 - 1 = 5$ basic variables) is

$x_{11} = 300$	$x_{12} = 300$	$x_{13} = 100$	$x_{14} = 0$	northwest
$x_{21} = 0$	$x_{22} = 0$	$x_{23} = 300$	$x_{24} = 200$	corner rule

Depending on the values of c_{14} and c_{24} that one assigns, the optimal solution could indicate some allocation of supply to the dummy sink. Suppose, for example, that the optimal solution required that $x_{14} = x_{24} = 100$. This means that each source has an excess of 100 units of supply which either must be sent to an unspecified external sink or which remain as untransported quantities.

In all fairness it should again be stated that occasional pathologies do occur in the solution process because of a special structure that the problem may have. For instance, if source 1 has an excess of 100 rather than 200 units, one would only have four, not five, basic variables. However, this and similar irregularities can often be easily accommodated as is discussed in the referenced literature.

NOTES

In our view, the most useful introductions to linear optimization, as well as to a number of other topics discussed in this book, are found in the well-known books by

F. Hillier and G. Lieberman, *Introduction to Operations Research*, 2nd ed., Chapters 2–4, Holden-Day, San Francisco, 1974,

H. Wagner, *Principles of Operations Research*, Chapters 2–5, Prentice-Hall, Englewood Cliffs, New Jersey, 1969.

Integer programming is well-discussed in Chapter 17 of the Hillier–Lieberman book and also by

D. Plane and R. McMillian, *Discrete Optimization*, Prentice-Hall, Engelwood Cliffs, New Jersey, 1971.

Computer codes for linear (and integer) programming problems can be found in Plane and McMillan as well as in several texts on the Fortran or Basic languages. Most computing centers have prepared codes with user manuals and IBM systems utilize the standard MPS package. A survey of available computer codes (ca. 1973/1974) for the kind of linear optimization problems as discussed in these lectures is given by

B. Salkin and W. Balinsky, "Integer Programming Models and Codes in the Urban Environment," Rep. No. 279, Dept. Operations Res., Case Western Reserve Univ., Ohio, 1972.

B

Integer Programming

Consider a slightly modified version of the problem described by [A.2] in which the third constraint now reads as

$$x_1 + 2.8x_2 \leqq 90.$$

The feasible region can be drawn by the reader and a graphical argument gives the optimum at the vertex point in which $x_1 = 12.3$, and $x_2 = 27.7$. Suppose, however, that one wishes a solution in *integers*. One might think that the integer solution is obtained by rounding off the fractional solution. However, $x_1 = 12$, $x_2 = 28$ leads to an infeasible point and other integer approximations may be nonoptimal, even if feasible. Another approach might be to enumerate explicitly all lattice points within the feasible region and to choose that one which maximizes the objective. However, even in our modest example there are already hundreds of lattice points to examine and so a more efficient procedure is called for. A number of algorithms have been devised in recent years, but perhaps the most widely used are variants of what is known as the *branch and bound method*. We will illustrate the main elements of the method by using it to solve our modified sample problem.

The idea is not to enumerate explicitly all integer possibilities within the feasible set, but rather to enumerate implicitly by partitioning the feasible region into smaller and smaller subsets (branching) and then prune away (bound) those partitions in which a further search for the optimum would prove to be fruitless. An essential aspect of the pruning process is the easily grasped notion that *as a feasible set is further and further restricted* (by adding more constraints) *the corresponding optimum values of the objective function can never improve in value and may become decidedly worse* since the range of choices have been reduced. That is to say, if A, B are feasible regions with $A \subseteq B$ and if f is any objective function, then the maximum of f over A is less than or equal to the maximum of f over B.

One begins, then, with the fractional solution to the modified problem which, as we noted, is given by $x_1 = 12.3$, $x_2 = 27.7$. The value of $f(x) = c^T x$ there is 2154 and it provides an upper bound for all subsequent solutions. This is in accordance with the principle stated previously since, as the feasible set is further reduced, the corresponding maxima can never exceed 2154. Therefore, if the original solution happened to be an integer, we would have

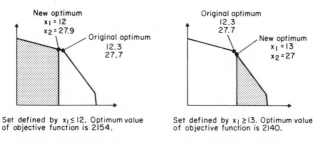

Set defined by $x_1 \leq 12$. Optimum value of objective function is 2154. Set defined by $x_1 \geq 13$. Optimum value of objective function is 2140.

FIG. B.1 Partitioning for an integer optimum.

been done. That not being the case, one first partitions the feasible set into two regions by adding the restrictions that $x_1 \leq 12$ and $x_1 \geq 13$. It is clear that the integer optimum must occur in one of these two subsets. Now find the maximum of $c^T x$ in each of these sets. Drawn (roughly) in Fig. B.1 are the two partitions and their corresponding optima. We see that an integer solution is available when $x_1 \geq 13$. Is this the best one can do? Unfortunately we do not yet know because in the region $x_1 \leq 12$, the objective function has a value greater than in the set defined by $x_1 \geq 13$ and so a further partition of this subset could reveal an integer optimum which is at least as good as the integer optimum obtained in $x_1 \geq 13$ (if the objective function in $x_1 \leq 12$ had been less than or equal to 2140, then no further improvement would be possible and the process would have terminated by accepting $x_1 = 13$, $x_2 = 27$). So, let us partition the region $x_1 \leq 12$ into subsets in which $x_2 \leq 27$ and $x_2 \geq 28$. Each has a feasible region pictured in Fig. B.2 with the corresponding optima. The integer solution in the case $x_2 \leq 27$ is

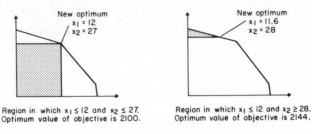

Region in which $x_1 \leq 12$ and $x_2 \leq 27$.
Optimum value of objective is 2100.

Region in which $x_1 \leq 12$ and $x_2 \geq 28$.
Optimum value of objective is 2144.

FIG. B.2   Further partitioning improves the optimum.

discarded since it is not better than one previously obtained but the region with $x_2 \geq 28$ needs to be further partitioned since its optimum is still greater than the previous integer optimum of 2140. Thus, let $x_1 \leq 11$ and $x_1 \geq 12$. However, the feasible set for $x_1 \geq 12$ is empty (and so cannot be further considered) whereas for $x_1 \leq 11$, the optimum objective value is 2132 (with $x_1 = 11$, $x_2 = 28.2$) and so we can finally prune it away since any subsequent partitions cannot yield any improvements on this value, which is itself less than the earlier integer optimum of 2140. Therefore $x_1 = 13$, $x_2 = 27$ is indeed the desired integer solution. We invite the reader to verify graphically that this is in fact the optimum.

The branching and pruning process can be summarized by a tree diagram given in Fig. B.3 which justifies the use of such arboreal terminology.

We note here that in the previously discussed transportation problem (Appendix A) it can be shown that as long as the supplies a_i and demands b_j are integer-valued, the optimum x_{ij} values will also be integers. In the particular case of the assignment problem, the x_{ij} will of course always be either zero or one.

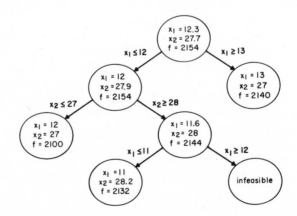

FIG. B.3   Branch and bound solution to the integer problem.

SET COVERING

Throughout the text one frequently encounters integer programs of the type

$$\text{minimize} \quad c^\mathsf{T} x$$
$$\text{subject to} \quad Ax \geqq b \qquad \qquad \text{[B.1]}$$

where A is an m by n matrix whose entries are zero or one and b is a column vector with positive integer components b_i. A solution vector x is sought which is nonnegative and with integer-valued entries. This is called the *multiple set-covering problem* or, in the case in which the b_i are all unity, simply as the *set-covering problem* (this terminology is explained in the text in Section 2.3). The inequality in [B.1] may be an equality in some applications. Although branch and bound methods can be used to solve such integer programs, special codes have been tailored to the specific form of [B.1]. We will not go into that here.

There are a few short remarks about set covering which are useful to make. We assume the simple case in which b_i are all one. First, note that if one row of A is zero, say the ith one, then the problem is infeasible because the relation $\sum a_{ij} x_j \geqq 1$ will fail to hold. Also if two rows r and s are such that every element of row s is also an element of row r (that is, $r \geqq s$) then one can safely delete the rth row from A since $\sum a_{sj} x_j \geqq 1$ automatically implies that $\sum a_{rj} x_j \geqq 1$. Finally, in an optimal solution it is always true that the components x_j of x are either zero or one. Indeed if $x_j > 1$ in some optimal vector, then $\sum a_{ij} x_j$ must necessarily be greater than one. Therefore by reducing x_j to have the value $x_j = 1$, we continue to have a feasible solution but at a lower cost—that is, at a lower value for $c^\mathsf{T} x$. The result follows from this observation.

UNIMODULARITY

We want to make an additional remark of a more theoretical nature here, which can be safely omitted by a reader inexperienced with matrix algebra. This material is not used anywhere in the text, but it does help explain something of the reason why integer problems are distinguished from ordinary garden variety linear programs.

It will be assumed that [B.1] holds with equality constraints and that A has maximal rank m (with $m \leqq n$). After permuting the rows of A, we can write it as (Q, N) where Q is a nonsingular m by m matrix (the first m columns of the permuted A) and N is the remaining $n - m$ columns. Let now the vector x be written as (x_Q, x_N) where x_Q has m components. Then $Ax = b$

is the same as

$$Qx_Q + Nx_N = b$$

from which

$$x_Q = Q^{-1}b - Q^{-1}Nx_N$$

Suppose that one finds an optimum solution x to the linear program [B.1] without insisting on its being integer-valued. Then, as we know, x is basic feasible and so its components can be arranged so that $x_Q \geqq 0$ and $x_N = 0$. Now since A has integer entries, every m by m nonsingular submatrix Q has a determinant $|Q|$, which is also an integer, and we say that A is *unimodular* if, for every such Q, $|Q| = \pm 1$. In such a case, it follows that Q^{-1} is also integer-valued since the adjoint of Q has integer entries and

$$Q^{-1} = \text{Adjoint}\, Q/|Q| \qquad \qquad \text{[B.2]}$$

Therefore, if x is an optimum solution, it is *also integer-valued* whenever A is unimodular for one has

$$x_Q = Q^{-1}b$$

and since both b and Q^{-1} are integer-valued, so is $x = x_Q$.

Note that $|Q|$ is of course always an integer but unless its value is plus or minus one, the quotient [B.2] need not itself be integer-valued.

NOTES

See the references given at the end of Appendix A for further readings. Most of the nonstochastic models in this book revolve around either the plant location fixed-charge problem (or some variant of it) which can be formulated as a mixed-integer program, or the set-covering (and multiple set-covering) zero–one programs. For this reason the reader is urged to regard closely the material given in this appendix.

APPENDIX

C

Random Processes

POISSON ARRIVALS

In this section we briefly review some elementary facts concerning random processes as background material for the discussion of urban emergency services.

To begin, consider a model for incidents that occur at random in time as shown in Fig. C.1. By this we mean that:

i. Incidents happening in disjoint intervals of time are independent of each other.

ii. The probability of no occurrence in a time interval is dependent only on the length of that interval and not on where it begins.

iii. In any sufficiently small interval, at most one incident can occur.

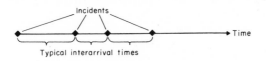

FIG. C.1   A random arrival process.

Break the unit time axis into N small time intervals of length $h = 1/N$. Then, by (iii) there is either one or no event in each such subinterval. Let p be the probability of a happening. Since events in subsequent intervals are independent, by (i), then the average number of occurrences is $\lambda = Np$ or $p = \lambda h$. In actuality λ is found empirically from observed data and so p is determined. Now let $P(t)$ be the probability of no incidents in an interval of length t: prob(interarrival time $\geq t$). Using (i) we have

$$P(t+h) = P(t) \cdot P(h)$$

and by (iii), $P(h) = 1 - \lambda h$. Therefore, in the limit as $h \to 0$,

$$dP/dt = -\lambda P$$

and, since $P(O)$ is clearly one, one can solve to find

$$P(t) = e^{-\lambda t} \qquad\qquad [C.1]$$

Finally, by virtue of (ii), $e^{-\lambda t}$ is the probability distribution of gap length greater than t *between any two incidents.*

Let $f(t)$ be the probability density of interarrival times. Then from [C.1]

$$e^{-\lambda t} = \int_{t}^{\infty} f(\zeta)\, d\zeta$$

or differentiating,

$$f(t) = \lambda e^{-\lambda t} \text{ is the probability of a gap of duration } t \atop \text{between incidents} \qquad [C.2]$$

Note that

$$\int_{0}^{\infty} \lambda t e^{-\lambda t}\, dt = 1/\lambda$$

and so the mean interarrival time is $1/\lambda$. The variance of these times is similarly computed as $1/\lambda^2$.

The exponential [C.2] has the property that small gap lengths occur more frequently than long ones. This gives rise to the "clumping" effect which is often visible in random processes.

Let us now ask for the probability $P_k(t, \lambda)$ of exactly k occurrences in a time interval t given that the interarrival distribution is exponential with

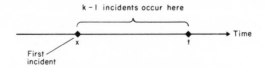

FIG. C.2   Successive random incidents.

mean $1/\lambda$. Well, if x is less than t, then

$$\lambda e^{-\lambda x} \cdot P_{k-1}(t-x, \lambda)$$

is the probability of the event displayed in the Fig. C.2. Therefore $P_k(t, \lambda) = \int_0^\infty \lambda e^{-\lambda x} \cdot P_{k-1}(t-x, \lambda)\, dx$. Since $P_0(t, \lambda)$ must clearly be $e^{-\lambda t}$ then

$$P_1(t, \lambda) = \int_0^\infty \lambda e^{-\lambda x} e^{-\lambda(t-x)}\, dx = \lambda t e^{-\lambda t}$$

$$P_2(t, \lambda) = \int_0^\infty \lambda^2 e^{-\lambda x}(t-x) e^{-\lambda(t-x)}\, dx = [(\lambda t)^2 e^{-\lambda t}]/2$$

and so on, from which it recursively follows that

$$P_k(t,\lambda) = [(\lambda t)^k e^{-\lambda t}]/k! \qquad\qquad\qquad [C.3]$$

which is the *Poisson* distribution. Conversely, if arrivals are governed by [C.3] then the probability of no arrival in an interval of time t is the same as the probability of gap lengths never less than t. But, from [C.3], this is given by $e^{-\lambda t}$ by setting k to zero. Therefore we have established the complete equivalence between the relations:

$$\text{Poisson arrivals} \leftrightarrow \text{exponential interarrival} \qquad\qquad [C.4]$$

Note that the mean number of incidents per unit time is given by

$$\sum_{k=0}^{\infty} k P_k(t, \lambda) = \lambda$$

as would be expected (since the average incident rate is simply the reciprocal of $1/\lambda$). Similarly, the variance of a Poissonly distributed variable is λ^2.

These arguments could be repeated to derive a distribution for k random occurrences in a space of area A to generate a *spatial Poisson* distribution given by

$$P_k(\lambda, A) = [(\lambda A)^k e^{-\lambda A}]/k! \qquad\qquad\qquad [C.5]$$

Here the parallel assumptions are that (i) events which occur in nonoverlapping sectors are independent, (ii) the probability of no event in a spatial sector is dependent only on the area of that sector and not on its location or shape, and (iii) at most one incident can occur in sufficiently small areas.

The exponential has an exceptional attribute, which is its memoryless character. That is, if t time units have already elapsed since the last arrival, then the probability distribution of the time remaining until the next arrival is again exponential with the same average interarrival rate. That is,

prob(gap length $\geq t + x \mid t$ time units already elapsed)

$$= \frac{\text{prob(gap length} \geq t+x)}{\text{prob(gap length} \geq t)} = \frac{e^{-\lambda(t+x)}}{e^{-\lambda t}} = e^{-\lambda x}$$

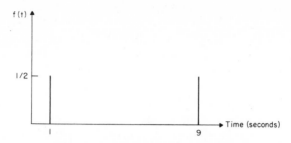

FIG. C.3   A simple interarrival density.

Thus, the exponential is unaffected by its past history and the time remaining before a new incident occurs is independent of when we start looking. Put into more picturesque terms, if cars randomly pass an intersection at some average rate λ then a pedestrian is just as likely to be hit when crossing that intersection immediately after a car passes as to cross it at some arbitrarily chosen time.

This memoryless property is not shared by other distributions, however. Consider, for example, a simple interarrival density given by $f(1) = f(9) = \frac{1}{2}$, as shown in Fig. C.3.

Here the process of random incidence would bring one into contact with the larger gap length nine times more frequently than with the smaller gap. Therefore, the probability density $g(w)$ of the lengths w of gaps entered into by random incidence will favor these longer interarrival times. It is thereby reasonable to suppose that $g(w)$ is proportional to w and so we let $g(w) = kwf(w)$ where k is determined from the requirement that $\int_0^\infty g(w)\,dw = 1$.

The constant k is found to have the value $1/E(w)$, where $E(w)$ is the expected value of gap lengths. In the previous example, $g(1) = \frac{1}{10}$ and $g(9) = \frac{9}{10}$ (see Fig. C.4). It is apparent now that for random incidence the distribution of the remaining waiting time until the next incident is likely to be quite different from the original distribution of gap lengths. Indeed the expected length of the *remaining* gap for such randomly entered processes

FIG. C.4   Distribution of gap lengths for the density of Fig. C.3.

could be *larger* than the expected length of the gaps themselves! However, we do not show this here and instead only point out one application of the concept of random incidence in statistical data analysis. Suppose that $F(x)$ is the distribution of the number of crimes committed by a population of criminals in some file. If a crime is picked at random, then it is more likely that the individual identified with that crime has an extensive crime record than of having a meager one. That is because random incidence biases in favor of choosing longer crime careers than short ones and so one might be tempted to conclude, without justification, that the "average" criminal is likely to have a long history of arrests.

Now consider n independent and concurrent Poisson arrival processes (with mean arrival rates, λ_i) in a given time period. Suppose that following a given incident, one looks at the successive interarrival times t_i of each of the random processes. The very next event will occur at a time $\tilde{t}$ given by

$$\tilde{t} = \min(t_1, ..., t_n) \qquad [C.6]$$

Therefore, the probability that the next arrival has a gap length $\geq t$ equals

$$\text{prob}(\tilde{t} \geq t) = \text{prob}(t_1 \geq t, t_2 \geq t, ..., t_n \geq t)$$

which by independence can be computed as

$$\text{prob}(t_1 \geq t)\,\text{prob}(t_2 \geq t) \cdots \text{prob}(t_n \geq t) = e^{-\lambda_1 t} \cdots e^{-\lambda_n t} = e^{-\lambda t}$$

where

$$\lambda = \sum_{i=1}^{n} \lambda_i \qquad [C.7]$$

This shows two things. First, the distribution of the variable given by [C.6] is exponential and second, because of this, the sum of independent Poisson processes is again Poisson with a mean equal to the sum of the individual means.

On the other hand consider n successive interarrival times, t_i, each from the same Poisson distribution having mean λ. We want the distribution of their sum. Now $\text{prob}(\sum_{i=1}^{n} t_i > t)$ is the same as the prob(at most $n-1$ incidents occur in the interval of length t) which, in turn, is given by using the fact that the probability of a sum of mutually exclusive events is the sum of the respective probabilities,

$$G(t) = \sum_{k=0}^{n-1} \frac{(\lambda t)^k e^{-\lambda t}}{k!} \qquad [C.8]$$

The corresponding density function $g(t)$ is found by differentiating the expression

$$G(t) = \int_t^\infty g(\zeta)\, d\zeta$$

to get

$$g(t) = \frac{\lambda^n t^{n-1} e^{-\lambda t}}{(n-1)!} \qquad\qquad [C.9]$$

which is known as a *gamma distribution*. For our purposes it will be convenient to assume that the original arrival process had an average inter-arrival time of $1/n\lambda$ rather than of $1/\lambda$. Then, the sum of the n independent gap times has a mean equal to $n \cdot 1/n\lambda = 1/\lambda$ and a variance of $n \cdot 1/(n\lambda)^2 = 1/n\lambda^2$. The corresponding density function is given by the family of *Erlang distributions*:

$$\frac{(n\lambda)^n t^{n-1} e^{-n\lambda t}}{(n-1)!}, \qquad n = 1, 2, \ldots \qquad [C.10]$$

When $n = 1$, the Erlang reduces to the exponential density function with mean $1/\lambda$ but as n increases, the variance tends to zero. Therefore, as n increases, we get a family of probability distributions which represent less and

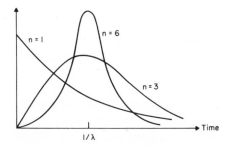

FIG. C.5   Erlang density functions.

less variability about their mean $1/\lambda$. The limiting case as $n \to \infty$ is that of constant interarrival times with value $1/\lambda$. Typical Erlang distributions are exhibited in Fig. C.5. The corresponding distributions [C.8]—with λ replaced by $n\lambda$—look like those shown in Fig. C.6. The Erlang can be interpreted in this way. Suppose one considers a sequence of n tasks, each of which takes a certain time to complete and that this time is a random variable exponentially distributed with mean $1/n\lambda$. As each task is completed, the next one immediately commences. The total completion time of all the tasks together is now distributed according to [C.10] with a variability which is less than that experienced in the completion of each individual task!

In actual data gathering experiments one empirically computes the value of the mean, $\hat{\lambda}$, and standard deviation, $\hat{\sigma}$, of an arrival process. A quick and dirty test of whether the process is Poisson is to compute the ratio $\hat{\lambda}/\hat{\sigma}$. If this number is close to one, it lends credence to the Poisson assumption.

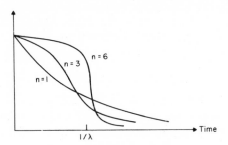

FIG. C.6 Erlang distributions.

But if the ratio is considerably less than one, it is more reasonable to conclude that the data comes from an arrival process whose interarrival times are Erlang, since theoretically $1/\sigma = 1/\sqrt{n} < 1$.

We want to point out quickly one other application of the above ideas to the statistical analysis of data. This comes about in trying to fit automobile accident data to a simple model in which each person is assumed to enter into an accident at random—that is, according to a Poisson distribution—with average rate, λ. This random model allows one to test whether a statement of the type "50% of all accidents are caused by 15% of all the drivers" means that 15% are chronic offenders and should be removed from the road or whether the 15% could be accounted for within a random accident hypothesis. This is, one can check what percentage of accidents the 15% would reasonably be expected to be involved in. However λ itself is subject to some variation and so a person chosen at random has an accident rate of λ according to a distribution $g(\lambda)$. That is, there is some degree of accident-proneness in the population described by $g(\lambda)$, which is usually modeled as a gamma distribution. Thus, the probability that a generic driver has k accidents in a time period t is given by

$$\int_0^\infty P_k(t, \lambda) g(\lambda) \, d\lambda$$

QUEUEING

A final topic for this appendix concerns waiting lines or "queueing" systems. Applications of this material is worked out in Chapter 3. Suppose that one has a Poisson process of arrivals into a "service system" in which the arrival is processed or serviced and it then exits. Assume also that service times are exponentially distributed and that $\Pi_n(t)$ denotes the probability of exactly n units (or "calls" or "arrivals") in the system consisting of the service block plus waiting. Let λ_n be the arrival rate and μ_n be the service rate of the process when n units are in the system. If h is a sufficiently small time interval, then the probability of one arrival in time h is $1 - e^{-\lambda_n h} \sim \lambda_n h$ and for one departure it is approximately $\mu_n h$. Consistent with the assumptions made earlier regarding Poisson arrivals, we insist that during a very small interval h, *at most* one arrival or departure can occur, each independently of each other. That is, in a system with n units at time t, the only transitions in this next interval of length h is to a system with either $n-1$ or $n+1$ units, as we display in the rate transition diagram shown in Fig. C.7. Therefore, for $n \geq 1$, if the system is in "state" $n-1$ (meaning that it has $n-1$ units) then in the next instant it moves to state n with probability $\lambda_{n-1} h$ whereas the transition from $n+1$ to n occurs with probability $\mu_{n+1} h$. The only other way of getting to state n consists in being there to begin with and not moving out. Shifts from n to $n-1$ and n to $n+1$ occur, respectively, with probabilities $\mu_n h$ and $\lambda_n h$ so that $1 - (\mu_n + \lambda_n)h$ is the probability of staying put. From the assumed independence of arrivals and departures in the system it then follows that

$$\Pi_n(t+h) = \Pi_n(t)(1 - \lambda_n h - \mu_n h) + \Pi_{n-1}(t)\,h + \Pi_{n+1}(t)\mu_{n+1}h$$

and, from this relation,

$$[\Pi_n(t+h) - \Pi_n(t)]/h = -\Pi_n(t)\lambda_n + \mu_n + \Pi_{n-1}(t)(\lambda_{n-1}) + \Pi_{n+1}(t)\mu_{n+1}$$

and if the transition probabilities are sufficiently smooth, one obtains as $h \to 0$ that

$$[d\Pi_n(t)]/dt = -\Pi_n(t)(\lambda_n + \mu_n) + \Pi_{n-1}(t)\lambda_{n-1} + \Pi_{n+1}(t)\mu_{n+1}$$

Moreover, for $n = 0$, one similarly obtains

$$[d\Pi_0(t)]/dt = -\Pi_0(t)\lambda_0 + \Pi_1(t)\mu_1$$

We now examine these equations in the case of *steady state*. That is, we assume that as $t \to +\infty$ the system reaches an equilibrium in which the transition probabilities no longer depend on time. In this case, the previous derivatives can be set to zero and one finds that

$$\lambda_0 \Pi_0 = \mu_1 \Pi_1$$
$$(\lambda_n + \mu_n)\Pi_n = \mu_{n+1}\Pi_{n+1} + \lambda_{n-1}\Pi_{n-1}, \qquad n \geq 1$$

[C.11]

FIG. C.7   Rate transition diagram in queuing.

It is simple to solve this set of algebraic equations recursively and thereby to find that

$$\Pi_1 = \frac{\lambda_0}{\mu_1} \Pi_0$$

$$\Pi_2 = \frac{\lambda_1 \lambda_0}{\mu_2 \mu_1} \Pi_0 \qquad \qquad [\text{C.12}]$$

$$\vdots$$

$$\Pi_n = \frac{\lambda_{n-1} \lambda_{n-2} \cdots \lambda_0}{\mu_n \mu_{n-1} \cdots \mu_1} \Pi_0 \equiv C_n \Pi_0$$

Now it is apparent that there are either zero or one or two, etc. units in the system at any time, and so

$$\sum_{n=0}^{\infty} \Pi_n = 1$$

That is,

$$\Pi_0 + \Pi_0 \sum_{n=1}^{\infty} C_n = 1$$

or

$$\Pi_0 = \left(1 + \sum_{n=1}^{\infty} C_n\right)^{-1} \qquad \qquad [\text{C.13}]$$

In order for the steady-state probabilities to have any meaning, the sum in [C.13] must be convergent. In all the examples of Chapter 3, this will be the case. There the relations [C.11] or, as they are called, the "balance equations" are interpreted in several significant urban contexts.

SOME SPECIAL CASES

I Consider the simple setting of a *single-server queueing system* in which $\lambda_n = \lambda$ and $\mu_n = \mu$ for all n. Then, from [C.12], $C_n = \rho^n$ with $\rho = \lambda/\mu$ and the sum in [C.13] converges if $\rho < 1$. Solving for Π_n gives

$$\Pi_n = \rho^n \Pi_0$$

and from [C.13],

$$\Pi_0 = 1 - \rho \qquad \qquad [\text{C.14}]$$

(which means that ρ is the probability of the server being busy), so that

$$\Pi_n = (1-\rho)\rho^n \qquad \qquad [\text{C.15}]$$

Using [C.15], the average number of units in the system is given by

$$L = (1-\rho) \sum n\rho^n$$

$$= (1-\rho)\rho \sum \frac{d}{d\rho}\rho^n$$

$$= (1-\rho)\rho \frac{d}{d\rho} \sum \rho^n$$

$$= (1-\rho)\rho \frac{d}{d\rho}\left(\frac{1}{1-\rho}\right)$$

$$= \frac{\rho}{1-\rho}$$

Therefore

$$L = \lambda/(\mu-\lambda) \qquad\qquad [C.16]$$

Now the number of calls in the system at any time is a random variable, u_n, which equals the product of the random variables v_n and w_n, where v_n is the number of calls arriving per unit time and w_n is the total time in the system that each call is held before service is completed. It is reasonable to suppose that *in an equilibrium state*, v_n and w_n are *independent* and so the expected value of u_n is the product of expected values of v_n and w_n. Thus, *in the steady state* one has

$$L = \lambda W \qquad\qquad [C.17]$$

where W is the mean waiting time in the system. This *heuristic* argument can be made rigorous, but the reader can follow that up himself by consulting the reference. In a similar way one shows that if L_q and W_q are, respectively, the average number of units waiting in queue (prior to service) and the average waiting time in queue (prior to service) then,

$$L_q = \lambda W_q \qquad\qquad [C.18]$$

It is also clear that

$$W = W_q + 1/\mu \qquad\qquad [C.19]$$

and so all the quantities W, W_q, L, L_q can be determined once one of them is known. In our example, since L is given by [C.16], then $W = 1/(\mu-\lambda)$ and

$$W_q = \lambda/[\mu(\mu-\lambda)] \qquad\qquad [C.20]$$

II   For a second special case, consider a system with s *identical servers working from a single queue* (Fig. C.8). Here each server has a service time exponentially distributed with a mean service time of $1/\mu$. Therefore we know from [C.6] and [C.7] that if n of the s servers are busy, they become

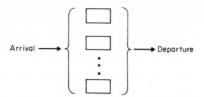

FIG. C.8 Schematic of a multiserver queue.

free at a rate which equals $n\mu$—that is, the set of n servers taken together behaves as a single server whose service time is exponential with a mean service time of $1/n\mu$. Therefore, the model expressed by Eqs. [C.11] is applicable with μ_n given by

$$\mu_n = \begin{cases} n\mu, & n < s \\ s\mu, & n \geq s \end{cases}$$

If we also assume that $\lambda_n = \lambda$ then

$$C_n = \begin{cases} \rho^n/n!, & n < s \\ \rho^n/(s!\,s^{n-s}), & n \geq s \end{cases}$$

It follows that

$$\Pi_0 = \left[\sum_{n=0}^{s-1} \frac{\rho^n}{n!} + \frac{\rho^s}{s!} \sum_{n=s}^{\infty} \left(\frac{\lambda}{s\mu} \right)^{n-s} \right]^{-1}$$

where the infinite sum converges provided that $(\lambda/s\mu) < 1$, as we assume. Now

$$\sum_{n=s}^{\infty} \left(\frac{\lambda}{s\mu} \right)^{n-s} = \sum_{j=0}^{\infty} \left(\frac{\lambda}{s\mu} \right)^j = \left(1 - \frac{\lambda}{s\mu} \right)^{-1}$$

and so

$$\Pi_0 = \left[\sum_{n=0}^{s-1} \frac{\rho^n}{n!} + \frac{\rho^s}{s!} \frac{1}{1-(\lambda/s\mu)} \right]^{-1}$$

From [C.12] it also follows that

$$\Pi_n = \begin{cases} \dfrac{\rho^n}{n!} \Pi_0, & n = 1, \ldots, s-1 \\[2ex] \dfrac{\rho^n}{s!\,s^{n-s}} \Pi_0, & n \geq s \end{cases} \qquad [C.21]$$

Note that the probability that the servers are busy is $\sum_{n \geq s} \Pi_n$ which for $s = 1$ equals $1 - \Pi_0 = \rho$. For $s = 2$, this probability is $1 - \Pi_0 - \Pi_1 = 1 - (1+\rho)\Pi_0$.

For $s > 1$, it is easier to compute L_q than L. In fact

$$L_q = \sum_{n=s}^{\infty} (n-s)\Pi_n$$

which follows since there are no waiting units in line when $n \leq s$ and $n-s$ wait when $n \geq s$.

Using [C.21] one can compute L_q as

$$L_q = \sum_{j=0}^{\infty} j\Pi_{s+j} = \frac{\Pi_0 \rho^s}{s!} \sum_{j=0}^{\infty} j\left(\frac{\lambda}{s\mu}\right)^j = \frac{\Pi_0 \rho^s(\lambda/s\mu)}{s!(1-\lambda/s\mu)^2}$$

For $s = 2$ one finds Π_0 to be

$$\Pi_0 = (2-\rho)/(2+\rho) \qquad\qquad [C.22]$$

and so for $s = 2$,

$$W_q = L_q/\lambda = \lambda^2/(2\mu^2 + \lambda\mu) \cdot 1/(2\mu - \lambda) \qquad\qquad [C.23]$$

NOTES AND REMARKS

The material of this appendix is treated in a number of places, one of which is the book by Hillier and Lieberman referenced in Appendix A. The observation about random incidence and crime data was made available to the author by Professor R. Larson of MIT while the material on accident data is a brief abstract from an extensive study done by

J. Ferreira, "Drive Accident Models and Their Use in Policy Evaluation," in *Analysis of Public Systems* (A. Drake, R. Keeney, and P. Morse, eds.), MIT Press, Cambridge, Massachusetts, 1972;

J. Ferreira, "The Effect of Removing Accident Repeaters from the Road," *Urban Anal.* 1 (1972), 45–62.

The relation $L = \lambda W$ was established by

S. Stidham, "A Last Word on $L = \lambda W$," *Operations Res.* **22** (1974), 417–421.

D

Nonlinear Optimization

Our purpose here is to give a brief introduction to nonlinear optimization by examining a special kind of problem which occurs with some frequency in practice and which appears several times in this book.

The problem is to maximize an objective function $f(x_1, \ldots, x_n)$ of n variables subject to $x_i \geqq 0$ and an equality constraint of the type $\sum_{i=1}^{n} x_i = X$. Many allocation problems are of this form in which, as in linear programming, x_i are activity levels and X is some maximum resource level. Our approach to this is to formulate a set of necessary conditions for the optimum which are, in fact, a generalization of the duality relations in linear programming.

THE PENALTY ARGUMENT

In approaching constrained optimization in the nonlinear case we will utilize a simple device, treated here in a somewhat heuristic fashion, known as the penalty argument.

Suppose that f and g are continuously differentiable functions on R^n and one wishes to find that x^0 in R^n which yields the maximum of $f(x)$ subject to $g(x) = 0$ and $x \geq 0$. Ignore, for the moment, nonnegativity restrictions. The idea is to replace this problem by a sequence of unconstrained ones in which the objective f is augmented by introducing additional terms as follows:

$$F_k(x) = f(x) + kg^2(x), \qquad k > 0.$$

It appears plausible that if F_k is minimized to yield an optimum vector $x^k = (x_1{}^k, ..., x_n{}^k)$, then the quantities $g^2(x^k)$ will be small for large values of k since the product $kg^2(x^k)$ cannot be very large; indeed as k increases without bound one expects $g^2(x^k)$ to tend to zero. Under suitably mild conditions on f and g one can in fact show this to be true and that the optimizing vectors x^k tend to some x^0 which is the solution to the original constrained problem.

An example will illustrate what happens. Suppose one wishes to find the shortest distance from the origin in the plane to the line defined by $x + y - 1 = 0$. It is reasonably clear from geometric considerations that the minimum occurs where $x_1{}^0 = x_2{}^0 = \frac{1}{2}$. Let us see how the penalty argument arrives at the same conclusion. Incidently, the term "penalty function" for the terms kg^2 derives from the fact that each increase in the parameter k represents a correspondingly larger cost or penalty for violating the constraint $g = 0$. Since distance from the origin can be replaced by distance squared without loss of generality, the problem is to minimize $f(x_1, x_2) = x_1{}^2 + x_2{}^2$ subject to the constraint $g(x_1, x_2) = x_1 + x_2 - 1 = 0$. We therefore form the augmented functions $F_k(x_1, x_2) = x_1{}^2 + x_2{}^2 + k(x_1 + x_2 - 1)^2$ and find the unconstrained minimum by computing the gradient of F_k and setting it equal to zero:

$$\partial F_k/\partial x_1 = 2\{x_1 + k(x_1 + x_2 - 1)\} = 0$$
$$\partial F_k/\partial x_2 = 2\{x_2 + k(x_1 + x_2 - 1)\} = 0$$

[D.1]

The only solution to these algebraic equations is the vector x^k whose components $x_1{}^k$ and $x_2{}^k$ are equal, from which one obtains that

$$x_1{}^k = x_2{}^k = k/(1 + 2k)$$

which tends to $\frac{1}{2}$ as $k \to \infty$. Notice that although $g(x^k)$ goes to zero in the limit, the product $kg^2(x^k)$ tends to $-\frac{1}{2}$. Therefore, letting $x^0 = (\frac{1}{2}, \frac{1}{2})$ and labeling kg as the scalar λ one computes the value of [D.1] at the optimum as

$$[\partial f(x^0)]/\partial x_1 + \lambda = 0$$
$$[\partial f(x^0)]/\partial x_2 + \lambda = 0$$

[D.2]

which is a special case of the well-known *Lagrange multiplier rule*. The derivation in this case, using the penalty idea, differs from the usual approach and can be extended to the more general case of functions of n variables.

If one assumes that f, g are continuously differentiable, with gradient vectors ∇f, ∇g then, provided that f possesses a constrained minimum x^0, one can derive in analogous fashion that

$$\nabla F_k(x^k) = \nabla f(x^k) + 2kg(x^k)\,\nabla g(x^k) = 0$$

which extends the simple case of [D.1]. This describes a system of n equations in n unknowns since the gradient is a vector with n components. Provided that

$$\nabla g(x^0) = \left(\frac{\partial g(x^0)}{\partial x_1}, \ldots, \frac{\partial g(x^0)}{\partial x_n}\right) \neq 0$$

one shows that $x^k \to x^0$ and that there exists a scalar λ (the Lagrange multiplier) for which

$$\nabla f(x^0) + \lambda\,\nabla g(x^0) = 0 \qquad\qquad\qquad [D.3]$$

and this includes [D.2] as a special case.

The same argument applies to an inequality constraint of the form $g(x) \leqq 0$ except that now the penalty terms are modified to read as

$$kg^2(x)\,u(x)$$

where

$$u(x) = \begin{cases} 1 & \text{if } g(x) > 0 \\ 0 & \text{otherwise} \end{cases}$$

One sees immediately that $g^2 u = 0$ if and only if $g \leqq 0$ and so the inequality constraint is replaced by an equality and the method used can be reapplied. The astute reader will notice that even though u is discontinuous, the product $g^2 u$ is not only continuous but also continuously differentiable with gradient $2gu\,\nabla g$. Therefore one again has that [D.3] holds except that now λ is known to be nonnegative since it is the limit of quantities $2kg(x^k)u(x^k) \geqq 0$. In this form [D.3] is a version of the *Kuhn–Tucker multiplier rule*. In the equality case λ is undetermined in sign.

Suppose that we now additionally require that $x \geqq 0$. Consider what can happen in the simple case of a function $F(x_1, x_2)$ in which $x_1, x_2 \geqq 0$. If, let us say, the maximum occurs where $x_1{}^0 = 0$ and $x_2{}^0 > 0$ (a similar argument applies to $x_1{}^0 > 0$ and $x_2{}^0 = 0$) then

$$F(x_1{}^0 + \delta_1 x_2{}^0) - F(x_1{}^0, x_2{}^0) \leqq 0$$

for all positive δ sufficiently small. Therefore, when F is differentiable one has

$$(\partial F/\partial x_1)(x_1{}^0, x_2{}^0) \leqq 0 \qquad \text{and} \qquad (\partial F/\partial x_2)(x_1{}^0, x_2{}^0) = 0$$

since $x_1{}^0 > 0$. If $x_1{}^0 = x_2{}^0 = 0$ then both partial derivatives are nonpositive. These simple remarks apply in general and so if $x \geqq 0$ is added to the problem of maximizing f with $g = 0$ (or $g \leqq 0$), then the penalty argument given above can be modified to immediately give the relation

$$\nabla f(x^0) + \lambda \nabla g(x^0) \leqq 0$$

or to be more specific,

$$[\partial f(x^0)/\partial x_i] + \lambda [\partial g(x^0)/\partial x_i] \leqq 0, \quad \text{if} \quad x_i^0 = 0$$

$$[\partial f(x^0)/\partial x_i] + \lambda [\partial g(x^0)/\partial x_i] = 0, \quad \text{if} \quad x_i^0 > 0$$

[D.4]

In the case of $g \leqq 0$ we note, additionally, that not only is $\lambda \geqq 0$ but that *if* $g(x^0) < 0$ *then* $\lambda = 0$ which follows from the fact that $g(x^k)u(x^k) = 0$ for all sufficiently large k.

AN IMPORTANT SPECIAL CASE

In a number of examples, as given in several chapters, f is of the special form

$$f(x) = \sum_{i=1}^{n} f_i(x_i)$$

in which the *objective is separable* in each variable, and in which

$$g(x) = \sum_{i=1}^{n} x_i - X = 0$$

Then the necessary conditions for an optima [D.4] reduce to

$$[\partial f_i(x^0)/\partial x_i] + \lambda \leqq 0 \quad \text{if} \quad x_i^0 = 0$$

$$[\partial f_i(x^0)/\partial x_i] + \lambda = 0 \quad \text{if} \quad x_i^0 > 0$$

[D.5]

In certain cases one wants a solution under the additional requirement that the x vector consist of integers. Assuming the separability of F, a simple solution method is discussed for this problem in Chapter 4 in connection with the square root law for the allocation of emergency vehicles.

DUALITY

The relations [D.4] represent necessary conditions for an optimum. When f is linear of the form $c^T x$ and g is linear of the form $a^T x - b \leqq 0$ then they reduce to

$$c_i + \lambda a_i \leqq 0 \quad \text{for all} \quad i = 1, ..., n$$

with $\lambda \geqq 0$. One recognizes this as a special case of the constraints for the dual problem in linear programming in the circumstance of only one inequality constraint in the primal, except that the dual multiplier is instead here denoted by λ. Thus we see that the dual constraints in linear programming constitute a set of necessary conditions for optimality. The relations [D.4] can be viewed as a duality statement for the nonlinear case and indeed λ continues to have the same economic interpretation as a shadow price. In fact, if the constraint is slack at the optimum (in the sense that $g(x^0) < 0$) then, as we saw, λ is zero, which is in accord with the economic metaphor of a "free good."

NOTES

The penalty argument and its consequences is detailed by

E. Beltrami, *An Algorithmic Approach to Nonlinear Analysis and Optimization*, Academic Press, New York, 1970.

APPENDIX

E

Graphs, Minimal Trees, and Shortest Paths

Graphs are sets of points, called *nodes* or *vertices*, linked together by *arcs* or *edges*. For example, Fig. E.1 represents a graph in which A, B, C, D are the nodes linked by five edges.

Let (V, E) denote a graph with a set V of vertices and a set E of edges (V, E are each assumed to be finite). Traverse the graph (V, E) by beginning at some vertex A. If A is not isolated we can move away from it along some edge to C, and so forth. If one eventually arrives at some vertex P then it is said that *P is connected to A*. Let us call such a route a *path*. If the starting and terminal vertex are the same the path is a *cycle*. If each vertex is connected to every other vertex by a path the graph is said to be *connected*. For example, the graph in Fig. E.2 is not connected. Note that the path from

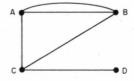

FIG. E.1   A typical graph.

210

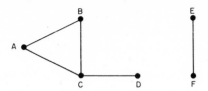

FIG. E.2   A graph that is not connected.

A to *B* to *C* and back to *A* is a cycle. A *directed graph* is one in which every edge is given an orientation or direction. This is usually indicated by an arrow along each edge. A *complete graph* is one in which every node is linked to each of the others.

Let the *number of edges incident to a vertex be called the degree of the vertex.* In the graph of Fig. E.2 for instance, vertex *A* has a degree 2 while vertex *C* has degree 3.

Theorem   In a connected graph the sum of all the degrees equals twice the number of edges.

PROOF   In adding up the degrees of all the nodes, we end up by counting each edge twice since each edge is incident to precisely two vertices. Therefore, the number of edges is one half the sum of the degrees, which is what we wanted to show. In Fig. E.1 for example the sum of the degrees is ten and there are five edges. ∎

A connected graph with no cycles is called a *tree*. In Fig. E.3 are two examples of trees.

Theorem   A tree with *n* nodes has *n* − 1 edges.

PROOF   Between two vertices there can be only one edge otherwise we have a cycle. The simplest tree has only one edge, with two vertices. Each time an edge is added at the end of a vertex, a new vertex is added. Eventually we reach the last vertex of the graph with a total of *n* − 1 edges. ∎

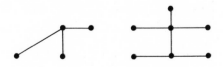

FIG. E.3   Some examples of tree graphs.

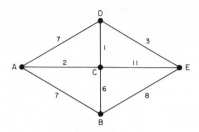

FIG. E.4 A graph used to illustrate the minimal tree algorithm.

A tree is said to span the n nodes it covers. There are many different ways of spanning a vertex set V, and of all of them one tree, called the *minimal spanning tree*, has the shortest total length for all the arcs. Incidentally, the "length" of an arc can be any nonnegative quantity and need not represent the actual distance between nodes. Although we do not prove it here there are a total of n^{n-2} trees spanning n nodes.

There is a procedure for constructing minimal trees which we shall describe, but a proof that the resulting tree is indeed minimal will not be given:

1.   Link together that pair of vertices that are closer together than any other pair. That is, choose the edge having the shortest length. If there is a tie choose any one of the competing edges.

2.   Now extend this single edge tree *to form a new tree* by joining to it that edge of smallest length among all those that remain.

3.   Continue in this manner until all the nodes have been joined.

An example will illustrate the algorithm. To this end consider the graph given in Fig. E.4 with the edge lengths as indicated. The shortest edge is the one linking C to D. Of all the remaining arcs, the one which joins node A to C is the smallest and, together with the one from C to D, forms a new tree. Next, we join on the edge from E to D, since it has the smallest length among those that are left. The only node which remains to be connected is B. Since

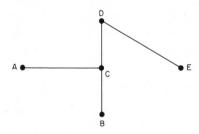

FIG. E.5 Minimal tree corresponding to the graph of Fig. E.4.

it is linked to the tree already formed by three edges we choose the smallest one, namely the arc from B to C. The procedure terminates at this point since all nodes are now connected. The minimal tree is therefore the one exhibited below (Fig. E.5) and it has a total length of 12.

An analogous question concerns the finding of the *shortest path* from any given node to all other nodes. An algorithm for accomplishing this is best explained in terms of an example. For this purpose consider again Fig. E.4 and let A be the node from which the shortest distance to all other nodes is desired. Begin by joining A to the node closest to it, which happens to be C. This forms a simple tree consisting of a single edge. In each step of the algorithm, edges are added on one at a time to form increasingly larger trees until all nodes have been connected. In this sense the procedure bears some resemblance to that used to find the minimal tree but, as we will see, the results are generally different.

Denote by S_1 the set of nodes already linked to A in a tree and let S_2 be the set of all *adjacent* nodes to S_1. In the previous example, the first step resulted in $S_1 = \{A, C\}$ and $S_2 = \{B, D, E\}$. The shortest way of joining D to A is through C. All competing ways are longer, as one readily sees.

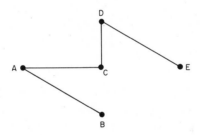

FIG. E.6   Tree of shortest paths based on the graph of Fig. E.4.

Since all other links between S_2 to A via S_1 are also longer, we choose to add D to the tree to form a new set $S_1 = \{A, C, D\}$, with $S_2 = \{B, E\}$. Of all the paths joining B to A the shortest is the direct link between them of length 7. However, E can also reach A along a path of length 6 by backtracking through D and C. Therefore the edge from E to D is added on to form $S_1 = \{A, C, D, E\}$ and $S_2 = \{B\}$. The last step is to let B connect to A directly. The resulting tree structure of total length 13 is shown in Fig. E.6 which is clearly different from the minimal tree of Fig. E.5.

The procedure in general is based on the rather self-evident principle of optimality which says that if a shortest path exists between A and some other node, say A_j, via a predecessor node, call it A_i, then the path from A to A_i must also be of minimal length. Therefore if L_i denotes the shortest path between A and any node i in the set S_1 and if δ_{ij} is the length of the edge linking node i with any node j in the set S_2 then one seeks that pair of nodes (i, j) for which $L_i + S_{ij}$ is minimized. Since the path from A to i is already optimal the search for an optimum reduces to finding a single link between the sets S_1 and S_2. It is then apparent that L_j is given by

$$L_j = \min\{L_i + S_{ij}\} \tag{E.1}$$

We leave it to the reader to verify how [E.1] was used in the simple example shown.

NOTES

The proof that the algorithm for a minimal tree is indeed optimal is given by

J. Kruskal, "On the Shortest Spanning Subtree of a Graph," *Proc. Amer. Math. Soc.* **7** (1956), 48–50,

whereas the shortest path method given here is due to

J. Dijkstra, "A Note on Two Problems in Connection with Graphs," *Num. Math.* **1** (1959), 269–271.

Index